The Book: An Actor's Guide to Chicago

Edited by Mechelle Moe

Fifth Edition

Published by Perform*ink* **Books, Ltd.**

PerformInk Books, Ltd.
3223 N. Sheffield
Chicago, IL 60657

ISBN: 1-892296-03-9

Carrie L. Kaufman, Publisher

Mechelle Moe, Editor

Design and production by Marty McNulty

Successor to "Acting, Modeling and Dance," Founding Editors: Allyson Rice-Taylor, Emily Gerson-Saines

Editors's Note

Welcome to the 5th edition of "The Book: An Actor's Guide to Chicago," a comprehensive resource guide for the actor, designer, director, producer, arts administrator and educator. Whether you've been working in the business for 20 years or are just starting out, we have something for everyone at every level. Hopefully the mysteries of working and living as an artist in Chicago will be unraveled, if only just a bit, within these pages.

For those long-time readers, the staff at PerformInk decided that after five long hard years "The Book" needed a bit of a face-lift. Well that's what happens when the editor quits to pursue greater things (something about managing a theatre company, go figure!), and you have a virgin staff ready to wreak havoc on the unsuspecting arts community.

Out with the old, in with the new!

In 2002, PI is all about streamlining; a little nip and tuck here and there. First, lets take a moment of silence for the lamentable loss of The Book Guy who was retired earlier this year. Some may say we lost our sense of humor, I'd like to think we just made room for more invaluable content. There are plenty of new and improved features, as well as expanded listings. (You may notice that some older articles were pulled or checklisted, but never fear, most can be found in full online at www.performink.com.)

Many thanks to the staff of PerformInk—Rob Mello, Jen Ellison, Adam Cook and Carrie L. Kaufman—for their creativity, expertise and guidance. A big thank you goes out to our proofreader Claire Kaplan and layout wizard Marty McNulty both of whom have been with this publication since the beginning. To former editor Kevin Heckman, who deserves a great deal of credit for laying the groundwork for this publication and carrying it as far as it has come, thanks for passing on the torch (I think). A special nod to all contributors: Jonathan Abarbanel, Chris Gatto, Jenn Goddu, Susan Hubbard, Carrie L. Kaufman, Kelly Kurtin, Ben Winters, Rachel Patterson and Dr. Amy Seham. And last but not least, thanks to the community at large who provided great insight and data while compiling this resource.

PerformInk is always looking for ways to improve and expand "The Book," so if you have any questions or comments, please feel free to contact us.

Enjoy!

Mechelle Moe

Table of Contents

Chapter 1

Coming to Chicago

The Hypocrites, "Ajax"

Threescore and ten I can remember well,
Within the volume of which time I have seen
Hours dreadful and things strange.

By Jonathan Abarbanel

Chicago always has been a theatre town, or at least highly theatrical. Just look at the City Council. Well, maybe that's just a comedy troupe (rim shot).

But seriously folks, theatre has been part of the city's life since the day in 1837 when Chicago actually became a city. By the time the Village of Chicago (1832) reincorporated as a city, touring professional actors already had made the semi-frontier outpost a semi-regular stop. Notable among them was Joseph Jefferson II, who headed west to escape the shadow of his famous actor father, just as good ole dad had moved to the United States from England in 1795 to escape the shadow of his own father, a famous London actor. Joe II was among the first important performers to bring theatre to the hinterlands. Here in Chicago, the uncorroborated story goes, Joseph Jefferson III—destined to become an even greater star than either his American father or grandfather or his English great-grandfather—first appeared onstage as a baby carried in Joe II's arms.

The baby bit probably isn't true, but it is a fact that Joe II was a member of the stock company at Chicago's very first theatre, the Rialto, which operated here for three years (1838-1840). Joe III no doubt acted here as well during that period, for he would have been nine years old in 1838 (which pretty much discredits the babe-in-arms story, at least in Chicago), having made his stage debut at the age of four. As an adult, Joe III returned many times to Chicago, appearing opposite players such as Mrs. John Drew and Laura Keene in *Our*

American Cousin, The Rivals, The Octoroon and in his legendary signature role in *Rip Van Winkle,* adapted by Dion Boucicault from the Washington Irving tale.

Because of the family's strong Chicago connections, and pioneering spirit in bringing culture to the west, our local theatre awards are named in honor of Joseph Jefferson. Which one? Well, Joe II actually.

Burning Down the House: Chicago Theatre in the Late 1800s

The Rialto Theatre was managed by John B. Rice, a gentleman who waxed big in Chicago's nascent performing arts world. A few years later, in 1847, he opened his own playhouse—Rice's Theatre—which was the venue for the first professional opera performance in Chicago, Bellini's *La Sonnambula,* in 1850. The city's cultural elite and not-so-elite dressed to the nines and tromped through unpaved, muddy streets to hear four genuine, Italian touring stars sing the lead roles, backed by a pick-up cast of locals and a small orchestra. It must have been a singularly curious experience, which the local newspapers proclaimed a sensation. They didn't know whether the singing was any good or not, but they knew that the occasion was special.

It was so special that Rice's Theatre burned down. The building was swept away in a conflagration that took several square blocks of downtown Chicago. No matter. Just about everything was still built of wood, and was quickly replaced. John Rice certainly bounced back; he was elected mayor of Chicago a few years later. See? The Chicago connection between theatre and politics started very early.

The next big step came in 1857, when John H. McVicker built a substantial and costly theatre of 2,600 seats on Madison Street as a home for the finest touring stars and stock companies. Abraham Lincoln saw plays at McVicker's, and James O'Neill was a young leading man there. The first McVicker's burned down in the Great Fire of 1871, with a new house erected on the same spot almost immediately. The second McVicker's was replaced by a third in the early 20th century—a house which hosted live theatre and, later, films into the 1970s, when it finally fell to the wrecker's ball for another Loop parking garage.

Few cities have the opportunity to start over from scratch the way Chicago did following The Great Fire. For the next 50 years, the metropolis remade itself, often with world-leading architecture, notably in the work of Holabird and Root, Adler and Sullivan and—out in the then-new suburb of Oak Park—Frank Lloyd Wright. Adler and Sullivan designed the magnificent, 4,200-seat Auditorium Theatre, which was opened in 1889 by President Grover Cleveland and opera star Adelina Patti. When *The Phantom of the Opera* played the restored and modernized Auditorium Theatre in the 1990s, it was the only time that grandiose musical—which is set in a great 19th century opera house—actually was performed in a great 19th century opera house.

Turning the Century on its Heel: Vaudeville to the Emergence of off-Loop Theatre

By the turn of the century, downtown Chicago included a thriving theatre district of two dozen legitimate theatres and vaudeville houses. The great stars of the era—among them William Gillette, Sothern and Marlowe, Minnie Maddern Fiske, DeWolfe Hopper, Lillian Russell (born in Chicago as Helen Louise Leonard), Edwin Booth, Joe Jefferson III, Maude Adams, James K. Hackett, Nat Goodwin, Weber and Fields, David Warfield, Otis Skinner, the Drews and the Barrymores, George M. Cohan—all played Chicago, along with the greatest vaudeville stars of the day such as Al Jolson, Eddie Cantor, Blanche Ring, Nora and Jack Bayes and Eddie Foy (who grew up in Chicago and began his showbiz career here at 15).

Foy was a major star when he appeared here in 1904, headlining *Mr. Bluebeard* at the Iroquois Theatre, and was on stage when a fire broke out. Despite his heroic efforts to calm the crowd, a panic ensued and over 400 people were crushed to death in the stampede to exit through auditorium doors that opened inward. The resulting rewrite of the building and fire codes gave Chicago the most stringent ordinances in the country, which still is true today. Chicago codes, for example, do not permit standing room, and the Iroquois Theatre fire is the reason why.

In addition to the Loop, Chicago's neighborhoods were dotted with small vaudeville venues, opera houses (the 900-seat Athenaeum may be the only such survivor), and so-called "Little Theatre" societies, which were the off-Loop of the day. Although not professionally organized, as is today's off-Loop industry, the Little Theatre movement in Chicago—and elsewhere in the country—was extremely influential. Businessman and playwright Kenneth Sawyer Goodman was a leading exponent of Little Theatre in Chicago during the early 1900s. His legacy may be found in the institutions established as a memorial to him: the DePaul University Theatre School (originally the Goodman School of Drama), the Kenneth Sawyer Goodman Memorial Theatre (built in 1925 by the Art Institute) and the new Goodman Theatre.

The city also contributed to the growth and development of theatre in ways that were entirely quirky. For example, Henrik Ibsen's *Ghosts* had its world premiere in Chicago in 1882, performed in its original Norwegian by Scandinavian immigrants who idolized Ibsen as their great national poet. *Ghosts* wasn't produced in Europe for another year, and was not seen in English until a private performance in London in 1891.

Just as well. The Chicago newspapers probably would have condemned the play as diseased filth, as most European critics did.

Another oddity: The Marx Brothers lived in Chicago for a year or so before World War I, getting their act together in the neighborhood vaudeville houses.

By the 1920s, the roster of legitimate and musical houses in downtown Chicago included the Adelphi, Blackstone (now the Merle Reskin), Cort, Erlanger, Garrick, Goodman, Great Northern, Harris, Illinois, LaSalle, Majestic (now the Shubert), McVickers, Playhouse, Princess, Selwyn and Studebaker theatres. There also were downtown houses that offered vaudeville or a combination of a film and a live variety show such as the Chicago, Oriental, Palace, Roosevelt, State-Lake and Woods theatres, plus two opera houses (the Auditorium and the Grand Opera House, owned by George. M. Cohan).

Not counting opera or vaudeville, the 1921-1922 season saw 50 plays and 30 musicals performed in the downtown theatres for a total of 360 weeks to paid attendance of about 4.5 million, according to O. L. Hall, dramatic editor of the JOURNAL OF COMMERCE (the long-defunct Chicago daily that first employed Claudia Cassidy as a critic). Nine years later, CHICAGO TRIBUNE critic Charles Collins counted 84 downtown shows during the 1930-1931 season, although he observed that was fewer shows than in previous seasons and that the Depression had put the squeeze on expensive musicals, reducing them to only a dozen.

A flourishing theatre district is not made up only of playhouses, of course. During the early decades of the 20th century, the Loop also was home to music publishers, costumers and tailors who catered to the theatre trade as well as theatrical photographers, who generally signed their work. Many surviving star portraits—"headshots"—of the era bear the signatures of Chicago photographers Maurice Seymour or Moffett.

But downtown theatre had reached its zenith and now began a rapid decline, as did theatre districts in cities across the country. Live theatre and vaudeville couldn't compete—especially during the Depression—with the much cheaper competition of movies and radio. Then, after World War II ended (1945), theatre and film alike faced competition from a new medium: television. This was coupled with the deterioration of city centers in general, as post-war prosperity in the late 1940s, the 1950s and the 1960s fed a population shift from city to suburbs. By the 1970s, the only remaining downtown houses still used for theatre (versus movies) were the Goodman, Shubert, Blackstone and Studebaker (in the Fine Arts Building, later converted into a cineplex), and the Auditorium and Civic Opera House on an occasional basis.

The neighborhoods, however, had taken up some of the slack. Even during the Depression, the Little Theatre movement continued, and amateur theatricals flourished. Ethnic communities also continued to play a role. For instance, Chicago had a lively Yiddish theatre community, and settlement houses such as the Hull House actively promoted and taught all the arts. It was during this period, when commercial theatre increasingly was fallow, that Viola Spolin, initially working through the Hull House, developed her theatre games and later passed them on to her son, Paul Sills.

Beating the Economic Engine: Second City to the Suburbs

A few signs of life stirred in the late 1950s and early 1960s with the emergence of The Second City, Playwrights at Second City, the Ivanhoe and Candlelight Dinner Playhouse on the commercial front, and the strong showings among community theatres of Theatre First, Encore Theatre, the long-established Old Town Players and the Hull House Theatres. There also was a lively summer stock circuit—late 1940s to late 1960s—including Tenthouse, Music Theatre, Chevy Chase Theatre (where producer Hope Abelson got her start), Melody Top (here, then Milwaukee) and the slightly later and much more serious Academy Festival Theatre.

The Second City, founded in 1959 by Paul Sills, Bernard Sahlins and Howard Alk, has achieved such justified international fame and influence in the field of comedy, cabaret and improvisation that it now, wrongly, often is given status as a pioneer of Chicago off-Loop Theatre. Rather, it was an Equity company from the start and it was not until long after off-Loop theatre had begun to grow and professionalize itself that The Second City was absorbed into the larger off-Loop industry.

Ditto, Candlelight Dinner Playhouse, founded in the near southwest suburbs in 1959 by 20-something William Pullinsi. Now defunct, Candlelight grew to be a large and well-respected operation that was the model for the development of the dinner theatre industry across the nation. To its last day, Candlelight—and its sister Forum Theatre—offered both artistic fare and food far, far above the dinner theatre standard found elsewhere. Pullinsi produced American and world premiere plays and musicals in addition to standard repertory. The success of Candlelight spawned other suburban ventures, not all of them dinner operations, including the Arlington Park Theatre (particularly ambitious), Pheasant Run Dinner Theatre, Country Club Dinner Theatre and Drury Lane Evergreen Park.

The companies that really spawned the off-Loop theatre scene were ones such as the Old Town Players, Theatre First, the dynamic Hull House Theatres under director Robert Sickenger, the Experimental Black Actors Guild (X-BAG, co-founded by Chuck Smith) and—from the late 1960s—Chicago City Players and the New Chicago City Players, Café TOPA, Kingston Mines Theatre Company, the Drama Shelter (the city's first gay-oriented troupe) and the Body Politic (which produced Paul Sills' Story Theatre and brought the Organic Theatre to town). These troupes introduced a new, radical political energy to theatre and a large collective of newer, younger theatre artists. They were baby boomers who attracted other boomers in the decade before yuppification and gentrification, and they were able to establish new patterns of theatre-going in Chicago.

From the 1970s on, the explosive growth of off-Loop theatre from a movement to an industry is well documented, although its definitive history remains to be written. The emergence of a Chicago school of playwriting out of the success of David Mamet, the development of a distinctive local acting style modeled after early Steppenwolf, the successful establishment of theatre industry trade associations, the development of a flexible and Chicago-specific Equity contract, the rewrite of city codes to legalize found theatre spaces, the national growth of the not-for-profit arts industry and local and national recognition of Chicago theatre all have been important contributing factors in the success of contemporary theatre here. Furthermore, the success of off-Loop theatre has been the direct impetus for the revival of a modest downtown Theatre District.

However, with all its achievements and even with an estimated 12,000 performances a year by some 200 theatre companies throughout the metropolitan region, Chicago still is far from matching that figure from 80 years ago of 4.5 million tickets sold. Just a reminder that Chicago has a history as a great theatre town.

Desire for a Street Car

a tragi-comedy

Synopsis

A group of perky and budding young actors wrestle with the choice of owning automobiles in the bustling city of Chicago. The group is initially enticed by the benefits of car ownership from an overzealous car salesperson. But then the sobering realization of car expenses tempers their judgement. After weighing the pros and cons, they happily make their decision and celebrate.

The Pros of Car Ownership

No hauling groceries on the eL, train or bus.

Numerous offers of acting gigs come from distant suburban theatres.

Wider choice of neighborhoods to live in.

Less accessible neighborhoods are usually cheaper neighborhoods. In this case, owning a car can actually save you money.

Flexibility.

The Cons

High insurance rates.

Poorly maintained streets.

Tollways.

High gas prices.

Other Chicago drivers and road rage.

Difficult parking.

Street cleaning (watch for the orange signs).

Confusing highway systems.

The Highwaymen

The Chicagoland interstate highway system has honorary names that designate an entire interstate, or a portion of one, or a merged combination of two or more. Although they can be confusing, these names are important to master because most traffic reports refer to them, as they are more specific than just the highway numbers. Here is a definitive list.

The Kennedy.......90 from O'Hare airport to the Loop (including the 94 merge)

The Eisenhower..290

The Stevenson..55
The Edens..94 north after 90/94 split
The Dan Ryan.. 94 south of the Loop and part of 57
The Bishop Ford..94 south after the split with 57
The Kingery..94 south after merging with 294 and 80
The Skyway................................90 south of the Loop after 90 and 94 separate
The Tri-State Tollway...294
The Northwest Tollway.....................................90 west of O'Hare and beyond
The North-South Tollway..355
The East-West Tollway...88

So you've passed Driver's Ed

If you're still planning on driving in Chicago (and many people do), there are some civic steps you're going to need to take.

Visit the Secretary of State

Within 90 days of your arrival in Chicago, you're supposed to switch over your license and registration. To get an Illinois license, you'll need to have your old license, a social security card, proof of your current address (a piece of mail addressed to you will suffice) and you'll need to take a written test. Additionally, you'll need $10. To transfer your registration, you'll need an Illinois license, $13 to transfer your title and $48 for plates. If you've owned your car "for a while"(vague terms courtesy of the Secretary of State's office), you shouldn't have to pay tax on the updated registration. Call 312/793-1010 for more information.

Visit the City of Chicago Department of Revenue

Chicago residents who own cars are subject to an annual "wheel tax" and must pay $75 and place a city sticker on their car's windshield. You must purchase one as soon as you establish residence in the city. If you don't get it right away, they'll penalize you, and if you don't get one at all, you can be ticketed. Additionally, some neighborhoods require that you have a residential parking pass, which is a completely different animal from your city sticker. For that you'll need a city sticker, proof of residence and $10. You may be able to take care of both these things at your local currency exchange. Check one out before you bother with the trip downtown. For more information, call 312/747-4747.

Chicago Transit

In the city, the eL, the bus, and your feet get you where you're going. Mastering the eL is quite fun and adventurous. CTA fares are $1.50 per ride. If taken within two hours, the first transfer is 30 cents, the second is free. Take an eL, then transfer to a bus and get to your destination on $1.80. The CTA doesn't use coins. All riders — bus and eL — use fare cards. Machines are set up in eL stations to purchase cards or add money onto existing ones. To get information about the CTA, check out their website at **www.transitchicago.com** or call **1-888-968-7282.**

What the "eL"?

The eL is a network of frequently-stopping trains that run on ***elevated*** platforms one-story above street level.

The color-coded eL lines culminate in the heart of the city and "loop" around downtown. Two exceptions, the Red and Blue Lines, descend into subways downtown and tunnel under the Loop.

See page 310 for a detailed map of all Chicago CTA eL stops.

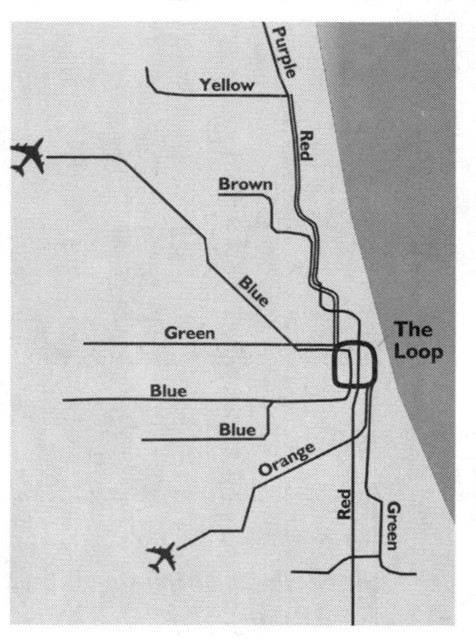

Metra: Training in from the suburbs

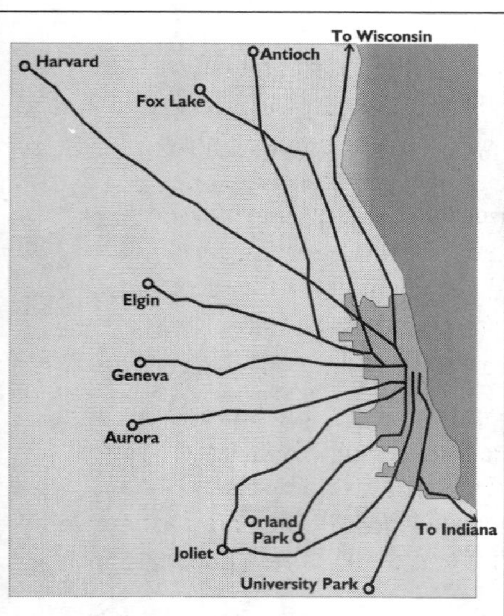

Metra trains can get you into Chicago from all corners of suburbia.

Metra is the train that runs from almost all the Chicago suburbs to the city. Metra riders swear by it and seem to feel sorry for folks dealing with traffic congestion on the highways. For under $10, you can travel from the farthest reaches of suburbia, and even parts of Indiana and Wisconsin. The trains are quiet, comfortable and great for reading.

For more about Metra, log on to **www.metrarail.com** or call **312/322-6777.**

Regional Transit Authority has a special hotline that can help you figure out how to get from any point A to any point B. Call the Hotline– **836-7000,** in any area code– and get advice regarding the use of Metra, CTA buses, eL trains, and the Pace suburban bus system.

This castle hath a pleasant seat. The air
Nimbly and sweetly recommends itself
Unto our gentle senses.

By Chris Gatto

Chicagoans live in neighborhoods. It's part of our identity: first name, last name, and neighborhood. The lines between such close-knit areas are loose at best; just ask any two people and they'll give you different boundary lines for every neighborhood. But what is clearly defined is that each community has an ever-evolving, specific, well…personality. Your mission, should you choose to accept it, is to find the neighborhood that best fits your personality and budget.

To find the right neighborhood, you'll first need to figure out how navigate the city and, depending on your mode of transport, this can vary in degree of difficulty. The layout of the city is relatively simple; Chicago is set up on a grid system with streets running directly north/south and east/west, with a few "diagonal streets" thrown into the mix. State Street is 0E/W and Madison Street is 0N/S and addresses are counted upward from there. Main thoroughfares can be found just about every four blocks running every direction, so you're never far from a bus or eL line.

If your preferred mode of transport is of the public variety, the CTA (Chicago Transit Authority) provides two viable options: the bus and the eL. Bus lines run along every main street and are usually named by street name and route numbers (i.e. the #8 Halsted Bus). The eL (subway or elevated) lines each have two names as well. They are each identified by color and by final stops. Thus, the red line is also known as the Howard-Dan Ryan.

And if you have the double-edged sword known as a car, further delights await you. Don't let people scare you about the weather; we have two seasons here—winter and construction. The most prolific example can be seen on the local interstates, which have both numerical designations as well as names. Which means that 290 is also known as the Eisenhower and 55 is the Stevenson. Learning the names is important if you want to be able to decipher a traffic report.

Now that you have a broad idea of how to get around, where do you start exploring? This is where "The Book" comes to the rescue. The following are breakdowns for select Chicago neighborhoods. These neighborhoods have been chosen for specific reasons: either they are neighborhoods that house a significant amount of theatre or they are neighborhoods that are popular with actors, either for living or playing.

Neighborhood descriptions are totally unscientific and based on the personal experience of local residents, as well as the staffers who have helped with this book. Also included are average rental rates and comparative violent and total crime "grades." These grades are based on the crime statistics posted on the Chicago Police Department Web site for 2000. Violent crime includes person-on-person crimes like assault, sexual assault, murder, battery, mugging, etc. Total crime includes that number plus things like vandalism, theft, arson, etc. So if you see a neighborhood with an "A" for violent crime and a "D" for total crime, you can assume that your body will be safe, but your property may not.

All in all, this guide is a starting place. Most importantly, you should go to a neighborhood that seems interesting and walk around. Experience the sounds, smells, and sights for yourself. What is fascinating and exhilarating to one may be irritating and intolerable to another. You make the decision.

Mastering the Chicago street number system

The streets of Chicago form a grid that is conveniently numbered for your navigational sanity. Mastering this system will greatly assist you in getting to know the neighborhoods and helping you get around town.

Madison and State Street are the starting lines for this system. The major streets that form the grid increase in number by hundreds. Streets are numbered and tagged with a N, S, E, or W.

Examples: Fullerton is 2400 N., or 24 blocks north of Madison. Halsted is 800 W., or 8 blocks west of State Street.

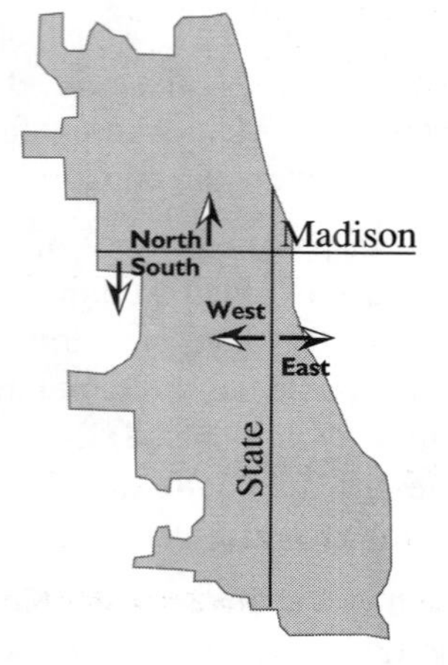

Andersonville

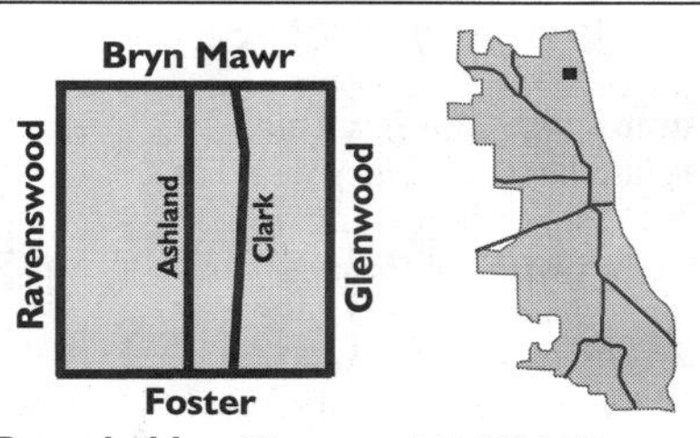

Bounded by: Glenwood (1400 W.), Ravenswood (1800 W.), Foster (5200 N.) and Bryn Mawr (5600 N.)

Rent: Studio: $590 1 Bedroom: $915 2 Bedroom: $1260

Violent Crime: A **Total Crime:** A

Comments: *Gentrification has been in full swing in this culturally diverse neighborhood. Andersonville has gotten more expensive over the years, but maintains a close-knit community feel. Historically Scandinavian, Andersonville is now home to a diverse population, including large Latino and Asian groups. The multi-ethnic personality of this community is seen in the vast selection of restaurants, including Scandinavian bakeries, the original Ann Sathers (a great place for pastries and light meals), and Reza's, the Mecca of Middle Eastern food. Additionally, Andersonville is also home to a large lesbian population. Theatre in the neighborhood is an integral part of the community, housing the Neo-Futurists and the Griffin. Actor-friendly hangouts include Simon's Tavern, Konak's, Hop Leaf and Kopi.*

Bucktown

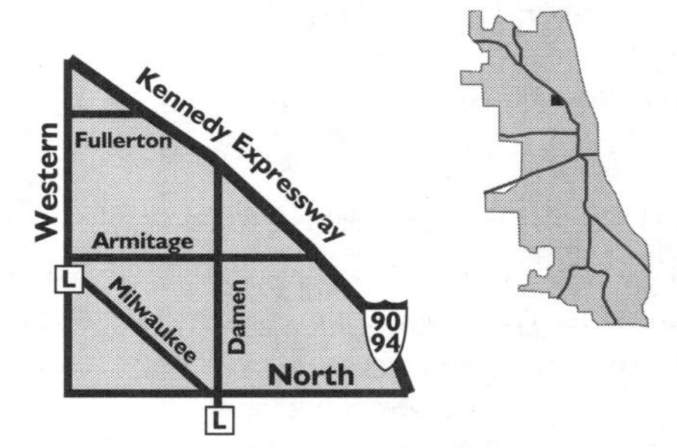

Bounded by: Kennedy Expressway, Western (2400 W.), North (1600 N.) and Fullerton (2400 N.)

Rent: Studio: $690
1Bedroom: $975 2 Bedroom: $1110

Violent Crime: C- **Total Crime:** D

Comments: *With an expressway and industrial corridor running along its northeast border, Bucktown has been called home by an increasing number of actors and artists. Gentrification, however, has made this neighborhood, like many others, increasingly expensive. Still, it maintains its bohemian flair (albeit at a slightly elevated dollar amount). Great theatre is located here, including Trap Door theatre company, which has recently expanded itself as casting a agency.*

Neighborhood Map Key:

M *–Metra Train Stop*	++++++++++++ *–Train Tracks*
L *– eL Train Stop*	**Street name** *–Streets*

Buena Park

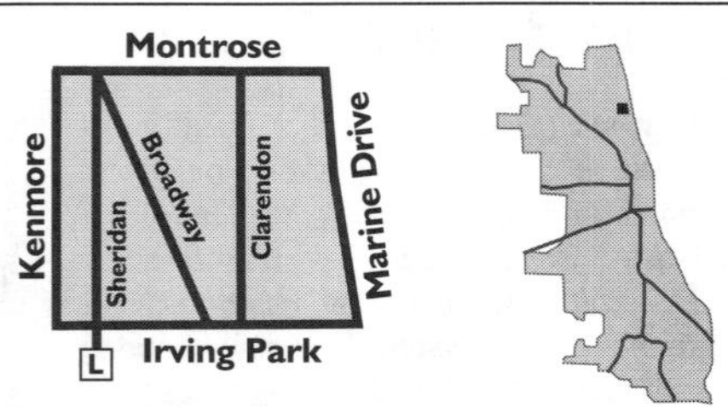

Bounded by: Marine Drive, Kenmore, Irving Park (4000 N.) and Montrose (4400 N.)

Rent: Studio: $640
1 Bedroom: $835 2 Bedroom: $1400

Violent Crime: A **Total Crime:** A

Comments: *This north side neighborhood is "homey for being urban," says one resident. The eastern portion of this neighborhood is lined with parks overlooking the lake as well as Lake Shore Drive, a convenient commuting artery. As you move west into the neighborhood itself, you find that Buena Park indeed has an urban personality, populated with apartment buildings, easy public transportation, but somewhat increasingly difficult parking. The many actors who live here have positive things to say, citing easy transportation access and accessible distance to theatres and theatre-related fare. National Pastime is one of several theatres in the neighborhood (Mary-Arrchie and Strawdog are located just south of the Irving Park boundary).*

Edgewater

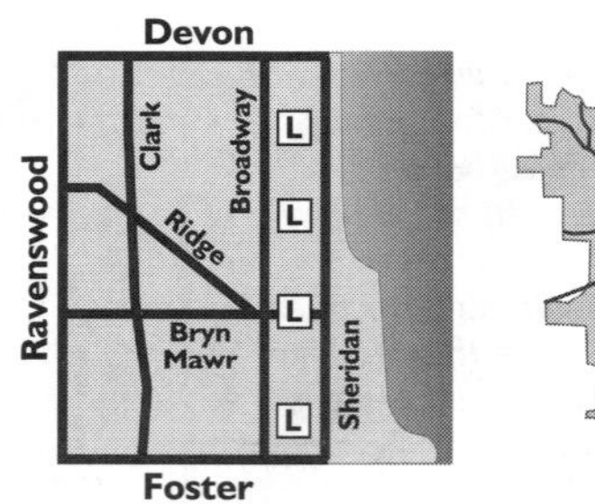

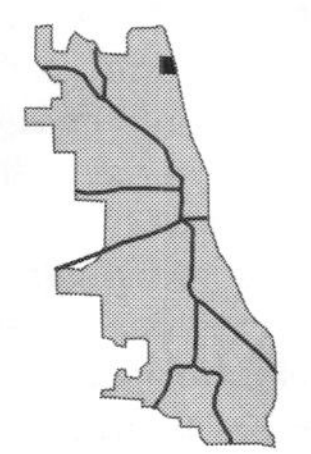

Bounded by: Lake Michigan, Ravenswood (1800 W.), Foster (5200 N.) and Devon (6400 N.)

Rent: Studio: $540
1 Bedroom: $735 2 Bedroom: $975

Violent Crime: A **Total Crime:** A

Comments: *Edgewater is an area that has seen incredible revitalization in recent years. Originally settled by German, Swedish, and Irish immigrants, this community started as a posh residential subdivision for some of Chicago's most prosperous families and entrepreneurs. Today it's a somewhat inexpensive area that is easily accessible by public transportation, so you don't necessarily need a car. Speaking of which, parking can range from spotty-good to OK, depending on what part of the neighborhood. The "Artists in Residence" building—a residence which solely houses artists of all persuasions—is located here.*

Neighborhood Map Key:

M *–Metra Train Stop*
L *– eL Train Stop*
++++++++++ *–Train Tracks*
Street name *–Streets*

Humboldt Park

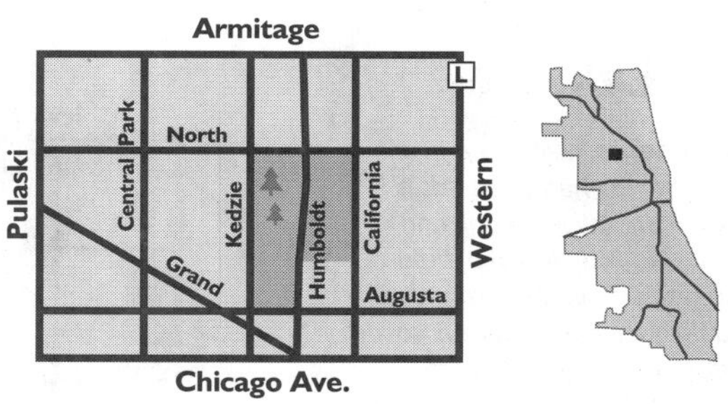

Bounded by: Western (2400 W.), Pulaski (4000 W.) Chicago (800 N.) and Armitage (2000 N.)

Rent: Studio: $510
1Bedroom: $685 2 Bedroom: $895

Violent Crime: D **Total Crime:** D

Comments: *Humboldt Park is home to a large number of young artists, partially due to its low rents. Something must be said for the neighborhood, however, which surrounds its namesake, Humboldt Park. The park itself is part of the vast boulevard system designed to link all of Chicago's parks from the north to the south sides, and really is beautiful and worth a visit during the spring, summer and fall months. This is a largely Latino community with a deep and strong sense of community. As for transportation, the area is extremely accessible by bus or car, especially since parking isn't terrible, but there is only one eL stop on the east side of the neighborhood. Unfortunately, the neighborhood is still dealing with problems associated with gang activity in the area.*

Hyde Park

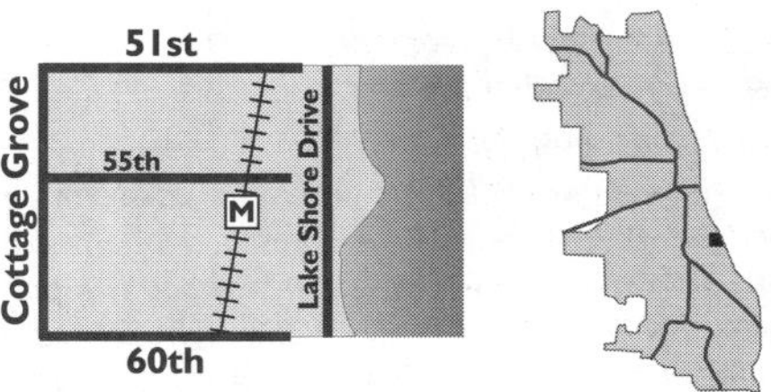

Bounded by: Lake Michigan, Cottage Grove, 60th (6000 S.) and 51st (5100 S.)

Rent: Studio: $455
1Bedroom: $565 2 Bedroom: $870

Violent Crime: B **Total Crime:** B

Comments: *This is a diverse college community tucked among the neighborhoods of the south side. It's prominent feature is the University of Chicago (famous for the first controlled nuclear reaction, among other things), and the neighborhood reflects the lifestyles of professors and students alike. Its diverse, has a lot of bookstores, and even has the highest percentage of Nobel prize winners living in the city. A short jaunt to the South Shore Cultural Center and the Museum of Science and Industry, Hyde Park is home to some of the most beautiful residential architecture in the city. While accessibility to and from Hyde Park is not a problem (although public transport can take a while with a few transfers), a car is somewhat recommended—especially for trips to and though surrounding areas, as they can be a bit dicey. Still, on a beautiful summer day (or night), you can slip a short distance over to Comiskey Park for a Sox game (complete with fireworks at an evening game), where the southsiders can credibly boast better Italian ice than their north side rivals. Court Theatre is located in Hyde Park.*

---

akeview

Comments: *Lakeview is one of those neighborhoods that is awake and alive all day and night. No matter what time of the day, people are around—partially because there is so much to do, not the least of which includes a large theatre scene. Bars, clubs, restaurants, theatres, and that north side ballpark—Wrigley Field—all feed into the life of Lakeview.*

If you're hungry, there is no lack of options. Penny's Noodles has expediently and inexpensively fed more than one actor before rehearsal or curtain call, the Pick Me Up café has great food in a great atmosphere, or if you're looking for a killer greasy spoon, The Diner is another inexpensive option. Other actor hangouts include the L&L Tavern and Bar San Miguel.

Bounded by: Lake Michigan, Ashland (1600 W.), Diversey (2800 N.) and Irving Park (4000 N.)

Rent: Studio: $720
1 Bedroom: $960
2 Bedroom: $1680

Violent Crime: A

Total Crime: B

Many young professionals, new college grads as well as actors live in Lakeview, which is perceived (with enough statistical proof) to be one of the safest neighborhoods in the city. Easily accessible by bus and especially the eL lines, the neighborhood is a parking nightmare for the very reasons that make it a great place to live—the nightlife and the ballpark. Lakeview is somewhat of a theatre hub, acting as home to the PerformInk offices, Sheil Park (a great rehearsal space resource), as well as theatres including Bailiwick Rep, WNEP, Stage Left, ComedySportz, ImprovOlympic, The Theatre Building and About Face. East Lakeview, primarily Halsted Street between Addison and Belmont, is known among the gay community as "Boys Town."

Lincoln Park

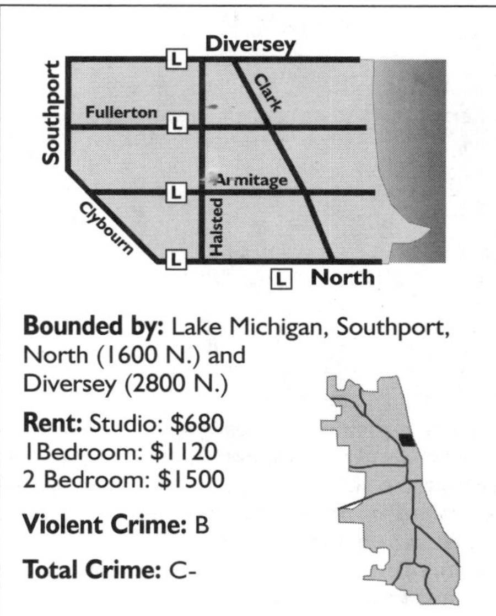

Comments: *The neighborhood landscape of Lincoln Park is beautiful; when you hear people refer to Chicago graystones or brownstones, Lincoln Park is one of the prime neighborhoods to browse these distinctive architectural mainstays of the city. Depending on one's preference or mood, Lincoln Park provides the best of urban life right alongside the best of outdoor and natural landscaping.*

Lincoln Park Zoo, one of the last free admission zoos, is open 365 days a year. Lincoln Park itself contains the Botanical Gardens, not to mention acres of bike paths, walking paths, refreshment stands, and playgrounds. On the other hand, the main thoroughfares running through the neighborhood of Lincoln Park are lined with all sorts of shops and boutiques, as well as restaurants and clubs, ranging from hip and trendy to high-end chic. This is an area easily accessible by public transportation, but extremely short on parking spots. Like its neighbor to the north, Lakeview, Lincoln Park is home to many young college-age adults attending nearby DePaul University, as well as young professionals.

The off-Loop theatre scene in large part started in Lincoln Park in the 1970s (ever hear of a little theatre called Steppenwolf?). Victory Gardens and the Royal George are also located here, as well as a much grown version of Steppenwolf. Sterch's and John Barleycorn are some notable actor hangouts in the neighborhood. The Biograph (where John Dillinger was shot) is located here as well. One of the most important resources for actors, Act I Bookstore, is located on Lincoln Avenue right next to the Apollo Theatre.

Lincoln Square

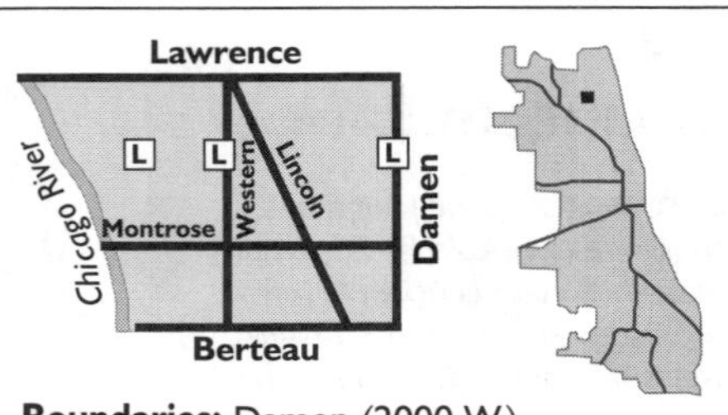

Boundaries: Damen (2000 W.), the Chicago River, Berteau (4200 N.) and Lawrence (4800 N.)

Rent: Studio: $525
1Bedroom: $785 2 Bedroom: $1245

Violent Crime: A **Total Crime:** B

Comments: *Once a north side, somewhat hidden secret, Lincoln Square has become a popular alternative to some of the more congested areas to the south. Lincoln Square is easily accessible by public transportation AND has generally decent parking. This is due in part to a mix of single-family homes and smaller apartment buildings. Historically, Lincoln Square was settled by German immigrants but is now a fairly even mix of Asian, Latino, and Caucasian families and young singles. Lincoln Avenue from Wilson to Lawrence is set up as a type of a town square, giving the area a real neighborhood, main street kind of feel. There are Greek, German, and American restaurants, antique shops, neighborhood bars, boutiques, and the Davis movie theatre on this section of Lincoln, as well as a little town square area, complete with a café, outdoor fountain and park benches. Don't forget to check out the fantastic German bakeries (and yes, there is a Starbucks). The Old Town School of Music is nestled here as well, and a number of theatres have set up shop in this area, including TinFish and Phoenix Ascending, to name a few*

Logan/Palmer Square

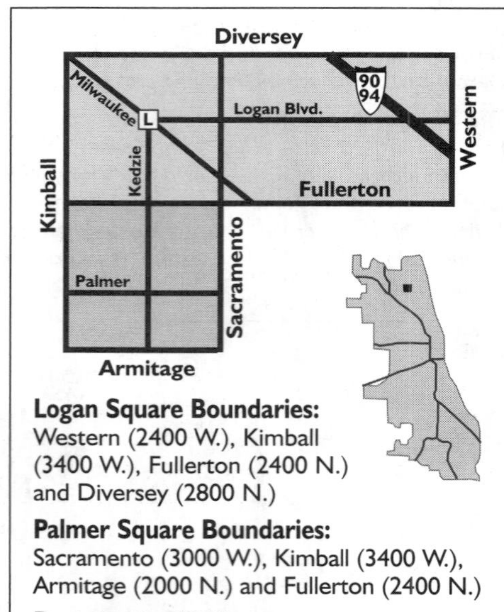

Logan Square Boundaries: Western (2400 W.), Kimball (3400 W.), Fullerton (2400 N.) and Diversey (2800 N.)

Palmer Square Boundaries: Sacramento (3000 W.), Kimball (3400 W.), Armitage (2000 N.) and Fullerton (2400 N.)

Rent: Studio: $550
1Bedroom: $785 2 Bedroom: $1320

Violent Crime: D **Total Crime:** D

Comments: *This area is extremely popular with artists of all persuasions. As a matter of fact, the artistic influx of the 1980-90s was one of the primary reasons for the area's increasing popularity and subsequent gentrification. This area is a tight community and diverse on all levels, including race, culture, class, you name it. Nineteenth century mansions still stand in the Palmer Square area. Logan Square is the starting point of the Boulevard system still in existence in Chicago. Redmoon Theatre Company is located in the Logan/Palmer area.*

Old Town

North
Larrabee
Clybourn
Wells
Clark
Division

Bounded by: Division (1200 N.), North (1600 N.), Clark (100 W.) and Larrabee (600 W.)

Rent: Studio: $680
1Bedroom: $965 2 Bedroom: $1700

Violent Crime: B **Total Crime:** D-

Comments: *The conjoined sister of Lincoln Park, Old Town is a well-established, fairly well-off neighborhood housing Chicago's Second City, A Red Orchid Theatre, and Zanies comedy club. Piper's Alley movie theatre is on the corner of North and Wells in the same building that houses Second City. Getting here is easy; parking, well, "fuggitaboutit," unless you pay. Lots of actor hangouts are in the neighborhood, including Corcoran's Grill and the Old Town Ale House, faves among the Second City crowd. Generally, this is a great, convenient location if you can afford it.*

Pilsen

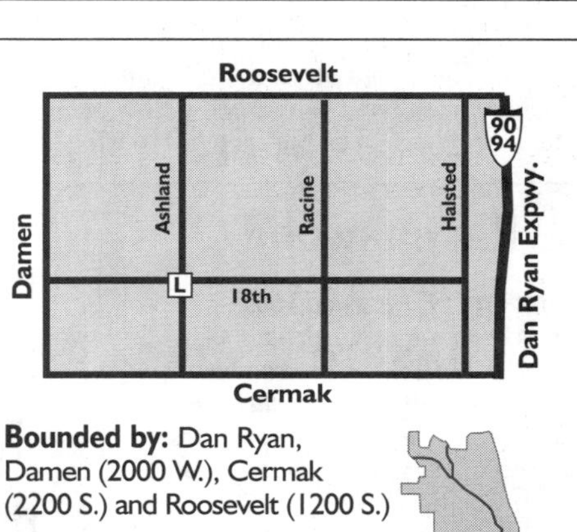

Bounded by: Dan Ryan, Damen (2000 W.), Cermak (2200 S.) and Roosevelt (1200 S.)

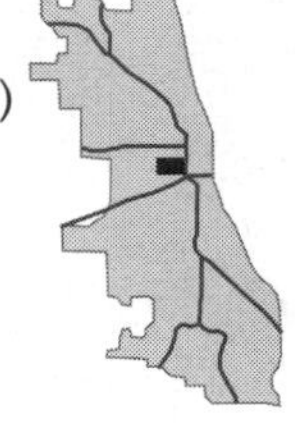

Rent: Studio: $375
1Bedroom: $580
2 Bedroom: $825

Violent Crime: D-

Total Crime: D

Comments: *Since its inception, Pilsen has been a hotbed for labor activism and social reform, as well as one of the doorways for generations of immigrants. Decades ago, Pilsen was mostly Irish and Polish, and the remnants of those cultures can still be seen. Now, Pilsen is the largest Mexican community in the United States and continues the tradition of struggle for political representation, educational reform, and worker's rights. There are lots of warehouses in the neighborhood which attract, among others, theatre companies, developers, and artists. Duncan YMCA Chernin Center for the Arts resides in this area and is the home to several small companies. The University of Illinois at Chicago (referred to as UIC or "Circle") anchors the area to the north.*

Neighborhood Map Key:

M *–Metra Train Stop*
L *– eL Train Stop*
++++++++++ *–Train Tracks*
Street name *–Streets*

Printer's Row/South Loop

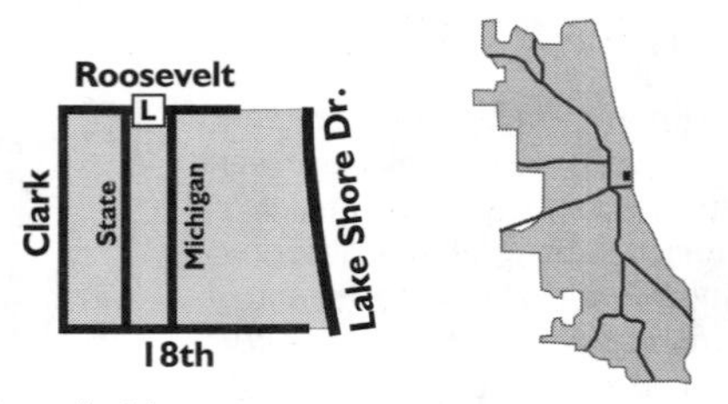

Bounded by: the Lakefront, Clark (100 W.), 18th (1800 S.) and Roosevelt (1200 S.)

Rent: Studio: $915
1Bedroom: $1480 2 Bedroom: $1870

Violent Crime: A **Total Crime:** B

Comments: *This area was a vast wasteland a mere 15 years ago. Abandoned freight yards, rising crime and visible prostitution were all symptoms of the decline of this former industrial hub. Recently, large-scale gentrification has turned this area into one of the city's newest desirables, listing Mayor Daley as one of its current residents. Transportation is readily accessible via bus or eL, but parking is scarce unless your residence of choice comes with attached parking. Practically speaking, however, you don't need a car if you live in this area. Not only is getting around easy, but also the area is in close proximity to many of the city's hallmarks, including Grant Park, Soldiers Field, the Planetarium, the Oceanarium, and the Art Institute. Printer's Row is also the site for the annual Printer's Row Book Fair, where publishers and authors alike come to sell their wares and avid readers come to meet writers and sift out great bargains. It's close enough to downtown to take advantage of all the Loop has to offer, but has a distinctively residential feel.*

Ravenswood

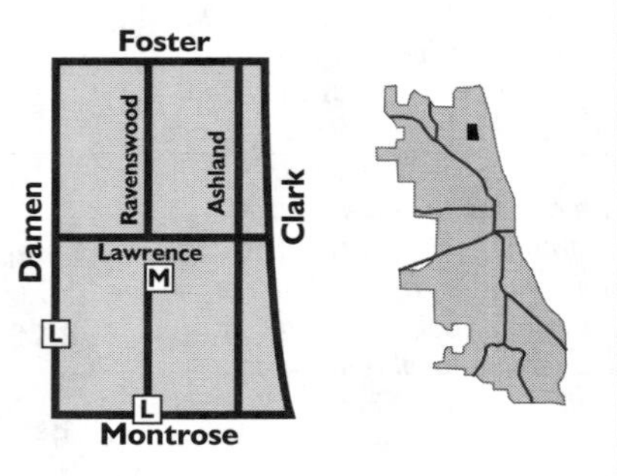

Bounded by: Clark, Damen (2000 W.), Montrose (4400 N.) and Foster (5200 N.)

Rent: Studio: $600
1Bedroom: $830 2 Bedroom: $1100

Violent Crime: A **Total Crime:** B

Comments: *Ravenswood has always been a family neighborhood. Since the 1940-50s, the area has been consistently working class, but recent gentrification of the area has changed the economic landscape of the neighborhood. Many young professional families and singles have arrived, consequently driving up real estate and rents. If you're looking for a small town neighborhood feel in a big city, this is the place. Like its neighbor to the west, Lincoln Square, public transportation is readily and dependably available and has some pretty good parking karma as city neighborhoods go. Pauline's, known for great breakfast fare, and the Zephyr, famous with locals for grotesquely large portions of fabulous ice cream, used to be the only viable hangouts in such a heavily residential neighborhood. In the past year or two, however, Montrose Avenue and the area just west of the Zephyr on Wilson Avenue have been developed, spawning numerous mom and pop shops, including coffee shops, a pizza joint (as we natives like to say), and an Italian restaurant.*

River West

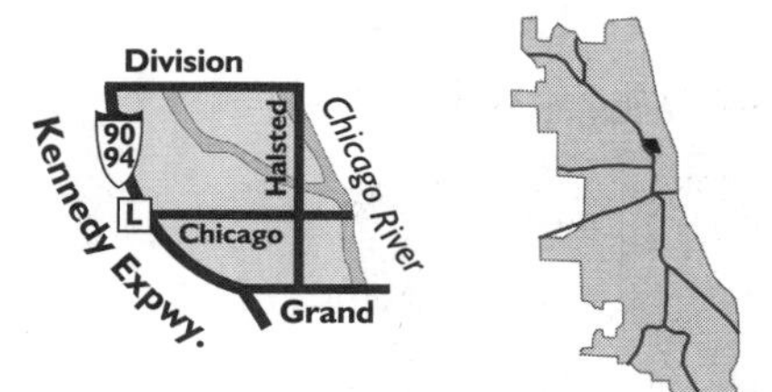

Bounded by: the Chicago River, the Kennedy Expressway, Grand (500 N.) and Division (1200 N.)

Rent: Studio: $700
1Bedroom: $990 2 Bedroom: $1500

Violent Crime: A **Total Crime:** A

Comments: *River West is bounded on the east by its namesake landmark the Chicago River-which was altered in 1900 by reversing the flow of the current, thereby preventing Chicagoans from choking on their own sewage, and is also dyed bright green (as opposed to the usual tint of fatigue green) for the annual St. Pat's Day celebration. Large warehouses and loft spaces make up River West, which has historically been an industrial and shipping corridor. These spaces, however, have long been abandoned for their intended uses and have been hungrily gobbled up by developers looking for property with chic and trendy potential. And so, an area of industrial grit and sweat has become one of the most trendy, sought after neighborhoods in the city. Clubs and restaurants are beginning to pop up; the Green Dolphin is a club on the far west side of this neighborhood which started as a trendy jazz club and grew to a top line restaurant and lounge, often requiring reservations.*

Chicago Dramatist Workshop is in the heart of River West, as is the Chicago Academy for the Arts—Chicago's answer to "Fame." Many filmmakers and companies make their homes here, to a greater extent than theatre artists do. Strangely, while the proximity to the Loop is close, public transportation is less accessible here, so a car is generally a good idea. The closest grocery store, for instance, is across the river in the Gold Coast.

gers Park

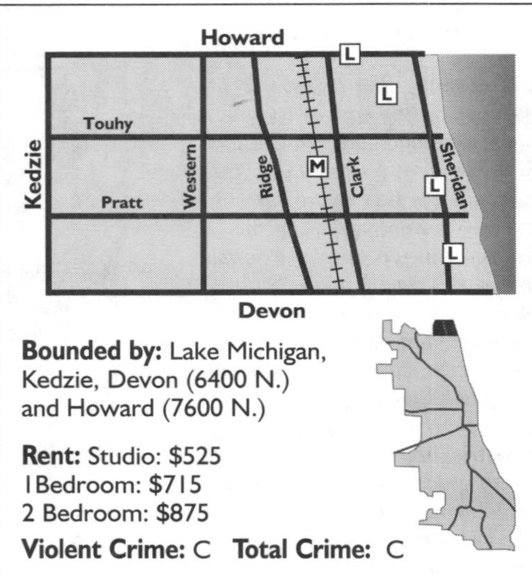

Bounded by: Lake Michigan, Kedzie, Devon (6400 N.) and Howard (7600 N.)

Rent: Studio: $525
1Bedroom: $715
2 Bedroom: $875

Violent Crime: C **Total Crime:** C

ents: *Rogers Park is the northernmost neighborhood in Chicago, bordering Evanston, and is extremely popular with actors and artists for many reasons, not the least of which include relatively cheap rents and good access to public transportation. Down side: Don't bother bringing a car here, especially if you intend to habitually arrive home after 9 p.m., as parking is brutal. Having said that, Rogers Park covers a huge area and feels as if it contains several neighborhoods with very distinctive personalities. The eastern most area, around Sheridan Road, is home to coffee shops and movie theatres as well as other small businesses and steady public transportation via bus. Many older professionals live in this area, which also seems to have a mixture of academia (probably the influence of Loyola University just south and Northwestern to the north) and a young artistic bohemian feel. Gradually west of that, the area is mixed, depending on your location north or south. In the northern reaches of the area, it can get a bit scary, especially at night, as there is some visible prostitution, vagrancy, and drug dealing. The southern parts are mixed in every sense: economically, ethnically, and culturally. The most western reaches boast a large working class Latino population, mostly families, which give the area a community feel. The Heartland Café is a popular artist and actor hangout as well as a performance space. Raven, Boxer Rebellion and Lifeline are some of the theatres in this area. As a matter of fact, Raven will soon be housed in a refurbished facility in a new Rogers Park Location.*

Roscoe Village

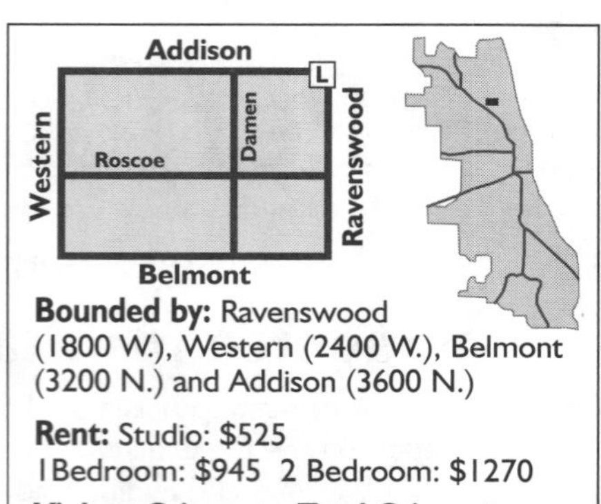

Bounded by: Ravenswood (1800 W.), Western (2400 W.), Belmont (3200 N.) and Addison (3600 N.)

Rent: Studio: $525
1Bedroom: $945 2 Bedroom: $1270

Violent Crime: A **Total Crime:** B

Comments: *This is a close-knit neighborhood, home to many families and young professionals, but for the most part, you'll need to take a short trip either east or north for the nearest entertainment and nightlife. Still, there are some actor hangouts here of note, particularly the Village Tap and the Four Moon Tavern, which is owned and managed by four actors. Roscoe Village also has many small boutiques and restaurants. Formerly a neighborhood where young newbies to Chicago could flee the higher rents of Lakeview and Lincoln Park, Roscoe Village and its sister neighborhood, St. Ben's, are now relatively competitive and as expensive as their nearby neighbors.*

Saint Ben's

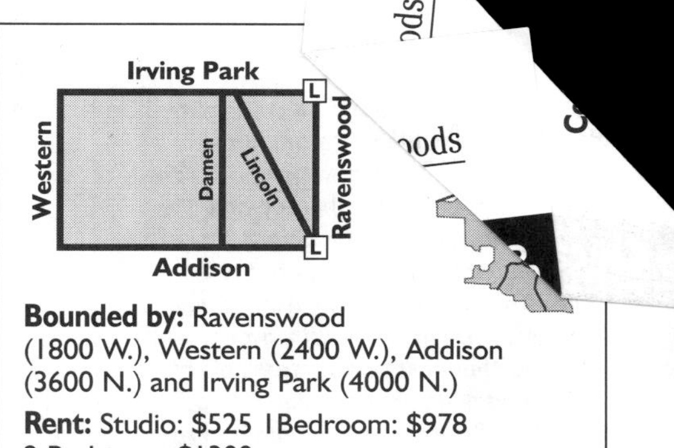

Bounded by: Ravenswood (1800 W.), Western (2400 W.), Addison (3600 N.) and Irving Park (4000 N.)

Rent: Studio: $525 1Bedroom: $978 2 Bedroom: $1300

Violent Crime: A **Total Crime:** B

Comments: *The sister neighborhood to Roscoe Village is named for the Catholic parish, St. Ben's, whose church spire can be seen as one of the distinctive landmarks of the area. Many families can be found here, living in single-family homes or two- and three-flats. Historically, the area has been working class, but with rising real estate values and rents, the population has become increasingly professional. American Theatre Company and Breadline Theatre Group are located in this neighborhood.*

Ukrainian Village

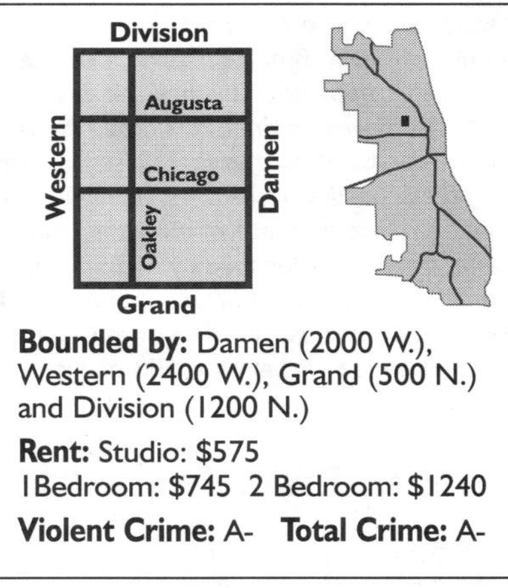

Bounded by: Damen (2000 W.), Western (2400 W.), Grand (500 N.) and Division (1200 N.)

Rent: Studio: $575 1Bedroom: $745 2 Bedroom: $1240

Violent Crime: A- **Total Crime:** A-

Comments: *Named for its large Ukrainian population, this neighborhood is also home to a number of other ethnicities, including Italians, Hispanics, and African-Americans. This diversity is due part to the heavily Hispanic influence of neighboring Humboldt Park, and the large Italian populations concentrated along Grand Avenue all the way to Taylor Street (known as "Little Italy"). These populations are augmented by artists who have flocked to housing in this area, which remains affordable although rents are rapidly on the rise. It's a close-knit community where people watch out for one another, which can be reiief or a nuisance depending on your point of view. Public transportation can be a hassle since only the buses, not the eL, serve the area but parking is generally OK, depending on where you're at.*

Uptown

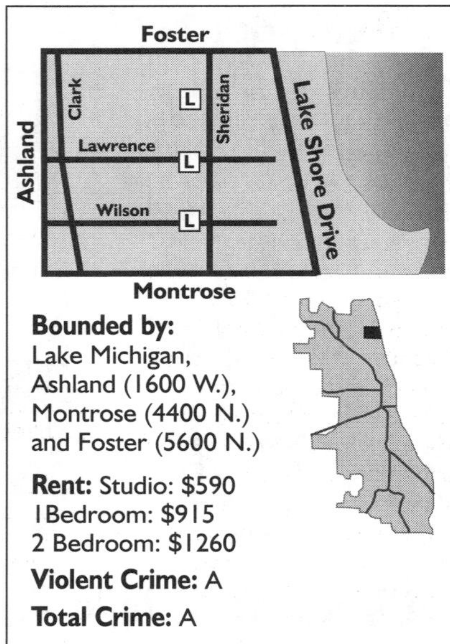

Bounded by:
Lake Michigan,
Ashland (1600 W.),
Montrose (4400 N.)
and Foster (5600 N.)

Rent: Studio: $590
1Bedroom: $915
2 Bedroom: $1260

Violent Crime: A

Total Crime: A

Comments: *Uptown is as culturally diverse as its neighbor to the north, Rogers Park. But while walking through Uptown, it becomes apparent that the neighborhood has held a unique place in the history and development of entertainers and their industry, as well as to the development of the city, over the last century. The massive structures of the old movie and dance houses along Broadway, including The Aragon Ballroom and the Uptown theatre, stand as a noble, if not presently tired-looking reminder to this old "Bright Light District's" past. The former Essanay Movie Studios (now St. Augustine College), one of the cradles of early American film, is located here and housed Charlie Chaplin's studio before he headed west. The Green Mill, a jazz club on the corner of Broadway and Lawrence, has been a popular club since the days when Al Capone roamed this area fostering drama to rival any movie plot line. Eventually, however, the area fell into a slump, attracting seedier types and diversions. Empty or run-down buildings, including the Goldblatt's Department Store just south of Lawrence, are evidence of a bustling neighborhood fallen to disrepair and neglect, only to be gradually awakened by recent rehab projects and community involvement. Public transportation is good in the area and parking is OK, if you can be assured that you'll have relatively close parking to your home if returning late at night. Pegasus Players is in the area, as part of Truman College.*

Wrigleyville

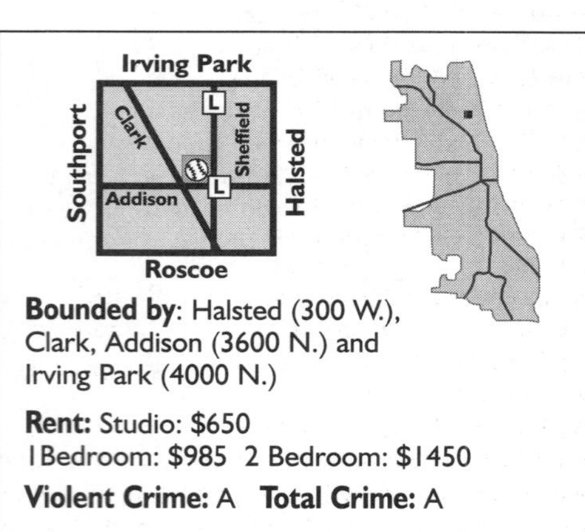

Bounded by: Halsted (300 W.), Clark, Addison (3600 N.) and Irving Park (4000 N.)

Rent: Studio: $650
1Bedroom: $985 2 Bedroom: $1450

Violent Crime: A **Total Crime:** A

Comments: *The home of the Cubs makes up the economic center of this neighborhood. Sports bars and clubs, restaurants and coffee houses flourish. You can get a great hot dog and sushi within a very short distance, which is a good thing since parking can be a nightmare during baseball season and Friday or Saturday nights year round. The area is also close to several theatres and much nightlife. Wrigleyville is home to many young families and yuppies. Technically, the neighborhood is part of Lakeview, but the distinct personality of the area gives Wrigleyville a feeling all its own.*

West Loop/ Greektown

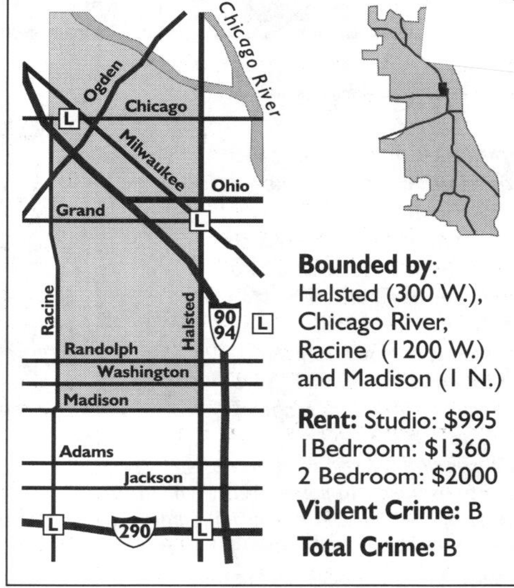

Bounded by: Halsted (300 W.), Chicago River, Racine (1200 W.) and Madison (1 N.)

Rent: Studio: $995
1Bedroom: $1360
2 Bedroom: $2000

Violent Crime: B

Total Crime: B

Comments: *This area is located exactly where you might suspect—directly west of downtown. This neighborhood is inclusive of both what is now known as Greek Town as well as the area adjacently north and west, which runs mostly along Randolph Street. Years ago, as far back as the Depression, Randolph was a bustling wholesale marketplace, selling goods such as meats, fish, and produce to local grocers and restaurateurs. Walking along Washington between Halsted and Racine, you can see the remnants of warehouses newly converted to loft condominiums and office buildings: Working class history meets gentrification. Because of this phenomenon, most of the converted residential property here has been turned into condominiums sprinkled with some rental property. Harpo Studios, owned by talk show queen, Oprah Winfrey, the Lou Conte Dance Studio, and Roadworks all have studios here. Note to chocolate lovers: On a good day, you can smell the chocolate wafting from the Fannie May Candies factory not far away!*

Wicker Park

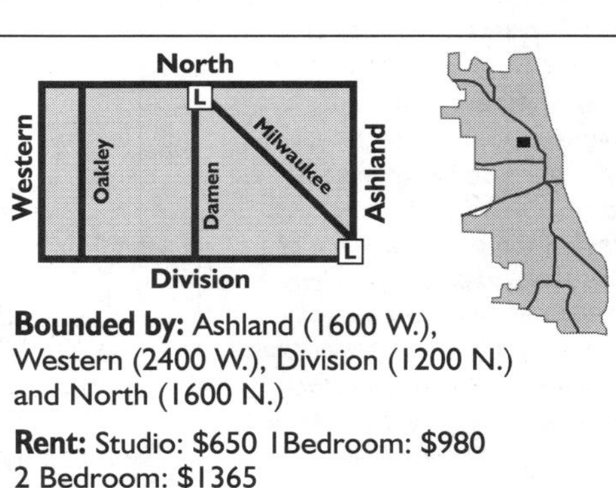

Bounded by: Ashland (1600 W.), Western (2400 W.), Division (1200 N.) and North (1600 N.)

Rent: Studio: $650 1Bedroom: $980
2 Bedroom: $1365

Violent Crime: D **Total Crime:** D

Comments: *Wicker Park is generally known as home to young trendy artists. Easily accessed by public transportation, this neighborhood has a lot of great bars and cafes, as well as superb small restaurants. One of the most popular hangouts in the area is the Subterranean. So trendy and hip is this neighborhood that the producers of Real World decided to bring their caravan to set up camp in Wicker Park during the summer of 2001, to the dismay of many local residents who worried about the commercialization of the area, as well as the practicality of reduced parking. Wicker Park is the area where Nelson Algren lived and wrote; the neighborhood is as tough and beautiful as an Algren book. There aren't a lot of theatres in the immediate area and if you want to get to Lincoln Park or Lakeview for rehearsal, let's say, you have take the eL to downtown and then come back north on a different eL line. Still, there is always bus transportation down North Avenue, Ashland and Damen.*

Select Suburbs

Evanston

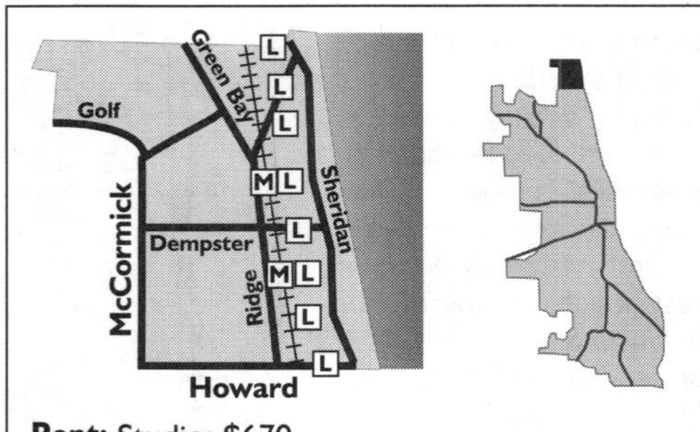

Rent: Studio: $670
1Bedroom: $850 2 Bedroom: $1020

Comments: *Evanston lies just to the north of the city, along the lake. Home to Northwestern University, which has produced such theatre and film names as Charlton Heston and David Schwimmer, Evanston is a "down to earth, well-rounded community," says one resident. The landscape of Evanston is made up primarily of houses and mansions. It can be quite exclusive in some areas, while remaining quite affordable around the university or west of the Ridge Street dividing line. Public transportation in Evanston includes buses as well as the "Purple" eL line that can get you from Evanston to Lakeview in 20-30 minutes. Living here is generally more expensive than living in the city; if you're in a buying mood, the taxes can total more than your mortgage payment. Fleetwood Jourdain is an African-American theatre that has been there for years. The famed Piven Theatre Workshop, from whence local talents Jeremy Piven, John and Joan Cusack trained, as well as The Actor's Gymnasium and Next Theatre are also located in the same Evanston facility. Additionally, the city is making good on its commitment to the arts by building a new cultural center.*

Forest Park

Comments: *Not to be confused with its south suburban sister of similar name, this WEST suburb sits west of the city on the hip of Oak Park, so to speak. The community itself is culturally diverse and is the home of the Jeff-winning Circle Theatre. Transportation into the city is a cinch; the blue line labeled "Forest Park" goes right to its Harlem Avenue border, not to mention the numerous bus lines servicing the area.*

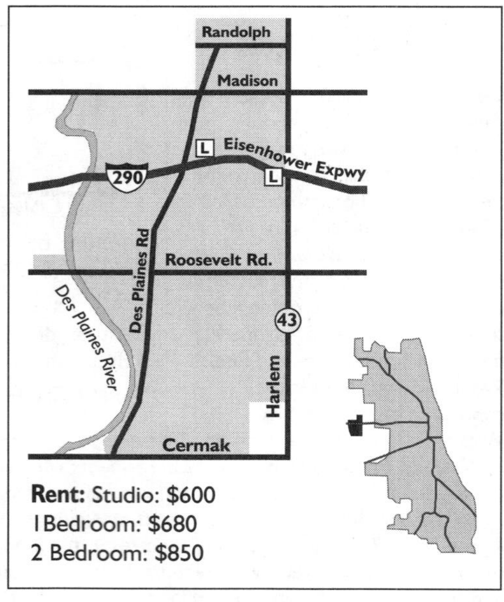

Rent: Studio: $600
1Bedroom: $680
2 Bedroom: $850

Oak Park

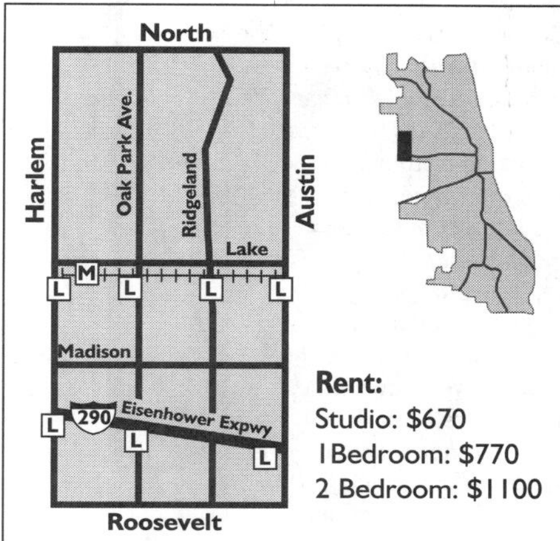

Comments: *Just west of the city, Oak Park is close, easily accessible, diverse, and fairly affordable. Famous for the architecture of Frank Lloyd Wright and as the home of Ernest Hemingway, Oak Park is home to many actors, including Steppenwolf company member John Mahoney. Oak Park has a village feel; you can walk anywhere. The downtown area, which runs along Lake Street just east of Harlem Avenue, has a main street feel. Coffee shops, restaurants, the movie theatre The Lake, stores and bookshops are all within walking distance for most residents. Both the "Green" and "Blue" eL lines go out to Oak Park, the former running directly into the Oak Park downtown area. The Metra lines and buses are also accessible. Taxes, once again, if you're in the mood to buy can be a bit stifling. There is a significant gay population in Oak Park. In fact, this progressive city is one of the few in the country who give domestic partnership benefits to gay spouses of city employees. Oak Park Village Players are located here as well as the Oak Park Shakespeare Festival, which is a staple for actors and theatregoers every summer.*

Northbrook

Comments: *This northern suburb is nestled approximately 25 miles from the Loop. Ensconced by forest preserves, Northbrook is located right between the Tri-State (294 for those of you keener on numbers) and the Edens (94) and is serviced by Metra, which makes this location extremely commuter-friendly. The community consists of a good deal of professionals, many with families. Demographically this is a high income, low crime area. Conveniently enough, Northbrook Theatre is located here.*

Rent:
1Bedroom: $800
2 Bedroom: $1100

Park Forest

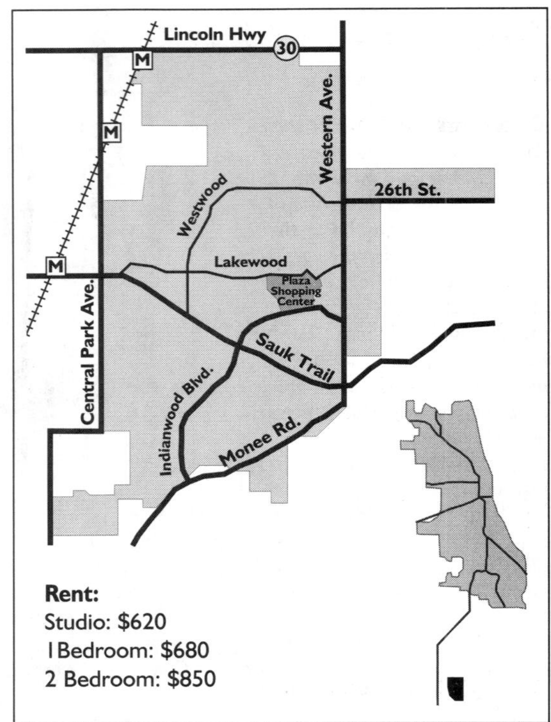

Comments: *Not to be confused with its west suburban sister of similar name, this SOUTH suburb is located a stone's throw from Interstate 57 and, to the interest of you avid shoppers out there, boasts one of the original "regional shopping malls." Don't flock out to see the mall just yet, however, as it has since been demolished but has served as the prototype for Oak Brook, Old Orchard and Water Tower Place. Among the old retail buildings now stands the new home of the equity theatre, Illinois Theatre Center (ITC for short), as well as the Tall Grass Arts Association Art Gallery and school. As for the rest of the mall structures, the town is working toward a more hometown feel, and the demolition has paved the way for Park Forest's "Main Street," which will be the main drag for retail, arts, and cultural organizations. The community itself is a mix of working class and professional, with a comparatively low crime rate (in comparison to other cities in the county).*

Skokie

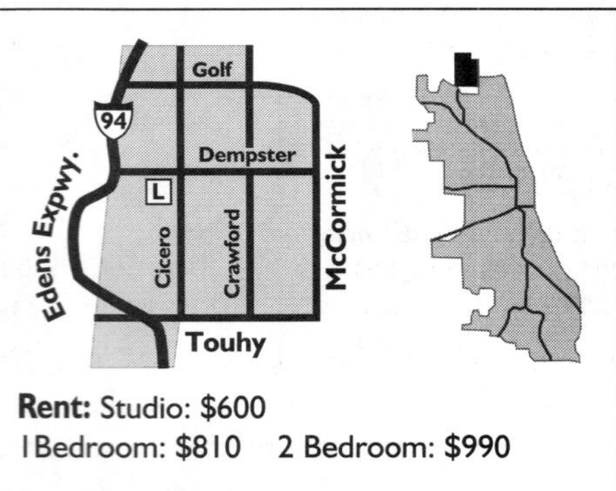

Comments: *Skokie is more diverse and less expensive than its neighbor to the east, Evanston. Traditionally, the area has been largely Jewish, but over the years has included a large number of Asians and Latinos. The schools have a solid reputation, and there is an active park district. Buses are available and make it easy to reach the Howard eL stop in Evanston. You can also take the "Skokie Swift," the one-stop extension of the eL that deposits riders at the Greyhound bus terminal. The Northshore Center for the Performing Arts is home to Northlight Theatre, along with the presenting company Centre East. Many companies also rent space in the North Shore Center.*

Helpful Phone Numbers

Police (NON EMERGENCY)
311

Examples: My cat is up a tree.

My boyfriend is up a tree.

Can you tell me where I can get my vehicle sticker?

Summertime: There's a hydrant open.

Winter: My street is rife with chairs and furniture debris. (If you're new to the city, wait one winter and you'll know what this means.)

Police (EMERGENCY)
911

Example: My rabid cat is holding my boyfriend hostage with a vehicle sticker in a tree.

Chicago Fire Department:
312/347-1313

City of Chicago Department of Housing, Tenant Hotline
773/292-4988

Water (not bottled)
312/744-7001

Office of Special Events
312/744-3315

(a.k.a "Hey, what's going on in my neighborhood this week?")

Chicago Park District
312/747-2200

Department of Revenue
312/744-PARK

This is where you pay parking tickets. Even the most anally vigilant of us can be afflicted with this orange scourge. Signs sometimes seem to be posted by invisible sprites while we are innocently parked. At any rate, be extra careful since a meter violation can carry with it a $50 fine, and parking in front of a hydrant a mere $100 and possible towing. Two words of advice: 1) Pay the parking lot, for God's sake, if you can't find a spot, and 2) You don't want the city towing your car. Think about it. Just trust us on this one.

RTA Travel Info
312/836-7000
Hearing Impaired: 312/836-4949
(www.transitchicago.com)

Information on RTA, CTA, PACE and Metra available seven days a week, including holidays, 4:45 a.m. to 1:00 a.m. Plan trips on the CTA, Metra commuter rail lines and Pace suburban bus by accessing this Web based itinerary planning service. Users receive a detailed transit itinerary.

People's Gas (heat/cooking gas utility)
866/556-6002 (toll free)

Com Ed (electrical utility)
1-800-EDISON-1

Ameritech (telephone utility)
1-800-244-4444

---

www.cityofchicago.org

Okay, this is a Web site, but it will give you loads of contact information, including which alderman belongs to your ward and any other information not included within these sage pages.

Coming to Chic

...tment Services

Century 21 - Amquest
2843 N. Halsted
Chicago, IL 60657
773/404-2100
773/404-6034 - fax
www.century21amquest.com

City Living Apartment Rentals
1300 W. Belmont
Chicago, IL 60657
773/525-6161

The Apartment People
3121 N. Broadway
Chicago, IL 60657
773/248-8800 • 773/248-1007 - fax
www.apartmentpeople.com

Apartment Source
2638 N. Halsted
Chicago, IL 60614
773/404-9900
773/404-0669 - fax

Oak Park Regional Housing Center
1041 South Blvd.
Oak Park, IL 60302
708/848-7150
members.aol.com/RENTinOP/oprhc.html

Cagan Management
3856 W. Oakton St.
Skokie, IL 60076
847/679-5512
847/679-5516 - fax

Realty & Mortgage
928 W. Diversey
Chicago, IL 60614
773/549-8300
www.aptrentals.com

Urban Equities R.E.C.
6240 N. Clark
Chicago, IL 60660
773/743-4141
773/465-4672 - fax

Apartment Connection
1000 W. Diversey
Chicago, IL 60614
773/525-3888
773/525-0210 - fax

Relcon Apartment Finders
21 W. Elm - 2nd floor
Chicago, IL 60610
312/255-9920
312/255-9928 - fax
www.relconapartments.com

Housing

Artist in Residence
6165 N. Winthrop
Chicago, IL 60660
800/LIVE-ART
773/743-8900
773/743-8259 - fax
www.artistsinresidence.com

Artist in Residence has been a home to artists since 1979. We rent solely to people active in fine or applied arts. We have facilities available for use by our residents, including rehearsal spaces, painter's and sculptor's workshops and darkroom. For more information and appointment, call 773/743-8900 or 1-800-LIVE-ART.

Eleanor Residence
Women Only
1550 N. Dearborn
Chicago, IL 60610
312/664-8245
312/664-0888 - fax
eleanorresidence.com

Three Arts Club (for women)
(men - June, July, August only)
1300 N. Dearborn
Chicago, IL 60610
312/944-6250
312/944-6284 - fax
www.threearts.org

Sovereign Apartments
1040 W. Granville
Chicago, IL 60660
773/274-8000
773/274-1321 - fax

Under the Ginkgo Tree (Bed & Breakfast)
Gloria Onischuk
300 N. Kenilworth
Oak Park, IL 60302
708/524-2327
708/524-2729 - fax

Under the Ginkgo Tree Bed and Breakfast Home: The Bed and Breakfast home in the historic district of Oak Park.

A spacious home ideally used for filming, photo shoots, etc.

Utilities

Chicago-based utilities Ameritech, ComEd and People's Gas are vilified by residents frequently and with great imagination. Poor service, uninformed representatives and order errors are all too common. The secret to a good (or tolerable anyway) relationship with these fine institutions is to call. Then call to confirm. You may want to follow up to confirm the confirmation.

Commonwealth Edison
800/334-7661
www.ceco.com/comed/main.asp

Peoples Gas Light & Coke Co.
130 Randolph
Chicago, IL 60601
312/240-4000

AT&T
800/222-0300

Sprint
800/877-7746

MCI
800/950-5555

Ameritech
800/244-4444

Temp Agencies

A Personnel Commitment
208 S. LaSalle #189
Chicago, IL 60604-1003
312/251-5151
312/251-5154 - fax

Active Temporary Services
25 E. Washington #1717
Chicago, IL 60602
312/726-5771
312/726-3273 - fax

Active Temporary Services
3145 N. Lincoln - Main Level
Chicago, IL 60657
773/404-5700
773/404-9635 - fax

Adecco Personnel Services
200 W. Madison #520
Chicago, IL 60606
312/372-6783
312/372-9732 - fax

Advanced Personnel
225 W. Washington - Ste. 500
Chicago, IL 60606
312/422-9333
312/422-9310 - fax
Michigan Ave. Branch
676 N. St. Claire
312/335-9111
www.advancedresources.com

Advanced Personnel is a staffing firm supplying office support employees to major financial, healthcare and Fortune 1000 corporations in Chicagoland. Our flexible scheduling helps match actors with temporary and full-time positions. Corporate positions, executive assistants, customer service professionals, production specialist, desktop publishers and administrative assistants.

Appropriate Temporaries
79 W. Monroe #819
Chicago, IL 60603
312/782-7215
312/704-4195 - fax

ASI Staffing Service, Inc.
333 N. Michigan #2106
Chicago, IL 60601
312/782-4690
312/782-4697 - fax

BPS Staffing
200 N. LaSalle #1750
Chicago, IL 60601
312/920-6710
312/920-6744 - fax

City Staffing
2 N. LaSalle #630
Chicago, IL 60602
312/346-3400
312/346-5200 - fax

Dunhill Staffing Systems
211 W. Wacker #1150
Chicago, IL 60606
312/346-0933
312/346-0837 - fax
www.dunhillstaff.com

Interim Office Professionals
11 S. LaSalle #2155
Chicago, IL 60603
312/781-7220
www.interim.com

Kelly Services
949C N. Plum Grove Rd.
Schaumburg, IL 60173
847/995-9350
847/995-9366 - fax
www.kellyservices.com

Larko Group
11 S. LaSalle #1720
Chicago, IL 60603
312/857-2300
312/857-2355 - fax
www.thelarkogroup.com

Loftus & O'Meara
166 E. Superior #410
Chicago, IL 60611
312/944-2102
312/944-7009 - fax

Mack & Associates Personnel, Ltd.
attn. Boula Proutsos
100 N. LaSalle #2110
Chicago, IL 60602
312/368-0677 • 312/368-1868 - fax
www.mackltd.com

Manpower Temporary Services
500 W. Madison #2950
Chicago, IL 60661
312/648-4555
312/648-0472 - fax
www.manpowerchicago.com

Olstens of Chicago, Inc.
123 W. Madison #500
Chicago, IL 60602
312/944-3880

Paige Temporary, Inc.
5215 Old Orchard Rd.
Skokie, IL 60077
847/966-0111
847/966-8479 - fax
www.paigepersonnel.com

Prestige Employment Service
19624 Governors Highway
Flossmoor, IL 60422
708/798-7666 • 708/798-9099 - fax
www.prestigeemployment.com

Profile Temporary Service
222 N. LaSalle #450
Chicago, IL 60601
312/541-4141
312/641-1762 - fax

Pro Staff Personnel Services
10 S. Wacker #2250
Chicago, IL 60606
312/575-2120
312/641-0224 - fax
www.prostaff.com

Proven Performers
70 W. Madison #530
Chicago, IL 60602
312/917-1111
312/917-0474 - fax
www.greatchicagojobs.com

Randstad, Inc.
542A W. Dundee Rd.
Wheeling, IL 60090
847/541-6220
847/541-6235 - fax
www.randstad.com

Right Employment Center
53 W. Jackson
Chicago, IL 60604
312/427-3136 • 312/427-3136 - fax
www.rightservices.com

Select Staffing
208 S. LaSalle #1244
Chicago, IL 60604
312/849-2229
312/849-2234 - fax

Seville Staffing
180 N. Michigan #1510
Chicago, IL 60601
312/368-1272 • 312/368-0207 - fax
www.sevillestaffing.com

Seville Staffing has been providing Chicago-area talent with temporary Office Support jobs such as: Administrative Assistant, Word Processor, Reception, Data Entry and Customer Service Clerk positions since 1979. We also offer weekly pay, vacation pay, health insurance, and respect for the work you do. Call 312/368-1272 for an appointment.

Smart Staffing
29 S. LaSalle #635
Chicago, IL 60603
312/696-5306 • 312/696-0317 - fax
www.smartstaffing.com

Temporary Opportunities
53 W. Jackson #215
Chicago, IL 60604
312/922-5400 • 312/347-1206 - fax
www.opgroup.com

Temporary Professionals
Personnel Staffing Services
625 N. Michigan #600
Chicago, IL 60611
773/622-1202 • 773/622-1303 - fax

Gloria J-M Piecha - Director
Registration policy: Submit H/R. Will contact if interested.
Soon to be moving to a new location! Call for mailing address.
Personnel staffing services for trade shows and promotions.
Models - Talent - Costume Characters - Samplers - Temporaries - Bi Lingual Personnel

Member of the Chicago Convention & Tourism Bureau

Mail Headshot and resumes. Agency will contact. No drop-ins.

Put your personality to work!

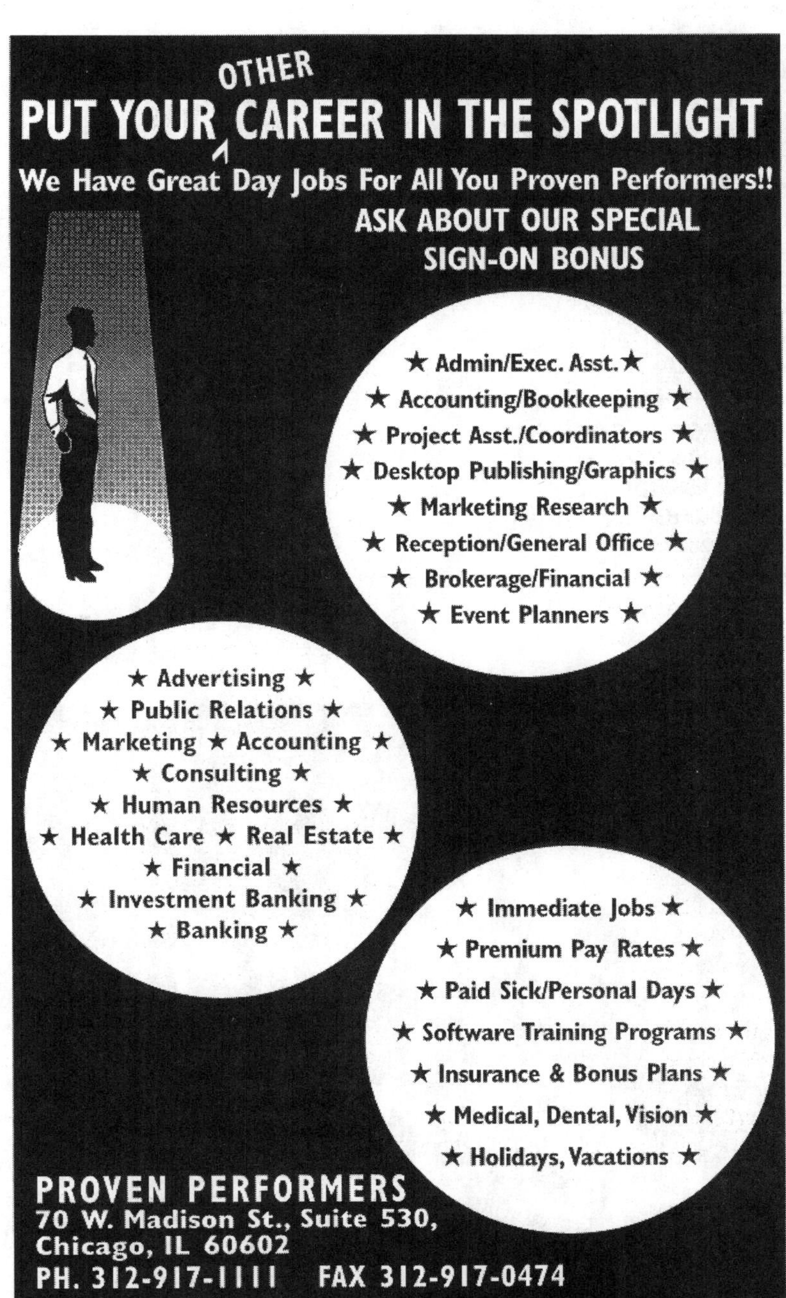

The Choice for Staffing
100 N. LaSalle #1900
Chicago, IL 60602
312/372-4500
312/853-4068 - fax
www.choicestaff.com

Today's Office Staffing
1701 E. Woodfield Rd. #903
Schaumburg, IL 60173
847/240-5300
847/240-5310 - fax

Unique Office Services
203 N. Wabash #608
Chicago, IL 60601
312/332-4183
312/332-2688 - fax

Watson Dwyer Staffing
25 E. Washington
Chicago, IL 60602
312/899-8030
312/899-8036 - fax
www.watsondwyer.com

Wordspeed
200 N. Dearborn #4006
Chicago, IL 60601
312/201-1171
312/201-1279 - fax

Actor-Friendly Jobs

A supportive job that allows you to pursue your career while still paying the bills is a rare and precious thing. These employers offer work that is particularly suited for the actor's schedule.

A Taste of California
2211 N. Elston
Chicago, IL 60614
773/235-9463
773/235-2633 - fax

Chicago Trolley Co.
1709 S. Prairie
Chicago, IL 60616
312/663-0260
312/663-0260 - fax

SST Communications (Associated with SST)
1840 S. Halsted
Chicago, IL 60608
312/563-1644
www.sstcommunications.com

Those Funny Little People Enterprises
7501 S. Quincy
Willowbrook, IL 60527
630/325-3320
630/325-8489 - fax
www.thosefunnylittlepeople.com

Ugly Duck
401 E. Illinois
Chicago, IL 60610
312/396-2205

Museum of Science & Industry
57th and Lake Shore
Chicago, IL 773/684-9844
773/684-0019
www.msichicago.org

Chicago Children's Museum
Tim Rey
700 E. Grand Ave.
Chicago, IL 60611
312/464-7711
www.chicagochildrensmuseum.org

Spirit of Chicago
Ed Carrella
River East Plaza
455 E. Illinois Street, Suite 461
Chicago, IL 60611
312/836-7888
www.spiritofchicago.com

Steppenwolf Theatre Telemarketing
Chuck Winans
1650 N. Halsted
Chicago, IL 60614
312/932-2462
www.steppenwolftheatre.org

The Princeton Review
Attn. Robb Rabito
2847 N. Sheffield
Chicago, IL 60657
773/868-4400
800/2REVIEW
www.review.com

Chicago Housesitting & Pet Care
1341 W. Fullerton #177
Chicago, IL 60614
773/477-0136
773/477-0896
www.chicagopetcare.com

Getting Started

I. GET READY…

First, make sure all your tools are in order. How recent are your headshots? Monologues ready to go? Resumé clean?

Headshots

Chicago headshots don't glorify their subjects. Glamour is out; reality is in. The headshot is your calling card, and if you're not happy with yours, you might consider getting new ones done locally. Check out the Actor's Tools chapter for information on finding a headshot photographer.

Resumés

Your resumé should mainly be clean and easy to read. Check the Resumé Checklist in the Actor's Tools section for tips on laying out your resumé.

Monologues

Most Chicago auditions will involve a monologue—so if you're auditioning for theatre, you need to have a few. You'll usually be asked for either one to two minutes, either comedic or dramatic and either classical or contemporary monologues. That means you should have selections available in each possible flavor.

II. GET SET…

Reference Materials

Your support materials are ready to go. Now what? Now you get informed about the Chicago scene. In your hands you have one great resource about all things Chicago—"The Book." PERFORMINK newspaper is another, available both as a subscription or online (www.performink.com). Also visit Act I Bookstore, Chicago's only theatre-oriented bookstore. Act I also carries the Act One Reports, which contain a lot of agent information available in "The Book," but it is updated three times a year, so it can be a good addition.

Site Visits

One of the best ways to get informed is to go see shows. Many small to mid-sized theatres have industry nights when professionals get in for a reduced price. Take advantage of those to see what everyone else is doing. Industry nights are advertised in PERFORMINK in the Hotlines section after the audition notices.

Mailings

Finally, once you're informed, get everyone else informed about you. Time to do a mailing. Some opt for the über mailing to every casting director, agent or theatre they can find. Others narrow their focus to agents or non-Equity theatres.

III. GO!!!

Time to get out there and make contacts. Like any scene, it's all who you know.

Audition

Many Chicago theatres have open auditions, so if they're casting, call up and reserve your slot. Auditions are published in PERFORMINK NEWSPAPER every two weeks and updated twice a week at www.performink.com.

Take a class

There are tons of good training centers here (check the Training chapter) and odds are there's one that would fit you. Taking a class gets you in with a group of peers who can help you out down the road. While you should never take a class just to meet the teacher, that person is presumably an experienced professional who's also in a position to give you advice when you need it.

Hang out

If you're the social type, use those skills to make friends and influence people. Actor bars and hangouts are noted in the neighborhood descriptions; odds are there is a theatre nearby.

TV & Film I & II Commercial Technique I
Industrial Film & Ear Prompter
Movement Scene Study
Meisner Technique I & II
Acting Instinctively
Audition Techniques I & II
Monologue Workshp
Masters Scene Class
Fundamentals Of Acting
If You're Serious About Acting
act one STUDIOS
Check out our
Conservatory Program
We have over thirty different classes for you to choose from. All taught by working professionals who really know the business. Classes for beginners to working actors.
Call for a free consultation.
312-787-9384
www.actone.com
You'll Never Act The Same Again
640 N. LaSalle, Suite 535 Chicago, IL 60610

Chapter 2

Training

Northlight, "Over the Tavern"

But in these cases
We still have judgement here, that we but teach
Bloody instructions, which, being taught, return
To plague th' inventor.

By Jenn Goddu

A person only needs to live in this city for one weekend to realize that Chicago is one of the major theatre centers in the country. Every Saturday night there are shows running in the glamorously refurbished Loop theatres, major theatres, studios, black box spaces, storefronts and creatively appointed hole in the wall venues. Now you want to know how you can best break into this world. What kind of training do you need to gain entry into this city's thriving professional theatre community? There are many options offered, many of them available right here in Chicago.

There are two main approaches to theatre training offered within the collegiate setting. There is conservatory training or university training. Since both are usually offered at a university, it can be confusing at first. But according to John Culbert dean of The Theatre School of DePaul University, the difference is the balance between specific professional training, a more general understanding of the world of theatre and an exploration of areas outside of theatre.

A conservatory program focuses more exclusively on professional skills. It is a way of teaching theatre that is modeled after the guild system of the Middle Ages. In a conservatory program, all the courses a student takes are geared towards making the student better at their chosen discipline. The liberal arts training at universities gives a solid base in theatre but also endeavors to expose its students to other areas of the liberal arts as well.

Quite often it is simply a matter of the difference between an undergraduate or graduate degree. Many programs have undergraduate degrees with a broader focus while at the graduate level the same theatre schools have a greater conservatory style.

Degrees Offered Out of State

The Yale School of Drama is a three-year graduate program with a conservatory focus. It promises potential applicants that, "the conservatory within the University teaches the crafts of the theatre, while the intellectual world of the University informs our critical aesthetic ideals." Yet, the university's undergraduate Theatre Studies program is a major integrated within the liberal arts curriculum.

UCLA's department of theatre offers a bachelor of arts (BA), a master of fine arts (MFA) or a doctor of philosophy (PhD). While the BA combines a liberal education with pre-professional training, the graduate level programs focus specifically on acting, production and design, playwriting or directing. New York University has a Drama program in the College of Arts and Sciences that focuses on dramatic studies and context. In the university's Tisch School of the Arts, there is a conservatory style program that offers BFA, MFA and PhD programs that combine professional training, theatre studies and liberal arts courses.

Chicago Programs

The entire spectrum of training options is available here in Chicago as well. DePaul and Roosevelt sit on the conservatory side of the spectrum, while Northwestern and Loyola have a more liberal arts style training. The theatre curriculum in the University of Illinois at Chicago's Department of Performing Arts balances practice and theory and offers a BA in Theatre. Columbia College is a liberal arts program in which all theatre majors learn the basics of all aspects of the profession in a program taught by working professionals.

Students in the theatre department at Northwestern study history and criticism as well as acting, directing and design. However, these courses represent only one-third of the student's studies. An undergraduate theatre major receives a Bachelor of Science (BS) from the School of Speech.

"I think the thing that we do is we sort of serve as a balance point between pure theatre conservatory education and universities that have theatre departments with less intensive study, particularly in the realm of acting," said Bud Beyer, chair of Northwestern's theatre department.

Northwestern has an intensive program of study for its theatre students, but it also encourages them to experience a "broad-based education," Beyer said. "It's the only time in a student's life, these four years, when their minds are sort of forcibly opened to all fields of knowledge."

Northwestern certainly encourages its graduates to continue their training in a conservatory setting at the graduate level, but at the undergraduate level the idea is to help students gain a "more profound viewpoint."

Loyola also boasts that its students get a "well-rounded education" in all aspects of theatre and in the liberal arts. It is exclusively an undergraduate program. There are courses in acting, directing and design but "the dramatic literature and the analysis of that literature in history are the foundation of our program," said Sarah Gabel, the department chair.

Students are involved in campus productions throughout the year, and there is a studio space that is turned over and devoted to students that the department supports financially and through advising. Students are also encouraged to work in productions in the city throughout the school year as well.

But the focus at Loyola is still on giving the students a strong foundation, Gabel said. "The ability to analyze literature with that solid historical background will prepare them for being able to see the script in the way the author wanted the audience to respond to it."

The Theatre School at DePaul is the Midwest's oldest theatre conservatory. It emphasizes "learning-by-doing," and offers a BFA or a MFA. "We are all the way at one end of the scale," said Culbert. "We're all the way over at fully specialized." DePaul is not better because it's a conservatory program, he was quick to add, it's just different. "The trade-off is you're not getting as much general education as you would otherwise," he said.

At the Theatre Conservatory of Chicago College of Performing Arts at Roosevelt University, a student can earn a BFA or MFA. The University offers a theatre BA and MA with a liberal arts bent, but there are few students who take that option. Most prefer to enroll for the more intensive program, said Joel G. Fink, the Theatre Conservatory's associate dean.

A conservatory program offers a "more intensified focus on the practical aspects of training," Fink said. The idea is that conservatory students will graduate with more of the specific professional theatre skills more fully developed. Instead of simply learning "about the theatre," conservatory students are "learning more how to do theatre," he said.

Finding the Right Fit

Picking the program that is right for you can be tough. "Not every place is right for every person," Beyer said.

Theatre faculty agreed that one style of program is not better than the other; they each simply offer different approaches to the teaching of theatre. The dedication can be equal.

Before enrolling in a conservatory program, for instance, you should be sure that the specific training is what you want. Especially at the undergraduate level, it can be a big decision for a young person to make. "That choice is definitely not for everyone," Culbert said.

Ask yourself how sure you are that you want to specialize in set design, directing, acting or dramaturgy. If you're not sure, he said, go to a program that gives you an option to try all of those things.

Kays suggests finding a program "that allows you to grow and change within the program and within the university itself." While she says she would have liked to train with more working professionals and learn more about the business of theatre, she felt Northwestern gave her a safe place to take risks.

The main thing a student should be looking for is "the right match," Gabel said. The student needs to feel the institution "fits them and that they can drive their education."

A training program should be judged on three things, said Dennis Zacek, artistic director at Victory Gardens. These factors are the facilities and the equipment available to you, the teachers you will study with and the education that you get from the other students.

"It is always a case of the individual," said Zacek, who has degrees from DePaul and Northwestern. "There are very talented people that have come out of both types of training programs, and some people who are not as gifted who have come out of both types of training programs."

What Ultimately Gets You the Job

Does it really matter which type of program you studied in? Do theatre producers or directors truly care where you got your training?

"What matters about where you went to school is the level of training you got in that program more than the name of that program," Fink said. As casting director for the Colorado Shakespeare Festival, Fink concedes that there are certain schools from which he will expect better-trained performers. That said, though, the final test is still a person's talent and how it is revealed in an audition.

As Culbert put it, "Ultimately no one is going to care where you got your degree. They are going to look at your work.

"I believe that we have a luxury of working in a field that doesn't care how you get there," Culbert said. "There are many paths…Our path works well for certain kinds of people."

While theatre professionals throughout the city agree with this assessment, they do concede that each program can confer its own advantages when you enter the professional world.

The contacts you make in a training program can also be pivotal.

"It's not exactly what you study, but who you meet along the way and how you cultivate those connections," said David Zak, artistic director of Bailiwick Repertory.

Sharon Evans, artistic director of Live Bait Theatre, says connections do exist. "There are artistic directors and directors who have strong ties with where they went to school," she said. Yet she says she doesn't really look at where someone was trained. "We need someone who can grasp difficult concepts in texts, so what I think we look for most is versatility," said Evans, a graduate of the School of the Art Institute. "If someone comes from a small college in Nebraska, we don't care as long as in the audition process they can handle all this material."

For actors, directors and designers, Evans is most interested in a resume that indicates that they are "well-rounded." Someone who is not university trained but who has been in many different types of productions or who has immersed him or herself in the industry is just as likely to get a shot at Live Bait, Evans said.

"We try as much as possible to give people a chance," Zak said. It really comes down to whether you have the drive and talent to make it. "You sort of learn on the job, and that's just as valid a way to go."

Acting Training Guide

Training should be an ongoing process in an actor's life. There are skills to be acquired and maintained. However, you'll get the most for your money if you ask yourself a few questions first.

What Are Your Skills?

These are the first questions you have to ask yourself. What are you already good at? What have you done? What do you list under special skills?

What Are Your Weaknesses?

What are you bad at? What skills do you need to acquire to make yourself more marketable?

What Are Your Goals?

Anyone can take a class, but if you've got a plan, you're more likely to get the best out of the money you spend on training. Most training goals fall into one of two categories:

1. Maintenance

What skills have you acquired but haven't used recently? These are the skills you may need to maintain through a class.

2. Acquisition

What skills would you like to acquire? What skills do you need in order to get work?

Choosing a Class

There are a lot of aspects to a positive class experience. Some you can control, some you can't. Instructors are the most important aspect of the class. If possible, audit a class they teach. They may have a fabulous reputation, but does their style mesh with yours?

Coaches

Getting a coach is quite different from taking a class. They're especially useful for prepping audition pieces or getting help with a particularly difficult role. As with a class, carefully interview a potential coach. They're expensive, so be picky.

Summer Programs

A summer program can provide a period of intensive training. Unfortunately, they're also expensive and time-consuming. This is a major investment, and one you should research before enrolling.

Graduate Programs

The ultimate amount of training, of course, is going back to school for your MFA or MA. An MFA is considered, by many institutions, to be a terminal degree, which means that once you've acquired the degree you can teach. Such a program can also hook you up with a peer group of serious artists that can lead to opportunities later.

Accompanists

Matthew Krause
773/334-6425

Bobby Schiff Music Productions
363 Longcommon Rd.
Riverside, IL 60546
708/442-3168
708/447-3719 - fax

Classes - Acting

Act One Studios, Inc.
640 N. LaSalle #535
Chicago, IL 60610
312/787-9384
312/787-3234 - fax
www.actone.com

Commercial Technique I - Get "camera-ready" for all types of commercial auditions.

Industrial Film & Ear Prompter - Learn to analyze and perform technical scripts and use an ear prompter.

TV & Film I, II & Workshop - Learn the "ins and outs" of the film and television world.

Fundamentals I, II & Scene & Monologue Workshop - Learn to make effective choices from the script.

Acting Instinctively - Flexibility, creativity, and imaginative freedom are explored.

Meisner Technique I, II & Workshop - Leads to a very truthful moment-to-moment style of acting.

Monologue Workshop - Prepare two to four monologues for auditions.

Audition Technique I & II - Learn the art of cold reading theatre auditions.

Shakespeare Beg. & Adv. - Approaches based on the work of Shakespeare & Co.

Masters Class - An on-going scene study class taught by Steve Scott.

Voice-Over I & II - Learn what it takes to be successful in the voice-over market.

Movement Scene Study - Learn to bring a physical life to your character.

Actors' Center of Chicago
Lance Gordon
3047 N. Lincoln #390
Chicago, IL 60657
773/549-3303
773/549-0749 - fax

Beginning Meisner Technique

Advanced Meisner Repetition

Advanced Meisner Technique

Master Meisner Technique

Movement (based on Williamson technique, adapted to Meisner)

Audition Skills (monologues, cold reading, audition technique)

Beginning Scene Study

Advanced Scene Study

Technique on Camera

TV/Film on Camera

The Actors Gymnasium & Performing Arts School
Noyes Cultural Arts Center
927 Noyes St.
Evanston, IL 60201
847/328-2795
847/328-3495 - fax
www.actorsgymnasium.com

Acro-Dance

Clown Theatre

Dance 101

Drum Performance

Gymnastics

Mime 101

The Lookingglasss Workshops

Pilates-Based Workshop

Viewpoints

Circus Arts

Your body is an instrument - we'll teach you to play it. A variety of physical performance skills, from trapeze to slap-stick, juggling to mime. Professional-level classes, run jointly with the Lookingglass Theatre Company. Convenient Chicago and Evanston locations. SAFD stage combat certification workshops. Master classes with renowned performers.

Actors Workshop
Michael Colucci
1350 N. Wells #F521
Chicago, IL 60610
312/337-6602
312/337-6604 - fax
www.actorsworkshop.org

Beginning Acting - On-Camera

Advanced Acting - On-Camera

Private Coaching: Ear Prompter, Monologue, Cold Reading, Commercial

Actors Workshop offers weekly ongoing classes for all levels. Each class starts with vocal warm-up, then commercials & scenes on-camera, which you can add to your demo reel. Call 1-888-COLUCCI to arrange a free visit and consultation with director Michael Colucci, author of ***Vocal Workout Booklet.***

The Artistic Home
1420 W. Irving Park
Chicago, IL 60613
773/404-1100

Technique 1, 2, 3

Advanced Repetition

Scene Study

Audition Intensive

Acting for Film 1 and 2

Voice for the Actor

Playwrighting Workshop

Musical Theatre Scene Study

Master Scene Study

The Audition Studio
(See our ad below)
20 W. Hubbard #2E
Chicago, IL 60610
312/527-4566
312/527-9085 - fax

Beginning Acting - Part 1 & 2: Weekly scene work, improvisation and script analysis help you build a strong foundation.

Cold Reading - The twelve guideposts are taught through weekly cold reading situations.

On-Camera - Strengthen your on-camera auditions. These courses cover all aspects of the commercial, industrial and film audition.

Scene Study (Beginning and Advanced) - In depth scene work, this class focuses on performance and the rehearsal process.

Monologue - Prepare audition pieces for theaters and agents. Actors will be assigned three pieces from classical to contemporary.

Voice Technique - Based on Kristin Linklater's vocal progression.

Voiceover (Beginning and Advanced) - Get an inside look into the world of voiceover. Explore various techniques for breaking down copy. Includes three sessions in a professional recording studio.

Shakespeare Workshop

Ongoing Workshop Series - Voiceover, Directing, Getting Started in the Business, Commercial On-Camera

List of Instructors: Kurt Naebig, Rachael Patterson, Jack Bronis, Linda Gillum, Chris Stolte, Jim Johnson, Pat Van Oss, Lawrence Grimm, Barb Wruck Thometz, Brighid O'Shaughnessy, Greg Vinkler, Molly Glynn Hammond, Jeff Lupetin, Deb Doetzer

Black Ensemble Theatre
4520 N. Beacon
Chicago, IL 60640
773/769-4451
773/769-4533 - fax

Jackie Taylor Workshop - Designed to upgrade performance skills by incorporating acting, dance and music.

Teaching Artists to be Teachers in the Classroom.

Bobby Schiff Music Productions
363 Longcommon Rd.
Riverside, IL 60546
708/442-3168
708/447-3719 - fax

Breadline Theatre Group
1802 W. Berenice
Chicago, IL 60613-2720
773/275-4342
www.Breadline.org

Chicago Actors Studio
1567 N. Milwaukee
Chicago, IL 60622
773/645-0222
773/645-0040 - fax
www.actors-studio.net

Scene Study

Film Tech

Commercials

Industrials

Characterization

Voice & Diction

Shakespeare

Auditioning & Marketing

The Ear Prompter

Trade Shows

Chicago Center for the Performing Arts Training Center
777 N. Green
Chicago, IL 60622
312/327-2040
312/327-2046 - fax
www.theaterland.com

Acting: Relationship with Energies

Acting: Understanding Action Within Conflict

Script Analysis

Improv to Scene Study Class

Improvisation

Scene Study: A Diagnostic Tool

Auditioning Strategies for the Stage

Monologues

Auditioning for Film and Television

Acting the Song

CTM Productions
228 State St.
Madison, WI 53703
608/255-2080
www.theatreforall.com

Acting for Adults

Dell Arte School of Physical Theatre
P.O. Box 816
Blue Lake, CA 95525
707/668-5663
707/668-5665 - fax
www.dellarte.com

One year full time physical theatre performance program and summer workshops.

Duncan YMCA Chernin Center for the Arts
1001 W. Roosevelt
Chicago, IL 60608
312/738-7980
312/738-1420 - fax

Beginning Acting

Youth Theatre Workshop for Teens

Eileen Boevers Performing Arts Workshop
595 Elm Pl. #210
Highland Park, IL 60035
847/432-8223
847/432-5214 - fax
www.appletreetheatre.com

ETA Creative Arts
7558 S. South Chicago
Chicago, IL 60619-2644
773/752-3955
773/752-8727 - fax
www.etacreativearts.org

Adult Acting - Beginning and Advanced

Sound

Lighting

Stage Management

How to Audition for Commercials

The Fourth Wall: Training for the Working Actor
Athenaeum Annex
2951 N. Greenview, 3rd Floor
Chicago, IL 60657
773/508-0397

Formerly Center Theater's Training Center

Professional Classes for beginners to advanced levels:

Scene Study • Monologues

Meisner Technique/Repetition

Camera Technique

Advanced Characterization

Audition Intensive • Shakespeare

Playwriting/Screenwriting

Career Guidance

Core Instructors: Dale Calandra, Peter Toran, Robin Witt

FIND YOUR CENTER!

Free Associates
2936 N. Southport #210
Chicago, IL 60657
773/296-0541 • 773/296-0968 - fax
www.freeassociates.org

GATE
Gregory Abels Training Ensemble
28 W. 27th St.
New York, NY 10001-6906
212/689-9371
www.GATEacting.com

Illinois Theatre Center
P.O. Box 397
Park Forest, IL 60466
708/481-3510 • 708/481-3693 - fax

Beginning Acting for Adults

Acting Workshop

Advanced Acting Ensemble (permission of instructor only)

The Improv Playhouse
847/968-4529
www.improvplayhouse.com

The Improv Playhouse, Libertyville. Foundational through advanced improvisation, Story Theater, radio drama, beginning through advanced dramatic arts classes for adults and youth. Staff are arts professionals from premier improv and drama programs. Professional performance opportunities available to students. Sponsor of ComedySportz North Suburban High School League. Several north suburban locations. Contact David Stuart.

Inner Urge to Move
Janet
801 Dartmouth
Island Lake, IL 60042
312/409-2277

It's Only A Stage
1847B W. Jefferson Ave.
Naperville, IL 60540
630/416-7974
www.onlyastage.com

John Robert Powers Entertainment Company
27 E. Monroe #200
Chicago, IL 60603
312/726-1404
312/726-8019 - fax
www.johnrobertpowers.com

TV 1, TV 2, TV 3

Image Development

Commercial Print • Runway

KV Studios
1243 N. Damen
Chicago, IL 60622
773/907-1551

New American Theatre
118 N. Main St.
Rockford, IL 61101-1102
815/963-9454
www.newamericantheater.com

SPRING CLASSES: Session #5: April 23–May 19

Discovering Drama: ages 5-7

Wednesdays, 4–5pm

Creative play that is the foundation of theater.

Theater Games: ages 8–10

Thursdays, 3:45–4:45pm

Games that stretch the imagination and inspire teamwork.

You're On!: ages 11–13

Mondays, 3:45–4:45pm

Improvisation: Get fast on your feet and have fun!

Monologue Class: adult

Saturdays, 10:00am–Noon

Learn how to shine when it's just you and the audience.

The Neo-Futurists
5153 N. Ashland
Chicago, IL 60640
773/275-5255
773/878-4514 - fax
www.neofuturists.org

Neo-Futurist Performance Workshop

Advanced Neo-Futurist Performance Workshop - both classes are studies in writing, directing and performing your own work.

Brenda Pickleman

535 N. Michigan #2914
Chicago, IL 60611
630/887-0529

Using intensive on-camera scene study and a variety of teaching methods, this workshop is designed to train serious actors to successfully compete in the LA market for Film and Television. Workshops are held on Tuesday evenings in the heart of Chicago.

Piven Theatre Workshop

927 Noyes
Evanston, IL 60201
847/866-6597
847/866-6614 - fax
www.piventheatreworkshop.com

This renowned training center offers beginning, intermediate and professional level classes in improvisation, theatre games, story theatre, and scene study. Submit H/R for intermediate and advanced scene study. Call for current class information.

Come learn to play again at the theatre school that launched John & Joan Cusack, Aidan Quinn, Lili Taylor, Jeremy Piven and many more! Classes for young people from 4th grade through high school. Call for current class information.

Plasticene

2122 N. Winchester #1F
Chicago, IL 60614
312/409-0400
www.plasticene.com

Summer Physical Theatre Intensive

Ongoing Workshops

Plasticene is an ensemble-based theater company that develops original works of physical theater for Chicago and national/international touring. Plasticene teaches actor-generated and action-based theater creation at Chicago Center for the Performing Arts. Combining physical acting technique, contact improvisation, and object work, Plasticene training is unique and essential.

Sarantos Studios

2857 N. Halsted
Chicago, IL 60657
773/528-7114

Feature Film Acting

Scene Study

Monologue Preparation

On-Camera Auditioning

Basic Acting Technique

The School at Steppenwolf

758 W. North Avenue - 4th floor
Chicago, IL 60610
312/335-1888 x5608
312/335-0808 - fax
www.steppenwolf.org

The Studio of The Moving Dock

2970 N. Sheridan #1021
Chicago, IL 60657
773/327-1572

Michael Chekhov Technique

Creative Movement Improvisation

Collaborative Creation

Ongoing Workshops

Sydney Moore

4736 N. Paulina
Chicago, IL 60640
773/728-8720

Meisner Techinique

Workshops

Private Coaching

Training

Victory Gardens Theatre
2257 N. Lincoln
Chicago, IL 60614
773/549-5788
773/549-2779 - fax
www.victorygardens.org

Basic Acting

Introduction to Scenes & Monologues

Musical Theater • Speech & Movement

Dialects • Building a Character

Monologues • Scene Study

Comedy Styles • Directing

The Victory Gardens Training Center is the educational arm of our theatre. Our eight-week sessions are taught by local professionals and are designed to serve both the beginner and the working professional. For more information or a brochure, please call 773/549-5788.

T. Daniel and Laurie Willets
c/o T. Daniel Productions
1047 Gage St.
Winnetka, IL 60093
847/446-0183
847/446-0183 - fax
www.tdanielcreations.com

Basic through Advanced Mime Techniques & Concepts

Mime Concepts & Techniques for the Disciplined Performing Artists

Mime as a Tool for the Verbal Storyteller

Mime Concepts Applied to the Fine Arts Students/Professional Artists

Understanding the Effectiveness of Corporeal Movement In Speech Presentations: For Business/Corporate People Only

Consulting and Classes on Movement and Staging for Magicians

Wisconsin Theatre Games Center
2397 Lime Kiln Rd.
Baileys Harbor, WI 54202
920/854-5072

Paul Sills One Week Summer Improvisational Theatre Intensives

Improv Classes

See the Improv Chapter for complete information on Improv training and groups.

ComedySportz
2851 N. Halsted
Chicago, IL 60657
773/549-8080

ImprovOlympic
3541 N. Clark
Chicago, IL 60657
773/880-0199 • 773/880-9979 - fax

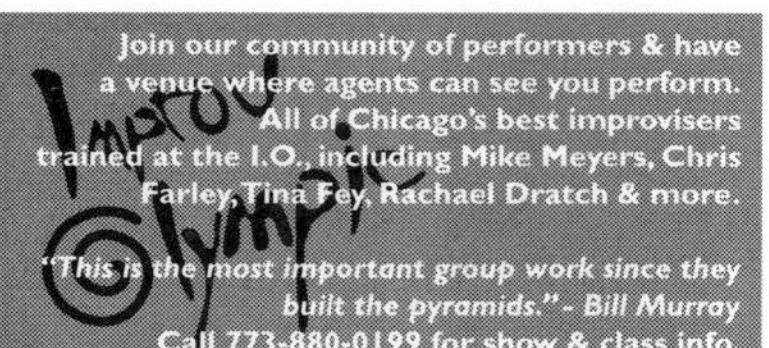

Low Sodium Entertainment
3741 N. Kenmore #2
Chicago, IL 60613
773/549-3250

Second City
(See our ad on page 54)
1616 N. Wells
Chicago, IL 60614
312/664-3959 • 312/664-9837 - fax
www.secondcity.com

The Improv Playhouse
847/968-4529
www.improvplayhouse.com

Classes - Dance

The Academy of Dance Arts
1524 Centre Circle
Downers Grove, IL 60515
630/495-4940
www.theacademy-ibt.com

Ballet (ages 3 to adult), Point, Jazz (ages 3 to adult), Hip-Hop, Tap (ages 3 to adult), Acrobat, Lyrical, Professional Ballet Program

---

Academy of Movement and Music
605 Lake St.
Oak Park, IL 60302
708/848-2329
708/848-2391 - fax

Ballet, Jazz, Modern, Creative Movement

American Dance Center Ballet Co.
10464 W. 163rd Pl.
Orland Park, IL 60462
708/747-4969
708/747-0424 - fax

Ballet, Point, Jazz, Hip-Hop, Modern, Tap, Swing

Authentic Mid East Belly Dance
Jasmin Jahal
P.O. Box 56037
Chicago, IL 60656-0037
773/693-6300
773/693.6302 - fax
www.jasminjahal.com

Traditional Middle Eastern & Classical Egyptian Dance

Ballet Chicago
218 S. Wabash - 3rd floor
Chicago, IL 60604
312/251-8833
312/251-8840 - fax
www.balletchicago.org

Ballet

Pre-Professional Program

Children's Ballet

Adult Ballet and Fitness Program

Barbara Dubosq
1068 Hillcrest
Highland Park, IL 60035
847/831-3383

Ballet, Tap, Creative

Belle Plaine Studio
2014 W. Belle Plaine
Chicago, IL 60618
773/935-1890
773/935-1909 - fax

Ballet, Jazz, Modern, Tap, Belly Dance, Flamenco, NIA

Beverly Art Center
2153 W. 111th
Chicago, IL 60643
773/445-3838
773/445-0386 - fax

Ballet, Jazz, Modern, Tap, Stretch and Strength, African

Boitsov Classical Ballet
410 S. Michigan #300
Chicago, IL 60605
312/663-0844
312/939-2094 - fax

Ballet - Vaganova Technique (Moscow Bolshoi Theatre system of training)

Boulevard Arts Center
6011 S. Justine
Chicago, IL 60636
773/476-4900
773/476-5951 - fax

Ballet, Modern, Tap, African

Chicago Human Rhythm Project
2936 N. Southport #210
Chicago, IL 60657
773/296-0869
773/296-0968 - fax
www.chicagotap.com

Adult tap instruction, all levels, specifically offered during their festival season in August.

Chicago Moving Company
3035 N. Hoyne
Chicago , IL 60618
773/880-5402
773/880-5402 - fax
www.chicagomovingcompany.org

Modern, Aerobic Jazz, Creative Movement, Special Populations, Special Summer and Spring Break Camps, Performance Opportunities

Chicago Multicultural Dance Center
806 S. Plymouth
Chicago, IL 60605
312/461-0030
312/461-1184 - fax
www.cmdcschool.com

Ballet, Jazz, Tap, Latin, Modern, Hip-Hop

Chicago National Association of Dance Masters
5411 E. State St. #202
Rockford, IL 61108
815/397-6052
815/397-6799 - fax
www.cnadm.com

Workshops only; no ongoing classes

Dance Center Evanston
610 Davis St.
Evanston, IL 60201
847/328-6683
847/328-6656 - fax
www.dancecenterevanston.com

Ballet, Jazz, Tap, Ballroom, NIA

Dance Center of Columbia College
1306 S. Michigan
Chicago, IL 60605
312/344-8300
312/344-8036 - fax
www.colum.edu

Ballet, Modern, Jazz, Tap, African

Dance Dimensions
595B N. Pinecrest Rd.
Bolingbrook, IL 60440
630/739-1195

Ballet, Jazz, Tap, Ballroom, Swing, Tumbling, Salsa

Dance Therapy Center
Fine Arts Building
410 S. Michigan
Chicago, IL 60605
312/461-9826
312/461-9843 - fax

Ballet, Modern

Dancecenter North
540 N. Milwaukee
Libertyville, IL 60048
847/367-7970
847/367-7905 - fax
www.dancecenterNorth.com

Classical Ballet, Point, Jazz, Tap, Irish Step Dance, Social Dance, Jazz and Funk

Diana's Dance and Fitness Dynamics, Ltd.
Diana Duda
429 Park Dr.
Glenwood, IL 60425
708/755-8292
708/799-7613 - fax

Ballet, Jazz, Tap, Ballroom

Discovery Center
2940 N. Lincoln
Chicago, IL 60657
773/348-8120
773/880-6164 - fax
www.discoverycenter.cc

Ballet, Jazz, Modern, Tap, Bacheta, Ballroom, Belly Dance, Contemporary Latin, Hip Hop, Salsa, Social Dance, Swing, Tango, Kardio Kickboxing

Domenick Danza
5116 N. Glenwood
Chicago, IL 60640
773/728-7305

Musical Theatre Dance

Dorothy's Stagecraft Academy
116 E. 115th
Chicago, IL 60628
773/821-6128

Ballet, Jazz, Tap, Acrobatic

Emergence Dance Theatre
804 1/2 Market
P.O. Box 186
DeKalb, IL 60115
815/758-6613

Ballet, Jazz, Modern, Tap, Drama

ETA Creative Arts
7558 S. South Chicago
Chicago, IL 60619-2644
773/752-3955
773/752-8727 - fax
www.etacreativearts.org

Adult Acting - Beginning and Advanced

Sound

Lighting

Stage Management

How to Audition for Commercials

Evanston School of Ballet Foundation
1933 Central St.
Evanston, IL 60201

847/475-9225

Ballet

Fluid Measure Performance Company
1720 W. Chase
Chicago, IL 60626
773/338-0519

Contact Improvisation Workshops, Summer Interdisciplinary Performance Workshops

Folk Dance Council of Chicago
914 Horne St.
St. Charles, IL 60174
630/232-0242

Folk Dances from around the world

Golden's School of Dance
1548 Burgundy Pkwy.
Streamwood, IL 60103
630/540-0996
630/540-9650 - fax

Ballet, Jazz, Tap, Ballroom, Clogging, Lyrical

Gus Giordano Dance Center
614 Davis
Evanston, IL 60201
847/866-9442
847/866-9228 - fax
www.giordanojazzdance.com

Ballet, Jazz, Modern, Tap, Hip-Hop, Ballroom, Pilates, East Indian, Children's programs

Hedwig Dances
Administrative Offices
2936 N. Southport #210
Chicago, IL 60657
773/871-0872
773/296-0968 - fax
www.enteract.com\~hedwig

Modern, African, Yoga, Hip-Hop, Tai Chi, Company Class

Jo's Footwork Studio
1500 Walker
Western Springs, IL 60558
708/246-6878

Ballet, Jazz, Modern, Tap, Hip-Hop

Joel Hall Dance Center
1511 W. Berwyn
Chicago, IL 60640
773/293-0900
773/293-1130 - fax
www.joelhall.org

Ballet, Jazz, Modern, Tap, Hip-Hop, African, Egyptian, Pilates

Judith Svalander School of Ballet
83 E. Woodstock St.
Crystal Lake, IL 60014
815/455-2055

Ballet, Jazz, Modern, Tap, Character Dance, Drama, Musical Theatre, Pointe

Lou Conte Dance Studio
(Home of Hubbard Street Dance Chicago)
1147 W. Jackson
Chicago, IL 60607
312/850-9766
312/455-8240 - fax
www.hubbardstreetdance.com

Ballet, Jazz, Modern, Tap, Dance Fitness, Hip-Hop

Mayfair Academy of Fine Art
1025 E. 79th
Chicago, IL 60619
773/846-8180

Ballet, Jazz, Modern, Tap, Tumbling

Milwaukee Ballet
504 W. National Ave.
Milwaukee, WI 53204
414/643-7677
414/649-4066 - fax
www.milwaukeeballet.org

Ballet, Jazz, Modern, Spanish Character Dance

Muntu Dance Theatre of Chicago
6800 S. Wentworth #3E96
Chicago, IL 60621
773/602-1135
773/602-1134 - fax
www.muntu.com

African, African-American

Najwa Dance Corps Studio
1900 W. Van Buren #0505
Chicago, IL 60612
312/850-7224
312/850-7019 - fax
www.ndc.org
Ballet, Tap, African, Caribbean

North Shore School of Dance
107 Highwood
Highwood, IL 60040
847/432-2060
847/432-4037 - fax
www.northshoredance.com
Ballet, Jazz, Modern, Tap, Hip-Hop, Irish, Yoga

Old Town School of Folk Music
4544 N. Lincoln
Chicago, IL 60625
773/728-6000
773/728-6999 - fax
www.oldtownschool.org
Ballet, Jazz, Tap, African, Aztec, Belly, Breakdance, Flamenco, Flat-Foot, Hip-Hop, Hula, Indian, Irish, Latin, Mexican, Swing, Tango, Brazilian, Capoeira

Patterson School of Ballroom Dance
1240 Sunset Rd.
Winnetka, IL 60093
847/501-2523
Ballroom Dance

Rockford Dance Company
711 N. Main
Rockford, IL 61103
815/963-3341
815/963-3541 - fax
www.rockforddancecompany.com
Ballet, Jazz, Modern, Tap, Ballroom, Tango Argentino, Irish, Folk

Royal Scottish Country Dance Society
Ree Grisham
3550 N. Lakeshore #227
Chicago, IL 60657
773/528-7824
Scottish Country Dance

Ruth Page Foundation
School of Dance
1016 N. Dearborn
Chicago, IL 60610
312/337-6543
312/337-6542 - fax
www.ruthpage.com
Ballet, Jazz, Tap, Pilates

School of Performing Arts
200 E. 5th Ave. #132
Naperville, IL 60563
630/717-6622
630/717-5131 - fax
www.schoolofperforming-arts.com
Ballet, Jazz, Modern, Tap, Hip-Hop, Fine Arts Adventures (Preschool)

Shelley's School of Dance and Modeling, Ltd.
450 Peterson Rd.
Libertyville, IL 60048
847/816-1711
847/816-1717 - fax
Ballet, Jazz, Modern, Tap, Hip-Hop, Lyrical, Pilates, Pointe

Teresa Cullen
729 Lake Ave.
Wilmette, IL 60091
847/256-6614
847/256-5318 - fax
Flamenco, Ballet

Tina Mangos Dance
773/282-5108
www.tinamangosdance.com
Ballroom, Latin, Movement for Performers, Swing

Von Heidecke School of Ballet
1239 S. Naper Blvd.
Naperville, IL 60540
630/527-1052
630/527-8427 - fax
www.chicagofestivalballet.org
Ballet

Classes - Kids

Ballet Chicago
218 S. Wabash - 3rd Floor
Chicago, IL 60604
312/251-8833
312/251-8840 - fax
www.balletchicago.org
Ballet
Pre-Professional Program
Children's Ballet
Adult Ballet and Fitness Program

Beverly Art Center
2153 W. 111th
Chicago, IL 60643
773/445-3838
773/445-0386 - fax
Ballet, Jazz, Modern, Tap, Stretch and Strength, African

Boitsov Classical Ballet
410 S. Michigan #300
Chicago, IL 60605
312/663-0844
312/939-2094 - fax
Ballet - Vaganova Technique (Moscow Bolshoi Theatre system of training)

Borealis Theatre Company
P.O. Box 2443
Aurora, IL 60507
630/844-4928
630/844-5515 - fax
www.borealis-theatre.org

Chicago Academy for the Arts
1010 W. Chicago
Chicago, IL 60622
312/421-0202
312/421-3816 - fax
www.chicagoacademyforthearts.org

Chicago Ballet Arts
Claire Carmichael - Director
7416 N. Ridge
Chicago, IL 60645
773/381-0000
847/657-8121 - fax

Chicago Theatre Company
500 E. 67th
Chicago, IL 60637
773/493-0901
773/493-0360 - fax
www.chicagotheatrecompany.com

Chicago Center for the Performing Arts Training Center
777 N. Green
Chicago, IL 60622
312/327-2040
312/327-2046 - fax
www.theaterland.com

Acting: Relationship with Energies

Acting: Understanding Action Within Conflict

Script Analysis

Improv to Scene Study Class

Improvisation

Scene Study: A Diagnostic Tool

Auditioning Strategies for the Stage

Monologues

Auditioning for Film and Television

Acting the Song

Chicago Moving Company
3035 N. Hoyne
Chicago , IL 60618
773/880-5402 • 773/880-5402 - fax
www.chicagomovingcompany.org

Modern, Aerobic Jazz, Creative Movement, Special Populations, Special Summer and Spring Break Camps, Performance Opportunities

---

CTM Productions
228 State St.
Madison, WI 53703
608/255-2080
www.theatreforall.com

Acting for Adults

Dancecenter North
540 N. Milwaukee
Libertyville, IL 60048
847/367-7970 • 847/367-7905 - fax
www.dancecenterNorth.com

Classical Ballet, Point, Jazz, Tap, Irish Step Dance, Social Dance, Jazz and Funk

---

DancEd
3131 Dundee Rd.
Northbrook, IL 60062
847/564-9120

DePaul University - Community Music Division
804 W. Belden
Chicago, IL 60614-3296
773/325-7262
773/325-4935 - fax
music.depaul.edu

The workshop is an intensive, performance-oriented program in musical theatre. Class sessions include vocal and physical warm-ups, theatre games, song preparation, interpretation of text, character analysis, and stage movement. Each student performs in group numbers and at least one solo or scene. Participants take an active role in the developmental process, working as an ensemble toward the final end-of-session performance.

Eileen Boevers Performing Arts Workshop
595 Elm Pl. #210
Highland Park, IL 60035
847/432-8223
847/432-5214 - fax
www.appletreetheatre.com

ETA Creative Arts
7558 S. South Chicago
Chicago, IL 60619-2644
773/752-3955
773/752-8727 - fax
www.etacreativearts.org

Adult Acting - Beginning and Advanced

Sound

Lighting

Stage Management

How to Audition for Commercials

Fieldcrest School of Performing Arts
11639 S. Ashland
Chicago, IL 60643
773/568-6706

Free Street Programs
1419 W. Blackhawk
Chicago, IL 60622
773/772-7248
www.freestreet.org

Golden's School of Dance
1548 Burgundy Pkwy.
Streamwood, IL 60103
630/540-0996
630/540-9650 - fax

Ballet, Jazz, Tap, Ballroom, Clogging, Lyrical

Illinois Theatre Center
P.O. Box 397
Park Forest, IL 60466
708/481-3510
708/481-3693 - fax

Beginning Acting for Adults

Acting Workshop

Advanced Acting Ensemble (permission of instructor only)

It's Only A Stage
1847B W. Jefferson Ave.
Naperville, IL 60540
630/416-7974
www.onlyastage.com

Northlight Theatre
9501 N. Skokie Blvd.
Skokie, IL 60077
847/679-9501 x3301
www.northlight.org

Oak Park Village Players
1006 Madison St.
Oak Park, IL 60302
708/524-1892
708/524-9892 - fax
www.village-players.org

Youth and adult classes in acting and improvisation.

Piven Theatre Workshop
927 Noyes
Evanston, IL 60201
847/866-6597
847/866-6614 - fax
www.piventheatreworkshop.com

This renowned training center offers beginning, intermediate and professional level classes in improvisation, theatre games, story theatre, and scene study. Submit H/R for intermediate and advanced scene study. Call for current class information.

Come learn to play again at the theatre school that launched John & Joan Cusack, Aidan Quinn, Lili Taylor, Jeremy Piven and many more! Classes for young people from 4th grade through high school. Call for current class information.

Roadworks
1144 Fulton Market #105
Chicago, IL 60607
312/492-7150
312/492-7155 - fax
www.roadworks.org

Shakespeare on the Green
Barat College - 700 E. Westleigh Rd.
Lake Forest, IL 60045
847/604-6344
847/604-6342 - fax
www.sotg.pac.barat.edu

Modeling

...rs
...npany
...e #200
Chicago, IL 60603
312/726-1404
312/726-8019 - fax
www.johnrobertpowers.com

TV 1

TV 2

TV 3

Image Development

Commercial Print

Runway

Model Image Center
1218 W. Belmont
Chicago, IL 60657
773/348-9349
773/348-9366 - fax
www.modelimagecenter.com

Shelley's School of Dance and Modeling, Ltd.
450 Peterson Rd.
Libertyville, IL 60048
847/816-1711
847/816-1717 - fax
Ballet, Jazz, Modern, Tap, Hip-Hop, Lyrical, Pilates, Pointe

Classes - Scriptwriting

Chicago Alliance for Playwrights
1225 W. Belmont
Chicago, IL 60657
773/929-7367 x60
773/327-1404 - fax

Chicago Dramatists
1105 W. Chicago
Chicago, IL 60622
312/633-0630
312/633-0610 - fax
www.chicagodramatists.org

New Tuners Theatre
1225 W. Belmont
Chicago, IL 60657
773/929-7367
Workshops in Writing for Musical Theatre

Victory Gardens Theatre
2257 N. Lincoln
Chicago, IL 60614
773/549-5788
773/549-2779 - fax
www.victorygardens.org

Basic Acting

Introduction to Scenes & Monologues

Musical Theater

Speech & Movement

Dialects

Building a Character

Monologues

Scene Study

Comedy Styles

Directing

Classes – Stage Combat

The Actors Gymnasium & Performing Arts School
Noyes Cultural Arts Center
927 Noyes St.
Evanston, IL 60201
847/328-2795
847/328-3495 - fax
www.actorsgymnasium.com

Acro-Dance

Clown Theatre

Dance 101

Drum Performance

Gymnastics

Mime 101

The Lookingglasss Workshops

Pilates - Based Workshop

Viewpoints

Circus Arts

Your body is an instrument - we'll teach you to play it. A variety of physical performance skills, from trapeze to slap-stick, juggling to mime. Professional-level classes, run jointly with the Lookingglass Theatre Company. Convenient Chicago and Evanston locations. SAFD stage combat certification workshops. Master classes with renowned performers.

Fencing 2000
328 S. Jefferson
Chicago, IL 60606
312/879-0430

R & D Choreography
7443 N. Hoyne #1N
Chicago, IL 60645
847/333-1494
www.theatrechicago.com/randd

Raoul Johnson
Loyola University
6525 N. Sheridan
Chicago, IL 60626
773/508-3841

Stunts & Swords
262/215-3983
www.stuntsandswords.com

Coaches - Acting

Dawn Arnold
2970 N. Sheridan Rd. #1021
Chicago, IL 60657
773/327-1572

Dawn Arnold is Artistic Director of The Moving Dock Theatre Company and teaches acting, movement for the actor, viewpoints, and improvisation at Roosevelt University. Her acting teaching and coaching is based on the Michael Chekhov Technique, a whole-bodied, imaginative approach to the actor's creative process.

Bud Beyer
1979 S. Campus Dr.
Evanston, IL 60208
847/491-3372

Belinda Bremner
773/871-3710

An audition is a job interview using someone else's words. The key to a successful audition is finding an author who tells your story in your words. Your choice of audition material speaks volumes. Decide what that message is and then craft your audition. Ideally suited for the well-trained actor looking for an edge.

Courtney Brown
3723 N. Southport
Chicago, IL 60613
773/878-3865

Bob Kulhan
3638 N. Pine Grove #1
Chicago, IL 60613
773/296-4887

Cecilie O'Reilly
2023 N. Damen
Chicago, IL 60647
773/486-3649
312/344-8077 - fax

Dale Calandra
773/508-0397

"Personal Training for the Total Actor"

Your Monologue is a SHOWCASE of your talent. ACT TO WIN! Contemporary to Classic, one-person shows, cold reading, on-camera, and callbacks. Over 500 actors privately coached since 1983. Creative Director, The Fourth Wall Training Center, Artistic Director, Oak Park Festival Theatre.

Dexter Bullard
2122 N. Winchester
Chicago, IL 60614
773/227-6487

Dexter Bullard is a Jefferson Cited Chicago director, Artistic Director of Plasticene Physical Theater, and a director for The Second City. Dexter has taught acting, improvisation, and audition technique for over six years at University of Illinois, Columbia College, The Actors' Center, The Audition Studio, and at The Second City Training Center. Gain immediate results for auditions or breakthroughs in acting over a few sessions. Very affordable sliding scale.

Michael Colucci
Actor's Workshop
1350 N. Wells #F521
Chicago, IL 60610
312/337-6602
312/337-6604 - fax
www.actorsworkshop.org

Illinois Theatre Center
Etel Billig
P.O. Box 397
Park Forest, IL 60466
708/481-3510
708/481-3693 - fax

Jaclyn Loewenstein
Evanston/Northbrook
847/866-8651

Janet B. Milstein
773/465-5804

Award-winning Acting Instructor, Janet has trained hundreds of actors, beginners to professionals. Her students continually get cast in Chicago theatre and have been signed by agents in Chicago, NY, and LA. Janet offers affordable private coaching in monologues and cold reading that will teach you the skills to audition powerfully and with confidence. Author of "111 One-Minute Monologues," "Cool Characters for Kids," and two forensics books due out this year.

Rick Plastina
1117 N. Taylor
Oak Park, IL 60302
708/386-8270

Jeremy Sklar's Monologue Workout
773/430-2827

Karen Vaccaro
1243 N. Damen
Chicago, IL 60622
773/201-0951

Kathryn Nash
312/943-0167

Kevin Heckman
1716 W. Albion #3A
Chicago, IL 60626
312/562-3748

Linda Gillum
773/878-3077

Tim Klein
Chicago Actors Studio
773/645-0222

Lori Klinka
916 Rainbow Dr.
Glenwood, IL 60425
708/709-0880
708/709-0881 - fax

Training

Ruth Landis, Inc.
773/991-7777
773/463-3683 - fax

We build inner safety so that creativity flows naturally and spontaneously while preparing the actor technically for auditions (monologues, on-camera, cold-reading) and performance experience. As a longtime acting coach and certified body-psychotherapist and hypnotherapist we explore mind/body/emotion awareness around performance anxiety, blocks, creating ease with self, using work rooted in Alexander, Feldenkrais, and Gestalt therapy. Ruth coaches actors, is in private practice, and has taught at Victory Gardens, Northwestern, Columbia and Roosevelt University.

Michael Menendian
Raven Theatre
2549 W. Fargo
Chicago, IL 60645
773/338-2177
773/508-9794 - fax
www.raventheatre.com

Richard Marlatt
773/338-8755

Monica Payne
773/404-2782

Kurt Naebig
20 W. Hubbard
Chicago, IL 60610
630/495-7188

Fredric Stone
5040 N. Marine #3A
Chicago, IL 60640
773/334-4196

A working professional actor/director with over 25 years experience (New York and Chicago), coaches actors in monologue and scene preparation for auditions - both contemporary and classical. He created and taught The Audition Workshop at Organic Theatre and currently teaches an 8 week Performing Shakespeare class at Victory Gardens Theatre.

T. Daniel and Laurie Willets
c/o T. Daniel Productions
1047 Gage St.
Winnetka, IL 60093
847/446-0183
847/446-0183 - fax
www.tdanielcreations.com

Basic through Advanced Mime Techniques & Concepts

Mime Concepts & Techniques for the Disciplined Performing Artists

Mime as a Tool for the Verbal Storyteller

Mime Concepts Applied to the Fine Arts Students/Professional Artists

Understanding the Effectiveness of Corporeal Movement In Speech Presentations: For Business/Corporate People Only

Consulting and Classes on Movement and Staging for Magicians

Coaches - Dialect

Martin Aistrope
3011 W. George Street
Chicago, IL 60618
773/276-4665

Native Brit. Standard, Regional (Cockney, Scots, Irish, Yorks, Scouse, Geordie, etc.), Colonial (Aussie, NZ, SA, etc.). All technique and no music? Aaargh! Taped personal coaching, customized drill, facial exercises, tapes. You have a better ear than you think: Find out which one it is!

Claudia Anderson
773/296-6929

25 years teaching and coaching experience. Dialect coaching for production. Designated Linklater voice teacher. "Freeing the Natural Voice" approach to improving your voice. One-on-one coaching for the individual. Coaching for heightened text, monologues, and songs.

Eric Armstrong
708/488-0131
faculty.roosevelt.edu/armstrong/

One-on-one: A complete approach to sharpen skills in the vocal area: voice work, dialect preparation, accent reduction or preparing a complex text. Individual attention in a supportive atmosphere helps you reach your goals.

Company coaching: productions with dialect/accent, voice or text needs. Reasonable rates.

Belinda Bremner
773/871-3710

Kate DeVore
4451 N. Hamilton
Chicago, IL 60625
773/334-7203
www.KateDeVore.com

Character-based dialect acquisition and coaching. The way we speak is an integral part of who we are; this principle informs technical coaching for sound changes, voice placement (resonance), and musicality of a dialect. Non role-specific dialect training also available, as is coaching in Standard American (accent reduction). Materials and personalized coaching tapes provided.

Cecilie O'Reilly
2023 N. Damen
Chicago, IL 60647
773/486-3649
312/344-8077 - fax

Coaches - Instrument

Academy of Movement and Music
605 Lake St.
Oak Park, IL 60302
708/848-2329
708/848-2391 - fax

Northwestern University
School of Music (ask for referrals)
711 Elgin Rd.
Evanston, IL 60208
847/491-7485
847/491-5260 - fax

Old Town School of Folk Music
4544 N. Lincoln
Chicago, IL 60625
773/728-6000
773/728-6999 - fax
www.oldtownschool.org

School of Performing Arts
200 E. 5th Ave. #132
Naperville, IL 60563
630/717-6622
630/717-5131 - fax
www.schoolofperforming-arts.com

Ballet, Jazz, Modern, Tap, Hip Hop, Fine Arts Adventures (Preschool)

Sherwood Conservatory of Music
1312 S. Michigan
Chicago, IL 60605
312/427-6267
312/427-6677 - fax

Wilmette Voice & Piano Studio
Wilmette, IL
847/251-7449

Coaches - Movement

Chicago Center for the Alexander Technique
Ed Bouchard
5415 N. Sheridan #1005
Chicago, IL 60640
773/728-3235

Courtney Brown
Alexander Technique
3723 N. Southport
Chicago, IL 60613
773/878-3865

Marina Gilman
5701 S. Dorchester
Chicago, IL 60637
773/955-0016
773/955-0016 - fax

Marina Gilman is a certified Feldenkrais™ Practitioner, licensed Speech and Language Pathologist, and holds an M.M. in Voice. She specializes in prevention and rehabilitation of voice professionals including singers, actors, and broadcast journalists. Her approach to teaching is a combination of somatic education and traditional voice training.

Nana Shineflug
847/724-1931

T. Daniel and Laurie Willets
c/o T. Daniel Productions
1047 Gage St.
Winnetka, IL 60093
847/446-0183
847/446-0183 - fax
www.tdanielcreations.com

Basic through Advanced Mime Techniques & Concepts

Mime Concepts & Techniques for the Disciplined Performing Artists

Mime as a Tool for the Verbal Storyteller

Mime Concepts Applied to the Fine Arts Students/Professional Artists

Understanding the Effectiveness of Corporeal Movement In Speech Presentations: For Business/Corporate People Only

Consulting and Classes on Movement and Staging for Magicians

Coaches - Singing

Tamara Anderson
1023 Barberry Ln.
Round Lake Beach, IL 60073
847/546-5548
847/546-5717 - fax

Learn the technique that many Grammy Award winners use. Personalized instruction. Breath Support, range, pitch, vocal freedom, control, confidence. Performance coaching, overcoming stage fright. Help for damaged voices, learn good vocal hygiene. Beginners to professionals. Specializing in contemporary styles of music.

Bridget Becker
773/381-9358

Randy Buescher
Chicago/Naperville, IL
312/671-3181
buzzcen@aol.com

Over 100 Grammy winners can't be wrong. Speech Level Singing is the technique to know if you are interested in a career in musical theater, pop, or other types of singing. For more information, call Randy Buescher at 773/384-8419 or 312/671-3181. Certified speech level singing instructor with studios in Chicago and Naperville. Also specializing in voice therapy; degreed in Speech Language Pathology.

Mark Burnell
2008C W. Potomac
Chicago, IL 60622
773/862-2665
773/862-2655 - fax
markburnell.com

Mark Burnell (773)862-COOL

Cabaret, jazz, Broadway, pop, R & B. Get your show together: repertoire, arrangements. Prepare your audition: style, phrasing, transposition, rehearsal tapes. Work your chops: technique, flexibility, improvisation, ornamentation. MFA and 10 years with Carnegie Mellon Music Theatre Department. markburnell.com

The Center For Voice
410 S. Michigan #635
Chicago, IL 60605
312/360-1111

Dr. Ronald Combs
917 W. Castlewood
Chicago, IL 60640
773/271-8425
773/271-0364 - fax

Lia Corinth
847/328-4202

David H. Edelfelt
1243 W. Foster
Chicago, IL 60640
773/878-SING

Dancecenter North
540 N. Milwaukee
Libertyville, IL 60048
847/367-7970
847/367-7905 - fax
www.dancecenterNorth.com

Matthew Ellenwood
4318 N. Sheridan Rd.
Chicago, IL 60613
773/404-2739

My studio practice focuses upon solid vocal technique paired with artistic interpretation and sensitive coaching which results in creating moving, captivating-memorable performances/auditions. 60 minute lesson for $40.00.

Jilann Gabriel
410 S. Michigan #630
Chicago, IL 60605
800/831-3139 • 773/237-0299 - fax
www.poporchshows.com

Marina Gilman
5701 S. Dorchester
Chicago, IL 60637
773/955-0016 • 773/955-0016 - fax

Marina Gilman is a certified Feldenkrais® Practitioner, licensed Speech and Language Pathologist, and holds an M.M. in Voice. She specializes in prevention and rehabilitation of voice professionals including singers, actors, and broadcast journalists. Her approach to teaching is a combination of somatic education and traditional voice training.

Matthew Krause
773/334-6425

Vincent Lonergan
773/761-0262

Richard Marriott
410 S. Michigan #920
Chicago, IL 60605
312/360-1728

Patricia Martinez
4072 N. Sheridan #3D
Chicago, IL 60613
616/469-1151

Music Workshop
Bob Kalal
4900 W. 28th Pl.
Cicero, IL 60804
708/652-4040
members.xoom.com\musicwkshop

Northwestern University
School of Music (ask for referrals)
711 Elgin Rd.
Evanston, IL 60208
847/491-7485 • 847/491-5260 - fax

Rak Vocal & Healing Clinic
6056 W. Irving Park
Chicago, IL 60634
773/283-8349

William Rush Voice Consultants
410 S. Michigan #920
Chicago, IL 60604
312/360-1039 • 630/620-1271 - fax

Old Town School of Folk Music
4544 N. Lincoln
Chicago, IL 60625
773/728-6000 • 773/728-6999 - fax
www.oldtownschool.org

Training

Patricia Rusk
1263 W. Foster
Chicago, IL 60640
773/784-7875

Chair of the musical theatre program at the Chicago Academy for the Arts.

School of Performing Arts
200 E. 5th Ave. #132
Naperville, IL 60563
630/717-6622 • 630/717-5131 - fax
www.schoolofperforming-arts.com

Sherwood Conservatory of Music
1312 S. Michigan
Chicago, IL 60605
312/427-6267
312/427-6677 - fax

Peggy Smith-Skarry
1347 W. Winona
Chicago, IL 60640
773/728-5240

Michael Thorn
400 E. Randolph #2927
Chicago, IL 60601
312/565-0862

The Voice Works
Ruth Allyn
Near North
Chicago, IL 60610
312/944-3867

What a Voice Productions
(The Vocal Studio)
Karyn Sarring
P.O. Box 558188
Chicago, IL 60655
708/388-5585
www.whatavoice.com

Wilmette Voice & Piano Studio
Wilmette, IL
847/251-7449

Frank Winkler
1765 George Ct.
Glenview, IL 60025
847/729-1893

Coaches - Voice-Over

Audio One, Inc.
325 W. Huron #512
Chicago, IL 60610
312/337-5111
312/337-5125 - fax

Bosco Productions
160 E. Grand - 6th floor
Chicago, IL 60611
312/644-8300

Helen Cutting
445 E. Ohio #1914
Chicago, IL 60611
312/527-1809

With over 25 years' experience as a professional Voice-Over Talent and Coach, Helen Cutting offers intensive training in Voice-Over Technique, Script breakdown and Demo Tape production.

Helen's coaching style is supportive yet challenging, with in-depth coverage of Television/Radio Commercials, Promotions, Animation and Narrations. All levels.

Call for private consultation.

Sound Advice

(See our ad on the next page)
Kate McClanaghan, Gina Mazza, Tyrone Dockery
2028 W. Potomac #2 & 3
Chicago, IL 60622
773/772-9539
www.voiceoverdemos.com

Get trained by two of Chicago's top former agents. Gina Mazza (CED) and Tyrone Dockery (Stewart) and Kate McClanaghan Producer at top Ad Agency (DDB Worldwide). Training includes the following:

Commercial technique

Cold reading

Vocal Technique

Audition technique

In studio voice-over workshop

Mastering the business of being a working talent

Sound Advice is the most complete, start-to-finish voice-over demo production service. We maintain no one does what you do. The copy is written/selected specifically for you by Professional Producers. Our mailing list and marketing plan is unparalleled. We coach, direct and produce you to get you completely poised to work. Get trained and produced by two of Chicago's top former Talent Agents, Gina Mazza (CED) and Tyrone Dockery (Stewart) and Kate McClanaghan-Producer at top Ad Agency (DDB Worldwide).

Voice Over U
Sherri Berger
773/774-9886
www.sherriberger.voicedemo.com

Voice Over U is one of the most recommended and highly regarded voiceover training programs in the Midwest with a complete "roadmap" into the business, a vairety of valuable recording workshops, and honest evaluations. Private coaching: Sherri Berger pinpoints a performer's strengths and weaknesses, keeps them abreast of trends, and helps them discover more interesting vocal nuances, style and range capabilities.

VoiceOver 101
Ray Van Steen
325 W. Huron #512
Chicago, IL 60610
312/587-1010
312/337-5125 - fax

Private, individual coaching sessions in voicing TV/Radio commercials, narrations. Employs record/playback method in recording studio environment. Basics through production of voice-over demo. Van Steen is a published writer on the subject, and has voiced thousands of commercials.

Phone for free, no-obligation brochure.

Coaches - Voice/Speech

Claudia Anderson

773/296-6929

25 years teaching and coaching experience. Dialect coaching for production. Designated Linklater voice teacher. "Freeing the Natural Voice" approach to improving your voice. One-on-one coaching for the individual. Coaching for heightened text, monologues, and songs.

Eric Armstrong

708/488-0131

faculty.roosevelt.edu/armstrong/

One-on-one: A complete approach to sharpen skills in the vocal area: voice work, dialect preparation, accent reduction or preparing a complex text. Individual attention in a supportive atmosphere helps you reach your goals.

Company coaching: productions with dialect/accent, voice or text needs. Reasonable rates.

Randy Buescher
Chicago/Naperville, IL
312/671-3181
buzzcen@aol.com

Over 100 Grammy winners can't be wrong. Speech Level Singing is the technique to know if you are interested in a career in musical theater, pop, or other types of singing. For more information, call Randy Buescher at 773/384-8419 or 312/671-3181. Certified speech level singing instructor with studios in Chicago and Naperville. Also specializing in voice therapy; degreed in Speech Language Pathology.

Lia Corinth
847/328-4202

Kate DeVore, M.A.
4451 N. Hamilton
Chicago, IL 60625
773/334-7203
www.KateDeVore.com

Over ten years experience as voice, speech and dialect coach; certified voice/speech pathologist specialized in performers' voice. Voice enhancement, exploration and development. Training in vocal projection, resonance, power, flexibility, ease and range. Vocal extremes (shouting and screaming) without injury. Vocal health and maintenance. Holistic approach to voice enhancement also available, incorporating energy and complementary healing techniques to free and strengthen the voice.

Marina Gilman
5701 S. Dorchester
Chicago, IL 60637
773/955-0016
773/955-0016 - fax

Marina Gilman is a certified Feldenkrais® Practitioner, licensed Speech and Language Pathologist, and holds an M.M. in Voice. She specializes in prevention and rehabilitation of voice professionals including singers, actors, and broadcast journalists. Her approach to teaching is a combination of somatic education and traditional voice training.

Deb Kowalczyk
773/255-8024
773/878-0503 - fax

M.A. in Speech/Language Pathology - over 20 years experience. Member ASHA (American Speech/Language/Hearing Association and VASTA (Voice and Speech Trainers Association). Studied with Patsy Rodenburg "The Actor Speaks: Voice and the Performer. Specializing in:

- *Standard American English pronunciation*
- *Voice and projection difficulties*
- *Dialect modification*

Trained theater professional

Richard Marriott
410 S. Michigan #920
Chicago, IL 60605
312/360-1728

Kathryn Nash
312/943-0167

Cecilie O'Reilly
2023 N. Damen
Chicago, IL 60647
773/486-3649
312/344-8077 - fax

Training

Professionally Speaking
2818 N. Ashland
Chicago, IL 60657
773/218-9183

William Rush Voice Consultants
410 S. Michigan #920
Chicago, IL 60604
312/360-1039 • 630/620-1271 - fax

Ann Wakefield
1500 N. LaSalle #3C
Chicago, IL 60610
312/751-9348

Ear Prompter Coaches

Rick Plastina
1117 N. Taylor
Oak Park, IL 60302
708/386-8270

Speech Therapy

Randy Buescher
Chicago/Naperville, IL
312/671-3181
buzzcen@aol.com

Over 100 Grammy winners can't be wrong. Speech Level Singing is the technique to know if you are interested in a career in musical theater, pop, or other types of singing. For more information, call Randy Buescher at 773-384-8419 or 312-671-3181. Certified speech level singing instructor with studios in Chicago and Naperville. Also specializing in voice therapy; degreed in Speech Language Pathology.

Center for Stuttering Therapy
9933 Lawler Ave.
Skokie, IL 60077
847/677-7473 • 847/677-7493 - fax
www.cfst.com

Kate DeVore, M.A., CCC-SLP
4451 N. Hamilton
Chicago, IL 60625
773/334-7203
www.KateDeVore.com

As a voice, speech and dialect trainer as well as a speech pathologist specialized in professional voice, Kate has created a unique combination of artistic and scientifically based techniques for vocal rehabilitation and speech training. She is also specialized in working with people who stutter, using similar principles to facilitate a feeling of ease and control in speech.

Krause Speech & Language Services
Sue Ellen Krause, Ph.D., CCC-SLP
233 E. Erie #815
Chicago, IL 60611
312/943-1927 • 312/943-2692 - fax

Kathleen E. Long
11142 S. Campbell
Chicago, IL 60655
773/239-8089

Professionally Speaking
2818 N. Ashland
Chicago, IL 60657
773/218-9183

Rak Vocal & Healing Clinic
6056 W. Irving Park
Chicago, IL 60634
773/283-8349

Bonnie Smith, Ph.D., CCC-SLP
Division of Speech Pathology
University of Illinois
at Chicago Medical Center
1855 W. Taylor
Chicago, IL 60612
312/996-6520 • 312/996-8106 - fax
www.otol.uic.edu/speech.htm

Universities (with MFAs in Theatre)

American Conservatory Theater
30 Grant Ave - 6th Floor
San Francisco, CA 94108
415/439-2350 •415/834-3300 - fax
www.act-sfbay.org

MFA's offered in Acting.

Arizona State University
Department of Theatre
P.O. Box 872002
Tempe, AZ 85287-2002
602/965-5359
602/965-5351 - fax
www.asu.edu/cpa/theatre

MFA's offered in Acting, Theatre for Youth and Scenography.

Boston University
School for the Arts
855 Commonwealth Ave. #470
Boston, MA 02215
617/353-3390
617/353-4363 - fax
http://web.bu.edu/SFA/

MFA's offered in Directing, Education, Theatre and Design.

Brandeis University
Theater Arts Program
P.O. Box 9110 MS 072
Waltham, MA 02454-9110
781/736-3340
781/736-3408 - fax
www.brandeis.edu/theater

MFA's offered Acting, Dramaturgy, Playwriting and Design.

California Institute of the Arts
Theatre School
24700 McBean Parkway
Valencia, CA 91355
661/255-7834 • 661/255-0462 - fax
www.calarts.edu

MFA's offered in Acting, Directing, Design, Management and Technical Direction.

Columbia University
Hammerstein Center/Theatre
School of the Arts
New York, NY 10027
212/854-3408 • 212/854-3344 - fax
www.columbia.edu/cu/arts/theatre

MFA's in Acting, Directing, Dramaturgy, Playwriting and Management

DePaul University
The Theatre School at DePaul University
2135 N. Kenmore
Chicago, IL 60614
773/325-7999
http://theatreschool.depaul.edu
MFA's offered in Acting, Directing, Costume Design, Lighting Design and Set Design.

Eastern Michigan State University
Department of Comm. & Theatre Arts
103 Quirk
Ypsilanti, MI 48197
734/487-1153
734/487-3443 - fax
www.emich.edupublic/cta/theatre_Home_page.html
MFA's offered in Theatre for the Young.

Florida State University
School of Theatre 239 FAB
Florida State University
Tallahassee, FL 32306-1160
850/644-7234
850/644-7246 - fax
http://theatre.fsu.edu
MFA's offered in Acting, Directing, Music Theatre, Costume Design, Design/Technical Theatre, Lighting Design and Scene Design.

Illinois State University
Department of Theatre
Campus Box 5700
Normal, IL 61761
309/438-8783 • 309/438-7214 - fax
www.orat.ilstu.edu/theatre
MFA's offered in Acting, Directing and Design.

Indiana University
Dept. of Theatre & Drama
Theatre 200, 1211 E. Seventh St.
Bloomington, IN 47405
812/855-4503 • 812/855-4704 - fax
www.fa.indiana.edu/~thtr
MFA's offered in Acting, Directing, Playwriting, Costume Design, Lighting Design, Set Design and Theatre Tech.

Linenwood University
Department of Performing Arts
209 S. Kingshighway
St. Charles, MO 63301
314/949-4949
314/949-4910 - fax
MFA's offered in Acting, Directing and Design/Technical Theatre.

Michigan State University
Department of Theatre
149 Auditorium Building
East Lansing, MI 48824
517/355-6690
517/355-1698 - fax
http://pilot.msu/theatre/unit
MFA's offered in Acting and Production Design.

National Theatre Conservatory
1050 13th St.
Denver, CO 80204
303/825-2117
www.denvercenter.org/edu
MFA's offered in Acting.

Northern Illinois University
School of Theatre Arts
DeKalb, IL 60115
815/753-1335 • 815/753-8415 - fax

MFA's offered in Acting, Directing, and Design/Tech.

Northwestern University
Theatre Department
1979 S. Campus Dr.
Evanston, IL 60208
847/491-3170 • 847/467-2019 - fax
http://nuinfo.nwu.edu/speech/departments/theatre.html

MFA's offered in Directing and Stage Design.

Ohio State University
Department of Theatre
1849 Cannon Dr.
Columbus, OH 43210
614/292-5821 • 614/292-3222 - fax

MFA's offered in Acting and Design/Tech.

Ohio University
School of Theater
307 Kantner Hall
Athens, OH 45701-2979
740/593-4818
740/593-4817 - fax
www.ohiou.edu/~thardept

MFA's offered in Acting, Directing, Playwriting, and Production Design and Technology.

Pennsylvania State University
School of Theatre
103 Arts Building
University Park, PA 16802-2900
814/865-7586
814/865-7140 - fax
www.psu.edu/dept/theatrearts/

MFA's offered in Acting, Directing, Design and Tech.

Purdue University
Department of Visual
and Performing Arts
G-84 Stewart Center
West Lafayette, IN 47907
765/494-3074 • 765/496-1766 - fax
www.sla.purdue.edu/theatre

MFA's offered in Acting and Theatre Design and Technology.

Just 2 hours south of Chicago. Graduate MFA programs in Acting, Production Design & Technology (Costume, Scenery, Lights, Sound, Theatre Engineering, Theatre Technology); MA program in Stage Management. Assistantships with tuition waiver plus salary in excess of $10,000/year. Member: U/RTA, NAST, ACTF. Info: www.purdue.edu/theatre; e-mail: theatre@purdue.edu. EA/EOU.

Roosevelt University
Theatre Program
430 S. Michigan Ave.
Chicago, IL 60605-1394
312/341-3719 • 312/341-3814 - fax
www.roosevelt.edu

MFA's in Directing/Dramaturgy, Musical Theatre and Performance-Acting.

Southern Illinois University
Department of Theatre
Carbondale, IL 62901-6608
618/453-5741 • 618/453-7582 - fax
www.siu.edu/~mccleod/

MFA's offered in Directing, Playwriting, and Design.

Southern Methodist University
Theatre Division
1164 Owens Art Center
Dallas, TX 75275
214/768-2558
www.smu.edu/~meadows/

MFA's offered in Acting and Design/Directing.

State University of New York/Purchase
Division of Theatre Arts & Film
735 Anderson Hill Rd.
Purchase, NY 10577
914/251-6830
914/251-6300 - fax

MFA's offered in Directing/Stage Management and Stage Design/Theatre Technology.

University of Alabama - Tuscaloosa
Dept. of Theatre & Dance
Box 870239
Tuscaloosa, AL 35487-0239
205/348-5283
205/348-9048 - fax
www.as.ua.edu/theatre

MFA's offered in Acting, Directing, Playwriting/Dramaturgy, Costume Design, Costume Design/Production, Set Design/Technical Production, Stage Management, and Management/Arts Administration.

University of California - Los Angeles
Department of Theatre, UCLA
Los Angeles, CA 90024-1622
310/825-7008
310/825-3383 - fax
www.tft.ucla.edu

MFA's offered in Acting, Directing, Playwriting and Design & Production.

University of California, San Diego
Department of Theatre and Dance
La Jolla, CA 92093-0344
http://www.ucsd.edu

MFA's offered in Acting, Directing, Dramaturgy, Playwriting, Design and Stage Management.

University of Cincinnati
College-Conservatory of Music
P.O. Box 210096
Cincinnati, OH 45221-0096
513/556-5803
513/556-3399 - fax
www.UC.edu/www/ccm

MFA's offered in Acting, Directing, Musical Theatre, Costume Design, Lighting Design; Make-Up & Wig Design, Scenic Design, Sound Design, Theatre Production, and Stage Management.

University of Delaware
Professional Theatre Training Program
Mitchell Hall, Room 109
Newark, DE 19716
302/831-2201
www.udel.edu/theatre/pttp

MFA's offered in Acting, Stage Management and Technical Production.

University of Houston
School of Theatre
Houston, TX 77004-5071
713/743-3003
713/749-1420 - fax

MFA's offered in Acting, Directing, Costume Design, Scenic Design, and Playwriting.

University of Illinois, Urbana-Champaign
Dept. of Theatre
4-122 Krannert Center
500 S. Goodwin Ave.
Urbana, IL 61801
217/333-2371
217/244-1861 - fax
www.theatre.uiuc.edu/theatre/

MFA's offered in Acting and Design/Management/Tech.

University of Iowa
Dept. of Theatre Arts
107 Theatre Building
Iowa City, IA 52242-1705
319/335-2700
www.uiowa.edu

MFA's offered in Acting, Directing, Playwriting, Design, Dramaturgy, and Stage Management.

University of Massachusetts
Department of Theater
Room 112, Fine Arts Center
Amherst, MA 01003
413/545-3490 • 413/545-4312 - fax

MFA's offered in Directing, Dramaturgy, Costume Design, Lighting Design and Scenic Design.

University of Michigan
Dept. of Theatre & Drama
2550 Frieze Build.
Ann Arbor, MI 48109-1285
734/764-5350 • 734/647-2297 - fax
www.theatre.music.umich.edu

MFA's offered in Directing, Playwriting and Design.

University of Missouri-Kansas City
5100 Rockhill Rd.
Kansas City, MO 64110
816/235-2702 • 816/235-5367 - fax
www.umkc.edu/theatre

MFA's offered in Acting and Design/Technology.

University of Nebraska-Lincoln
Dept. of Theatre Arts & Dance
215 Temple Building 12th & R Sts.
Box 880201
Lincoln, NE 68588-0201
402/472-2072

MFA's offered in Acting and Design/Tech.

University of North Carolina/Chapel Hill
Department of Dramatic Art
CB#3230, Graham Mem. 052A
Chapel Hill, NC 27599-3230
919/962-1132

MFA's offered in Acting, Costume Technology and Technical Production.

University of Oregon
Dept. of Speech & Theatre Arts
216 Villard Hall
Eugene, OR 97403-1231
503/346-4171
541/346-1978 - fax
http://darkwing.uoregon.edu/~tadept/index.htm

MFA's offered in Costume Design, Lighting Design and Scenery Design.

University of Southern California
School of Theatre
Los Angeles, CA 90089-0791
213/740-1285
213/740-8888 - fax
www.usc.edu/dept.theatre/DramaNet

MFA's offered in Playwriting and Design.

University of Texas at Austin
Department of Theatre & Dance
College of Fine Arts
Austin, TX 78712
512/471-5793

MFA's offered in Acting, Drama and Theatre for Youth, Directing, Playwriting, Design and Theatre Tech.

University of Washington
School of Drama
Box 353950
Seattle, WA 98195-3950
206/543-5140
206/543-8512 - fax
http://ascc.artsci/washington.edu/drama

MFA's offered in Acting, Directing and Design/Tech.

University of Wisconsin-Madison
Theatre and Drama Department
6173 Vilas Hall
821 University Ave.
Madison, WI 53706-1497
608/263-2329
608/263-2463 - fax
http://polyglot.lss.wisc.edu/tnd/theatre.html

MFA's offered in Acting, Lighting, Set Design, Costuming and Technology.

University of Wisconsin/Milwaukee
Professional Theatre Training Prog.
P.O. Box 413
Milwaukee, WI 53201
414/229-4947
414/229-2728 - fax
www.uwm.edu/Dept/SFA/Theatre

MFA's offered in Acting, Costume Production, Stage Management and Technical Production.

University/Resident Theatre Association (U/RTA)
1560 Broadway #414
New York, NY 10036
212/221-1130
212/869-2752 - fax
www.urta.com

Wayne State University
Theatre Department
3225 Old Main
Detroit, MI 48202-3489
313/577-3508
www.comm.wayne.edu/theatre

MFA's offered in Acting, Costume Design, Lighting Design, Scenic Design, Stage Management and Theatre Management.

Western Illinois University
Department of Theatre
Browne Hall
Macomb, IL 61455
309/298-1543
www.wiu.edu

MFA's offered in Acting, Directing and Design.

Yale University School of Drama
P.O. Box 208325
New Haven, CT 06520
203/432-1507
203/432-9668 - fax
www.yale.edu/drama

MFA's offered in Acting, Directing, Playwriting/Dramaturgy/Dramatic Criticism, Design, Sound Design, Technical Design/Production and Theatre Management.

Chapter 3

Actor's Tools

A Red Orchid Theatre, "Bug"

Scale of dragon, tooth of wolf,
Witches' mummy, maw and gulf
Of the ravin'd salt-sea shark,
Root of hemlock digg'd i' th' dark.

By Susan Hubbard

Okay, so you're a skilled, versatile, flexible and talented actor. Now how about making a living? "The bottom line is when you get a degree in theatre, they don't teach you how to make yourself a working actor," says Kate McClanaghan of Sound Advice/Big House Production. "The theatre is not how you subsidize your career, sad as that may be. But through voice-over and on-camera work you can subsidize your career, provided you are willing to apply yourself and are committed to developing the necessary promotional skills."

Voice-Overs

According to agent Kathleen Collins, head of voice-over at Geddes, you can make a living strictly out of voice-over in Chicago. "Some talent only does voice-over. But most voice-over artists in Chicago are actors."

Voice-over work can be very lucrative. It is not unheard of for an actor to earn $40,000 from multiple airings of a single day's recordings of commercial spots and taglines. The exact return depends upon the number of airings and whether the talent is union or not.

"Chicago is a voice-over town," says McClanaghan. "Producers will shoot on-camera commercials in NYC or LA, but they'll do the voice-over here."

"We're still the midwest," concurs Baker and Rowley agent Vanessa Lanier. "And advertisers love real people talking to real people."

Approximately 45 percent of the voice-over industry in Chicago is in industrials and 55 percent in commercials. "Chicago has the talent," says Collins. "And producers on both coasts know it."

Says Lanier, "Everyone loves voice-over. The talent doesn't have to worry about what they look like that day, and it's often repeat work so that you work with the same engineers; there's a nice community. The residuals are healthy. And I love auditioning for voice-over because I love watching the process. Watching the actors go into character and bring it all down to the mic is so amazing."

Most voice-over professionals agree that the market is wide open for the 18-25 age group, particularly African-American and Hispanic voices.

The Voice-Over Demo & Training

To jump on this money bandwagon, actors need to cut an audio demo and get one minute of it on their talent agency's CD.

"A year ago it wasn't so clear that CD was the way to go, but now it is," says Collins. "We're hearing it from the producers." Collins sends producers all her talent on an agency CD, organized by actor's names. "It's easier for them because they get everyone in one place, one minute of each."

McClanaghan agrees. "Cassettes are archaic," she says.

After listening, producers send the agency invitations for the talent they want to see along with the script, the specs, and the record dates. "It's very efficient," says Collins. "They can say I want to hear these artists for this many takes. We record it digitally, change it to mp3 and send it back. They can e-mail the tracks they like to others in their office."

Bosco Productions, where Collins once worked, has been known to reduce demo-tape production costs for talent at agencies they have a relationship with. Rates have been as low as $70 an hour to record spots, add effects and edit. Since it takes about four hours to record and eight to 12 hours to edit a resulting two-minute reel, that translates to about $840, more if you need coaching or scripts written. "The benefit is you have the same engineers mixing for on-air who know the industry," says Collins. It's an investment talent should quickly recoup once they start getting bookings.

There are many voice-over training providers in Chicago, including Bosco, Audio One and Voice Over U, just to name a few. Most of these will try to give actors the practical experience of what they're going to encounter at the audition and on the job.

"Ninety-nine percent of auditions are going to be at the talent agency, not at the producers or ad agency, which was the standard just a few years ago," says McClanaghan.

"When you do get on the job, producers and copywriters are giving very minimal direction. Good training should help actors deconstruct that and get them ready to deliver beyond what is being articulated."

Sound Advice's In-Studio Workshop helps actors learn to vary delivery and master the "proximity effect." "Think about an on-screen close-up," says McClanaghan. "On voice-over, the equivalent would be very deep and close to the mic. Whatever you imagine, you have to put it into the mic. Where are you focusing sound? Are we in your head? Are you whispering to someone a foot away, engaging someone 3-5 feet away or further?" Training should also help actors learn to keep it "live." McClanaghan has studied with Royal Shakespeare Company, Improv Olympic and Second City but says commercials are different. "You have to be there that one take, not after two weeks of rehearsal. And they're not after one perfect take. They're after four or five perfect takes, all different. We help actors develop what we like to call "safe free-falling." In-Studio Workshop meets for four consecutive Wednesdays. Each workshop is taped so that actors have a record of all their sessions. Actors may sit in on one workshop for free. Cost for the four sessions is $275.

J-Card a.k.a. Trade Card & Web Site Marketing

What just six months ago was known as a "J-card," the liner from a voice-over cassette tape, has become a CD "trade card." But the rules for what goes on it still hold. For one thing, no headshots. "They don't want to see what you look like, they want to imagine what you look like," says McClanaghan. "With voice-overs, imagination is everything. What does that voice convey? Your trade card had better look like your CD sounds. It should offer the same experience."

"You have to remember that ad agencies are some of the most creative and visually arresting environments around," says Collins. "You're sending to creative people. The cover has to make them want to open that CD and listen to it." Studios that record your demo can refer you to graphic artists who know the business and industry standards.

"If you've just pressed a CD and it's aesthetically pleasing, send it to your agent and the casting houses," says Collins. "Follow up with a postcard featuring that same or spin-off artwork reminding them to check out your agency's reel online."

The newest, hottest way to market voice-over talent is just six months old. Geddes in March started posting their clients' voices at www.voicebank.net. Collins calls it "the AOL of voices. All the agencies are up there and all the agents and producers- in fact, anyone- has access [to the site]." The site helps level the playing field between big and small agencies, known and unknown talent. "You can listen to very famous people and see how they do it," says Collins. Geddes handles the monthly fees for their artists. But just one booking a month can cover that fee.

Chicago also has its own start-up online voice bank. Lou Johnson at Big City Voices put up their site two months ago at www.bigcityvoices.com. Johnson agrees that the market is wide open for African-American and Latino voices, but welcomes interested talent of any background to make an inquiry at info@bigcityvoices.com. Be prepared to have a minute of fine quality actual work that you can put up. "You can hear from who we have up there now that this is experienced talent with spots already recorded. What's new about us is that we can make that talent available live to producers worldwide via ISDN," says Johnson. ISDN is a "very expensive telephone line," he says "but most studios have it." Using ISDN, talent can be interviewed and auditioned live. "For example, Hispanic production in Miami, which is huge, can tap into our talent live," he says.

Talent's Responsibility to Market

"I always tell people to read 'The Guerrilla Marketers,' says Collins. "It's geared for people who want to go into business, but actors can glean so much from it about how to market themselves."

"Talent has to remember that the talent agency is not their publicist or manager," says McClanaghan. "Talent agencies want to feel in their hearts that they are serving their clients but really their job is to service the industry, the producers, copywriters. The agencies that are dependable and can provide what producers want are the ones producers will call, and that means more jobs for that agency's talent."

Once the voice-over demo is cut, actors have to take the lead on getting the CD artwork and on promoting themselves. They have to get an agent and keep themselves known to that agent by sending updated CDs and postcards with updates on what they are doing. "Talent sometimes complains that their agent should be sending them on everything because they can do everything," says McClanaghan. "But in this industry if you are everything, then you are nothing. You have to be who you are and be your type, and your agent has to understand that and recommend you accordingly."

Film Reels

Most agents agree that a film reel is not essential for getting on-camera work in Chicago. But agent Vanessa Lanier, who handles commercial, film and voice-over at Baker and Rowley, stresses that reels are essential for submitting to New York and LA and that even in Chicago they can sometimes give talent the upper hand. "If you have something on tape and it's professional, producers already know you can do it." But in Chicago reels are less necessary. "There are a limited number of casting directors who most agencies work with over and over, and they get to know the pool of talent." If an actor comes in wanting to pursue an on-camera career, Lanier advises them to audition for local, even student, independent films, but suggests looking at a director's prior work first. "It can't go on a reel if the look isn't professional," she says. Actors should also look again at any of their past on-camera work to see if anything can be used. Creating a reel is "a partnership between agent and actor," says Rowley.

Mickie Paskal, casting director at Tenner Paskal, notes that most of the talent she sees do not have a reel. "Most people in Chicago, if they have a reel, have three commercials and two lines from a movie they did. Reels are expensive, and we don't expect actors to get them made." Like most Chicago agencies, Tenner Paskal prefers to see talent in person. "It's different when they go to LA; then it's really important." Tenner Paskal's casting is made up of half film and television and half commercials. Most of their film casting is searches for an LA production when part of the shoot occurs locally.

Claire Simon of Simon Casting agrees that reels are nice "some of the time."

"I'll look at them," she says. "If an actor is unknown or from out of town, or an agent is trying to introduce them and they have a reel that looks good and shows a body of work, then it's good. Or if an actor is from LA and is relocating here." Simon presented an LA actor auditioning for a part in the television series "What About Joan" to Chicago producers using his reel, and the actor got the part.

Simon admits that she doesn't use reels much for Chicago, preferring to tape talent on site or have them meet directly with producers. But she stresses that for relocating to LA reels are essential. "That's what will get you in the door. If you have a body of work and the quality of the tape is impressive, then that will help get you an agent in LA"

Local talent auditioning for roles for LA-based productions can also be helped by a reel. "For *Save the Last Dance,* it was down to the wire between two actors for a role. I sent a local actor's demo to the producer in LA It was really good and that made the difference. She got the part."

Simon states that because talent in New York is often multi-listed as in Chicago, it is not quite as hard to get an agent in New York as in LA. "LA is more TV or film and usually talent works for one or the other." New York, like Chicago, is a big theatre town and agents in both places see theatre regularly.

"In Chicago, it's headshots, referrals from agents, and we see a lot of theatre. Seventy-five percent of our casting is for television and film, fifteen percent is commercials and the rest is theatre. Most of the film we cast for is shot here, like *High Fidelity, Save the Last Dance* and *Ali,* although that had multiple locations."

The film and television work that comes to Simon from NY or LA also includes searches where producers haven't found cast locally and are expanding the search. Simon puts together a tape of her suggestions for them.

Actors without on-camera experience have been known to create a fake or dummy reel. Lanier of Baker and Rowley says, "I've seen fake reels and they're not bad but my preference is to show legitimate work. If you have to put something on camera, do a monologue."

Your agent, casting director or headshot photographer should be able to refer you to a cinematographer to shoot a reel. There are many such providers in Chicago including Cinema Video Center and Video Replay, to name just two. Video reels can be very costly. If you are willing to chance a student cinematographer, put up a flyer offering payment for services at Columbia College film department. Ask to see what cinematographers have previously shot. Make sure the tape is shot on a higher quality format than VHS—digital beta cam or high 8 are good choices, so that it dubs well to VHS later without losing definition. Then ask that same student to help you edit down the tape.

But agents agree if you can't afford a reel, put your effort and your dollars into your headshot. "It's your calling card," says Lanier. "Keep it updated. List your union affiliations upfront, no guessing games. LA wants SAG because it shows a certain experience and quality. And never send your resumes and headshots in unstapled. That irritates every casting director I know. LA even wants them glued!"

Behind the Scenes of a Film/TV Audition

Says Claire Simon at Simon Casting, "The way the audition works is we get hired to help fill roles for a production; the director gives us a spec, his vision of the characters and the script. We read the script and send breakdowns to agents about the project and the characters. They send us back a list of talent. We go through the hundreds of submissions. Then we bring in talent for pre-reads if we don't know them well or if they are highly recommend by an agent and also review the talent we do know well. We'll narrow it down to six actors per role, put them on tape and send it to the producer and director. They come back saying who they want to see and where we need to continue to look and we'll go from there. Sometimes we tell them they really need to take another look at someone they didn't pick."

Actors can be best prepared by reviewing all the information they can. Above all, make sure you are on time and are available for the dates of production. Get a copy of the whole script, if possible, to fully understand the story and the character.

Making the Leap to LA

"When you have a substantial body of work," says Simon. "When you've worked at the great theatres here, Steppenwolf, the Goodman. When people start asking for you. Then you go out to LA for pilot season, January to April. Your agent is backing you, and you have a lot of meetings and auditions set up. If you have the support of an agent, a strong reel and are prepared and able to demonstrate to them what you did in Chicago, people in LA are always looking for fresh faces. And they do call us."

Ear Prompters

According to Lanier, owning and using an ear prompter is essential if you want to be in the trade industrials, which are essentially corporate training videos and are big business in Chicago. An ear prompter is a device, either wireless or not, worn in the ear that connects to a tape player and feeds actors their lines. Most in the business agree that it can be very useful for pages of technical dialogue delivered in measured tones, but that it can be death for any other kind of performance. Says Mickie Paskal, "They tend to flatten performance. I always tell people go ahead and go for it, but I can usually spot it and it usually detracts." It can also be a problem when recording commercials as well, says Paskal. "If the producer wants to try something three or four different ways and the actor is working off an ear prompter, we can't wait for them to re-record it and play it back to see if they can hear it well."

But for actors seriously thinking of getting into industrial voice-over, it might be advisable to explore investing in the equipment. Ear prompters are available at Radio Shack for about $200 each. Then it's wise to get them custom-fitted. Sargon Yonan on Madison Avenue is the only fitter in Chicago or go to www.ear-prompter.com.

The Photo Session

A good headshot is one of the most important investments an actor can make. It's your calling card, introduction and logo all rolled into one. As a result, it's important to be careful when choosing a photographer to ensure that the money you spend gets you the best shots possible.

1. Research

This is a big investment, so you want to do your research carefully. Though it may be tempting, DON'T SKIMP! Your headshot is your introduction to many casting people. You want it to look professional. Look for photographers whose style you like or who sound appealing to you. Some places to check:

PERFORMINK, This Book

Act One Studios–Act One has a portfolio of many photographers' work.

References– If a friend has had a good experience with a photographer, or if an agent recommends someone, check him or her out. Don't take this reference as gospel, though. What works for your friend may not work for you.

2. Consultation

Any legitimate photographer should offer a free consultation.
Look for the following things:

Space- Are you comfortable with the space the photographer shoots in?

Personality- Do you get along with the photographer? Do they listen to you and understand what you want to do? Are you able to be yourself?

Portfolio- Look at the photographer's work closely. Have they shot anyone who's similar to you in appearance? How are those shots? Do all the shots look the same, or does the photographer seem to change his/her style with each subject?

3. Make-up Artist

You may want to hire a make-up artist as well. The photographer may have someone available that they like to work with or you can hire your own. Do research. Make-up should enhance your look without changing it. In the end you want to look like you.

4. The Shoot

The day finally arrives. What can I do to ensure the best session possible?

Sleep- It's important to be well rested. Schedule your shoot at the time of day when you are at your best.

Clothes- Bring a lot of choices. In particular, bring clothes that show your shape without being too tight or revealing. One photographer recommends bringing clothing that is darker than your skin tone. Above all, bring clothes that you're comfortable in.

Music- Bring music that you love. It'll help you maintain positive energy and a positive mood.

5. Choosing Your Shot

Proof sheets are in hand, but how do you choose between all these tiny shots?

Get a Loupe- Though it may sound like a wolf of some sort, a loupe is actually a small magnifying eye piece that will help you get a better idea of what a shot will look like blown up.

Get Advice- See what shots your agent likes. If you have an experienced actor friend, see what they like.

Get a Concept- Know what sort of image you're looking to project and choose shots that reflect that. What are you trying to sell, and how are you going to project that?

Get Some Shots- If necessary, spend the extra money to get extra shots blown up. You'll never know exactly how a shot will look until it's in 8x10 format.

6. Retouching

If your shot's almost perfect—if one hair's out of place or if a wrinkle in your sweater is marring an otherwise perfect shot—get it retouched. This is a process, done either by hand or computer, that will remove those imperfections. Retouching should leave you looking like you, however. In the end, the shot has to represent how you look.

7. Reproduction

Now that you've chosen your shots, you have to get them reproduced.

Style- Matte finishes with a border are currently in style in Chicago. Ask your photographer and/or agent for their recommendations.

Font- Even the font your name is in can help express yourself. Print your name out in a bunch of different ones to find one that you like.

Lithographs- Lithographs are made by breaking a picture into dots, like printing a photograph in a newspaper. On the positive side, it's cheaper. On the negative, the quality is not as high. Lithographs might be useful for certain types of mass mailings, but most agents prefer the traditional photographic process.

8. Postcard

Finally, in addition to standard headshots, you may want to make a postcard. Postcards are used for invitations to agents and directors when you're in a show, thank you notes and other "Remember me?" purposes. Postcard photos can be much more wacky than traditional headshots and can even use more than one photograph. Anything that will help them remember you is suitable.

Photographers

Aaron Gang Photography
1016 N. Ashland
Chicago, IL 60622
773/782-4363
www.aarongang.com

Superior Headshots at Reasonable Rates. Polaroids included so you see what you're getting. Comfortable, fun atmosphere. Agent recommended. Excellent makeup/hair stylist available.

Allan Murray
1717 N. Hudson
Chicago, IL 60614
312/337-0286

Andrew Collings
1550 N. Damen
Chicago, IL 60622
773/384-2200
www.andrewcollings.com

Art Ketchum Studios
2215 S. Michigan
Chicago, IL 60616
312/842-1406
312/842-6546 - fax

Brad Baskin
850 N. Milwaukee
Chicago, IL 60622
312/733-0932
www.bradbaskin.com

Brian McConkey
(See our ad below)
312 N. May #6J
Chicago, IL 60607
312/563-1357
312/563-1615 - fax
www.gratefulheads.net

Camera I
Joe Weinshenker
3946 N. Monticello
Chicago, IL 60618
773/539-1119

Cat Conrad Photography
510 W. Belmont Ave., Ste. 1810
Chicago, IL 60657-4600
773/755-0612
773/755-0612 - fax
www.catconradphoto.com
HEADSHOTS - Quality New York photographer now in Chicago. You'll be relaxed and look your best. Top makeup/hair available.

Christopher Jacobs Studio
1443 W. Grand
Chicago, IL 60622
312/563-0987 • 312/563-0588 - fax
www.jacobs-photography.com

Classic Photography, Inc.
(See our ad below)
John Karl Breun
38 South Main St. #2A
Mount Prospect, IL 60056
847/259-8373 • 847/259-8474 - fax
www.classicphoto.com

Costume Images
3634 W. Fullerton
Chicago, IL 60647
773/276-8971 •773/276-0717 - fax
www.costume-images.com

Dale Fahey
773/973-5757

Dan DuVerney
1937 W. Division - 1st floor
Chicago, IL 60622
773/252-6639

Daniel Byrnes Photography
113 W. North
Chicago, IL 60610
312/337-1174

Actors, Models, Dancers, Musicians: Whether your needs are for headshots, portfolios, or promotional photos, we have the experience to give you individualized images to be remembered. 20 years experience in Chicago and Los Angeles. Ask about our Scene Stealers Portfolios. VISA and Mastercard accepted.

David Puffer Studio
773/267-6500

Deon Jahnke
228 S. 1st St.
Milwaukee, WI 53204
414/224-8360 • 414/224-8356 - fax
www.execpc.com\~deon

Edda Taylor Photographie
Courthouse Square #304
Crown Point, IN 46307 NO
219/662-9500
www.eddataylor.com

Elan Photography
5120 Belmont #A
Downers Grove, IL 60515
630/960-1400 • 630/969-1972 - fax
www.elanphotography.com

G. Thomas Ward
(See our ad on previous page)
1949 W. Leland #1
Chicago, IL 60640
773/271-6813
www.thepeoplephotographer.com

Gary Jochim
1470 W. Huron #2F
Chicago, IL 60622
312/738-3204
312/738-3204 - fax

Gary Trantafil
312 N. May #100
Chicago, IL 60607
312/666-1029
312/666-1259 - fax

Gerald Peskin Photography
681 Academy Dr.
Northbrook, IL 60062
847/498-0291

Gerber/Scarpelli Photography
1144 W. Fulton Market
Chicago, IL 60607
312/455-1144
312/455-1544 - fax

Guy J. Cardarelli
119 W. Hubbard - 3rd floor
Chicago, IL 60610
312/321-0694

Guy Tinklenberg Photography
847/604-4118

IronHorse Productions
3310 S. Aberdeen #1-A
Chicago, IL 60608
773/890-4355
773/890-4345 - fax

Isabel Raci
773/486-1980
isabelraci@core.com

Jai Girard
3428 N. Janssen
Chicago, IL 60657
773/929-2625

Jason Smith Photography
773/353-2033
www.jasonsmith.com

Jean Whiteside
6410 N. Glenwood #1S
Chicago, IL 60626
773/274-5545

Jennifer Girard
1455 W. Roscoe
Chicago, IL 60657
773/929-3730
773/871-2308 - fax

JLB Photography
(See our ad the next page)
350 N. Ogden
Chicago, IL 60607
312/339-3909

Joseph A. Nicita
1500 W. Ohio
Chicago, IL 60622
312/666-2443

Joseph Amenta Photography
555 W. Madison #3802
Chicago, IL 60661
773/248-2488

Keith Claunch
2540 W. Eastwood
Chicago, IL 60625
312/285-6074

Kenneth Simmons
3026 E. 80th St.
Chicago, IL 60617
773/684-7232

L.L. Rice Photography
773/404-9269

Larry Lapidus
2650 W. Belden #304
Chicago, IL 60647
773/235-3333
www.lapidusphoto.com

I am considered by many to be the most reputable "headshot" photographer in Chicago. My directorial technique sets me apart from other photographers. The rapport we develop is the most essential tool in capturing your true individuality. We will express your character in a fashion that is perfect for commercial purposes in theatre, television, or film. Recommended by top talent agents, casting directors, and acting teachers. Satisfaction guaranteed. Photographic fees: $425 includes 45 minute consultation, three rolls, and two 8x10 custom prints. Credit cards accepted.

475
200 Deposit at consultation

Laurie Locke
4018 S. Oak Park Ave.
Stickney, IL 60402
708/749-2444

Linn Ehrlich
312/209-2107

Mary Clare
1201 Laura Ln.
Lake Bluff, IL 60044
847/680-3686

Mary Rouleau Photography
1030 Forest Ave.
Evanston, IL 60202
847/328-0219

Max Photography
P.O. Box 14620
Chicago, IL 60614
773/477-6548

Michael Brosilow Photography
(See our ad below)
1370 N. Milwaukee
Chicago, IL 60622
773/235-4696
773/235-4698 - fax

Michael J. Kardas Studio
2635 N. Albany
Chicago, IL 60647
773/227-7925

Michael McCafrey Photography
109 W. Hubbard
Chicago, IL 60610
312/222-9776

Michael Vollan
800 W. Huron - 3rd floor
Chicago, IL 60622
312/997-2347

Pete Stenberg
Photography
312.421.8850
1048 W. Fulton Market St.
Chicago, IL 60607
email: pdsphoto@aol.com
specializing in:
actors headshots
modeling composites
children + adults
call for your FREE consultation!
credit cards accepted
over 20 years of experience!
agency recommended!

Mike Canale Photography
614 Davis St.
Evanston, IL 60201
847/864-0146

Moore Photographic
773/276-0249

Paladino Photography
105 E. Burlington
Riverside, IL 60546
708/447-2822

Papadakis Photography
17 Lexington Rd.
South Barrington, IL 60010
847/428-4400
847/428-4403 - fax
www.papadakisphotography.com

Patrick Harold Productions
1757 W. Augusta
Chicago, IL 60622
312/226-3831
312/226-3832 - fax

Paul Sherman Photography
955 W. Fulton - 3rd Floor
Chicago, IL 60607
312/633-0848
312/666-1498 - fax
www.paulshermanphotos.com

Payton Studios
Reginald Payton
2701 W. Fulton
Chicago, IL 60612
312/661-0049
www.paytonstudios.com

Pete Stenberg Photography
(See our ad on previous page)
1048 W. Fulton Market
Chicago, IL 60607
312/421-8850
312/421-8830 - fax
www.petestenberg.qpg.com

Photographing people at their best! Specializing in headshots for actors and composites for models. Renowned Chicago photographer for over 20 years.

Children and Adults.

Agency recommended.

Free consultation.

Make-up artist /hair stylist available.

Rush service.

Credit cards accepted.

Located in Chicago's West Loop area, near several agencies.

Relaxed, fun atmosphere.

Peter Bosy
6435 Indian Head Trail
Indian Head Park, IL 60525
708/246-3778
708/246-1080 - fax
www.peterbosy.com\faces.html

Photographic Creations
Robert D. Wright
15 Stratford Ct.
Indian Head Park, IL 60525
708/246-8043

Pret a Poser Photography
April Wilson
100 E. Hillside Ave.
Barrington, IL 60010
847/382-2211
847/304-9419 - fax

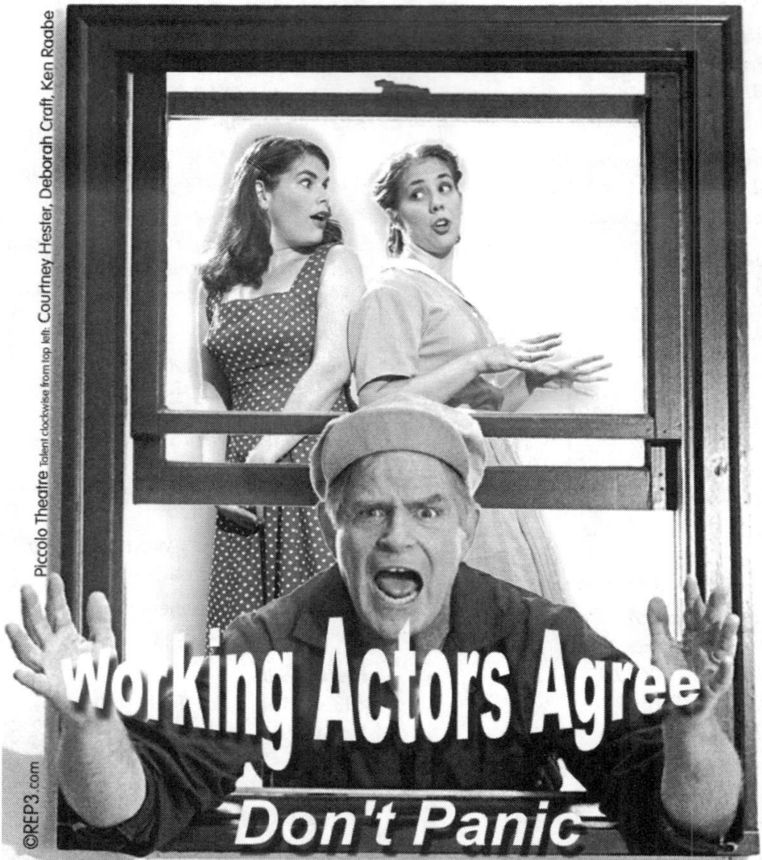
Piccolo Theatre Talent clockwise from top left: Courtney Hester, Deborah Craft, Ken Raabe
©REP3.com
Working Actors Agree
Don't Panic

ProShot Photography
1095 Willow Ct.
Aurora, IL 60504
708/820-6756

REP3.com aka
Robert Erving Potter III
(See our ad on previous page)
Chicago Photographer
2056 W. Superior
Chicago, IL
312/226-2060
www.REP3.com

"I recommend Rob (REP3.com) highly; his photographs, input and suggestions result in excellent, professional marketing devises for the Actor." -Joyce Sloane Producer Emeritus, The Second City.

REP3 dedicates Mondays to the Theatre Industry. Please make an appointment: Discuss your photographic & marketing needs, view REP3's portfolio & schedule a shoot.

Rick Mitchell, Inc.
652 W. Grand
Chicago, IL 60610
312/829-1700

Rubinic Photography
319 N. Western
Chicago, IL 60612
312/733-8901
312/733-8902 - fax
www.rubinic.com

Sandra Bever
1521 Dearborn St.
Joliet, IL 60435
815/723-3051
815/727-1687 - fax
www.sandrabever.com

Sara Levinson
1142 S. Michigan Ave.
Chicago, IL 60607
312/583-0338
www.saralevinsonphoto.com

Sharon White Photography
2941 W. Belmont
Chicago, IL 60618
773/539-0870
312/539-0434 - fax

Sima Imaging
Sid Afzali
1821 W. Hubbard #301
Chicago, IL 60622
312/733-1788
312/733-6890 - fax

Steve Greiner
1437 W. Thomas
Chicago, IL 60622
773/227-4375
773/227-4379 - fax

Steven Wright
1545 N. Larrabee
Chicago, IL 60610
312/943-1718

Suzanne Plunkett
3047 N. Lincoln #300
Chicago, IL 60657
773/477-3775
773/477-4640 - fax

Tom Krantz Photography
180 Marsh Ave.
Montgomery, IL 60538
800/898-6282

Triangle Studio
3445 N. Broadway
Chicago, IL 60657
773/472-1015
773/472-2201 - fax

Tyrone Taylor Photography
1143 E. 81st
Chicago, IL 60619
773/978-1505

Vic Bider Photography
1142 W. Taylor
Chicago, IL 60607
312/829-5540

Wayne Cable Photography
312 N. Carpenter
Chicago, IL 60607
312/226-0303
312/226-6995 - fax

Winkelman Photography
P.O. Box 531
Oak Park, IL 60303-0531
312/953-2141

Yamashiro Studio
2643 N. Clybourn
Chicago, IL 60614
773/883-0440
773/883-0453 - fax
www.yamashirostudio.com

Photo Reproduction Houses

A&B Photography
650 W. Lake - 2nd floor
Chicago, IL 60661
312/454-4554 • 312/454-1634 - fax

ABC Pictures
(See our ad on previous page)
1867 E. Florida
Springfield, MO 65803
417/869-3456 • 417/869-9185 - fax
www.abcpictures.com

Acme Copy Corp.
218 S. Wabash - 4th floor
Chicago, IL 60604
312/922-6975 • 312/922-6976 - fax

Bodhis Photo Service
112 W. Grand
Chicago, IL 60610
312/321-1141 • 312/321-3610 - fax

Composites International
12335 S. Keeler Ave.
Alsip, IL 60803
708/597-3449 • 708/597-3421 - fax

Minuteman Press
445 W. Erie
Chicago, IL 60610
312/368-0577
312/368-4989 - fax

National Photo Service
(See our on the next page)
114 W. Illinois
Chicago, IL 60610
312/644-5211 • 312/644-6285 - fax
www.nationalphoto.com

Photoscan
646 Bryn Mawr St.
Orlando, FL 32804
800/352-6367
www.ggphotoscan.com

Quantity Photo
Rich Pace
119 W. Hubbard - 2nd floor
Chicago, IL 60610
312/644-8290
312/644-8299 - fax
www.quantityphoto.com

Photo Retouching

Bob Faetz Retouching
203 N. Wabash #1320
Chicago, IL 60601
312/759-0933
312/759-0944 - fax

G. Mycio Digital Imaging
333 N. Michigan #710
Chicago, IL 60601
312/782-1472
312/782-9874 - fax

Irene Levy Retouching Studios
300 N. State #3431
Marina Towers
Chicago, IL 60610
312/464-0504
312/464-1665 - fax

John Bresnahan
3320 N. Clifton
Chicago, IL 60657
773/248-7211

Are you getting the right
exposure?
National
Photo Imaging
INCORPORATED
108 West Illinois Street
Chicago, IL 60610
toll free (800) 211-7978
phone (312) 644-5211
fax (312) 644-6285
email nps@nationalphoto.com
www.nationaltalent.com
Get all the exposure you need!
Make National Photo your source for
8x10 Head Shots,
Model Comp Cards,
Photo Postcards,
Photo Business Cards,
Digital Retouching,
CD Duplication
and our Free On-line Talent Database!
We can even store your negatives for easy re-ordering.
With over fifty years serving the acting and modeling community
National Photo has... everything you need to get exposed!

Makeup Artists

Andrea Nichols
312/851-6754

Anna Intravatolo
11350 Behrns
Melrose Park, IL 60164
847/455-2596
847/455-5772 - fax

Blair Laden
1864 Sherman Ave.
Evanston, IL 60201
847/328-1177

Cathy Durkin
1749 N. Wells #1106
Chicago, IL 60614
312/787-0848

Channings Day Spa
54 E. Oak
Chicago, IL 60611
312/280-1994
312/280-1929 - fax
www.channings.com

Che Sguardo Makeup Studio
500 N. Wells
Chicago, IL 60610
312/527-0821

Darcy McGrath
312/337-1353

Dawn Laurrie
312/837-6404

Denise Milito
(See our ad on previous page)
773/465-1134 - cell
tortoisedm@aol.com

Denise Milito is a make-up artist specializing in areas of print, film and television. Privately trained by a seasoned make-up artist of seventeen years, Denise has the ability to capture a range of looks from natural to more sophisticated artistic effects. Please call 773/456-1134 for price quotes.

Femline Hair Designs, Inc.
3500 Midwest Rd.
Oakbrook, IL 60522
630/655-2212

Gina McIver
Make-Up Artist
(See our ad on page 112)
708/268-4536

Being a professional make-up artist, Gina McIver has been working in Chicago for two years. Graduating from The Make-Up Designory in California, she has recieved training from the most qualified make-up artists. Her training is specialized in Beauty, Character, and Hairstyling. If interested, please call and book an appointment.

Jeanean-Lorrece Eldridge
P.O. Box 21397
Chicago, IL 60621
773/651-5690

Jenna Garagiola
Make-up & Hair
(See our ad on the previous page)
773/447-6550

A rising star in the industry, Jenna has commercial experience with headshots, model composites, and television. Jenna understands the importance of your photographs as your marketing tool and will give you the confidence and peace of mind to be the best you can be.

Jerry Malik
312/760-2515 - pgr.

Krissy Bailey
(See our ad below)
219/864-7822
219/781-5755 - Cel
Liplash@aol.com

Specializing in the art of make-up. I work with you to create a personalized look, specifically tailored to you and your features. I have worked for over 6 years as a make-up artist with renowned Chicago photographer, Pete Stenberg. All ages - All skin types - All Ethnicities. Portfolio available.

Marcus Geeter
655 W. Irving Park #207
Chicago, IL 60613
773/975-8242
773/296-2905 - fax

Make-up Artist

Stephanie Spero

- Beauty
- Print
- Character
- T.V.

Home: (708) 425-7449
Cell: (708) 404-7449

Make-up Artist

Gina McIver

All aspects of professional make-up.

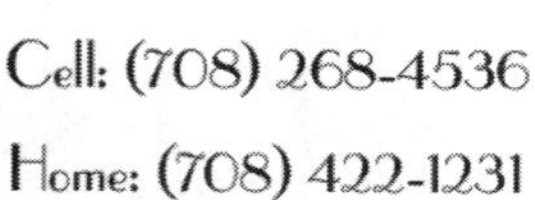

Cell: (708) 268-4536
Home: (708) 422-1231

Marianne Strokirk Salon
361 W. Chestnut
Chicago, IL 60610
312/944-4428
312/944-4429 - fax
www.mariannestrokirk.com

Marilyn Miglin Institute
112 E. Oak
Chicago, IL 60611
800/662-1120
312/943-1184 - fax
www.marilyn-miglin.com

Media Hair & Makeup Group
Maureen Kalagian
708/848-8400

Model Image Center
1218 W. Belmont
Chicago, IL 60657
773/348-9349
773/348-9366 - fax
www.modelimagecenter.com

Nancy P. Stanley
773/871-1396

Nouvelle Femme
1151 Wilmette Ave.
Wilmette, IL 60091
847/251-6698

Robyn Goldman
312/751-8994

Sandy Morris
773/549-4951

Sharleen Acciari
1007 W. Webster
Chicago, IL 60614
773/248-1273

Shelly Rolf
630/262-1142 • 630/262-0461 - fax

Stephanie Spero
Make-Up Artist
(See our ad on previous page)
708/404-7449 - cell
708/425-7449 - home
chirpspero@hotmail.com
Stephanie Spero has been a working make-up artist in Chicago for five years. She is a graduate of The Make-Up Designory in Burbank, California, where she was certified in Beauty and Character Make-Up and Theatrical Hairstyling. Call and book an appointment with Stephanie for a new look on make-up artistry!

Suzi Ostos
773/868-1738

Syd Simons Cosmetics, Inc.
6601 W. North Ave.
Oak Park, IL 60302
877/943-2333
www.sydsimons.com

Tammy McEwen
Make Up & Hair
630/226-9092

Transformations by Rori
146 N. Oak Park Ave.
Oak Park, IL 60301
708/383-8338 • 708/383-6796 - fax

Transformations by Rori
110 S. Arlington Heights Rd.
Arlington Heights, IL 60005
847/454-0600

By Kevin Heckman

The resumé that is glued, stapled or otherwise affixed (hopefully) to the back of your headshot is a key piece of your presentation. No one gets hired in this business based on their resumé, but a good one garners more respect and a bad one can lose you a job.

For information on what should go into a resumé, check out (appropriately) our checklist. If you'd like to know some of the things that shouldn't, read on.

Actually, these particular points I mention aren't all big no-no's, though some are. I also include things I or other directors have simply found strange. Each of these oddities has appeared in some form on actual resumés.

Joe Thesbyin

EMC

123 Strasberg Lane
Chicago, IL 60618
Pgr. 773/555-5555

Height: 5'10"
Hair: Brown
Eyes: Hazel
Voice:Tenor

The EMC Thang

I've never understood why actors list their EMC (Equity Membership Candidate) status under their name. I assume it's a spin-off of listing your union memberships there, but union membership affects casting and EMC doesn't. EMCs gather weeks by working as a non-Equity actor in certain Equity houses. Once they accumulate 50 weeks, they have to join the union with their next Equity job or drop their EMC status. The only situation in which EMC could influence casting is if Joe Thesbyin has close to 50 weeks. Otherwise, he's just emphasizing something that doesn't matter.

Anita Ajant

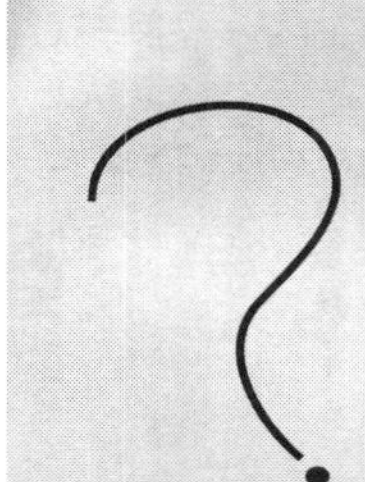

Height: 5'7"
Hair: Ochre
Eyes: Hazel
Voice: High Tenor

Call that actor...

Wow, Anita gave a great audition. I should definitely give her a call. Many directors separate your headshot and resumé from the cover letter that accompanied it. If your resumé doesn't have contact info, no one will contact you. Of course, many actors don't list an address or their home phone numbers as a security precaution, but you've got to give casting people some way to reach you.

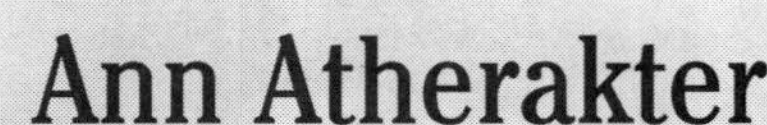
Ann Atherakter

23 Strasberg Lane
Chicago, IL 60618
Pgr. 773/555-5555

Height: 5'10"
Hair: Brown
Eyes: Hazel
Voice:Tenor

What does she look like?

If a casting director gets 200 headshots and resumés over a three-day span, and if two percent of the headshots are attached to their accompanying resumés with only a paper clip, what are the odds that the paper clip will successfully keep those resumés with their headshots? If you chose E. Not Good, you're correct!! Those resumés will probably get tossed. Staple, glue, whatever. Just make sure your resumé stays attached to your picture.

Production	**Role**	**Theatre**
Ten Little Indians	Tonto	Misaligned Theatre
You're a Good Man Charlie Brown	Calvin	Griffin Ascending
I'm 25 and Who the Fuck Cares	Bette	Stage Left
Dark at the Top of the Stairs	The Electrician	Goomdan Theater
Red Noses	The Pediatrician	Off-Stage Right

Who produced this show?

What's wrong with this picture? Only that Stage Left didn't produce *I'm 25 and Who the Fuck Cares.* It went up at Stage Left, but was produced by Irrelevant Players. Needless to say, if this resumé shows up at Stage Left, this actor's probably not going to get called in. Furthermore, any director who's familiar with Stage Left is probably going to think that this actor's lying about their work. Not the image she wanted to project.

Production	**Role**	**Theatre**
Ten Little Indians	Tonto	Misaligned Theatre
You're a Good Man Charlie Brown	Calvin	Griffin Ascending
I'm 25 and Who the Fuck Cares	Bette	Stage Left
Dark at the Top of the Stairs	The Electrician	Goomdan Theater
Red Noses	The Pediatrician	Audience Right Theatre
Tight-Ass Androgynous	The Queen	Theatre Pyu
Glass Meringue	Chef Tom	The Hyperactives
Six Degrees of Being Apart	Sydney Poitier	Eating Crow Theater
Billy Joe and the Remarkably Hued Overcoat	Billy Joe	Downtown Hilton Theater
Goddamn Car	Driver	Well-Known Window Productions
Always Cross-Hatched	Binky	Regal Porgie Playhouse
A Collection of Blue Hominids	The Blue One	Nettles Road Theatre

Get me my magnifying glass, Watson

The fact is, many directors look more closely at your training and skills than they do your credits. There's no reason to cram every show you've ever done on your resumé. Choose those credits that put you in the best light. Include name theatres, well-known shows or anything that got good press. You may even want to have different resumés for different genres: classical work, musicals, children's theatre, etc. Then you can emphasize work that particularly suits you for that genre.

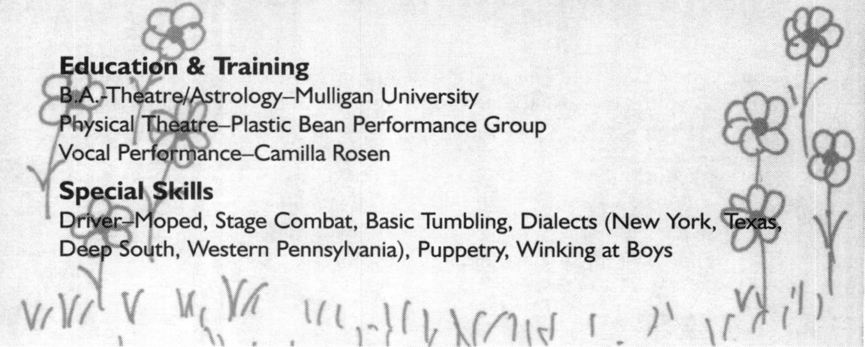

Education & Training
B.A.-Theatre/Astrology–Mulligan University
Physical Theatre–Plastic Bean Performance Group
Vocal Performance–Camilla Rosen

Special Skills
Driver–Moped, Stage Combat, Basic Tumbling, Dialects (New York, Texas, Deep South, Western Pennsylvania), Puppetry, Winking at Boys

Well isn't that special

Actors go to all sorts of lengths to be sure their resumé will be noticed. In this case, the actor has printed her resumé on pretty flower paper. Unfortunately, flowers, clouds or pink neon paper are more likely to upstage your resumé than call attention to it. They'll remember the paper but not the person. Present yourself as a professional. If your resumé feels sparse, do a student film, take a class, or work for one of Chicago's dozens of small theatres who might see your potential to build your resumé. A cheap attention grabber can annoy casting people and that will hurt instead of help.

Additionally, beware of the cute special skill. First of all, be sure it's a skill. "Winking at boys" isn't really that difficult, and listing it won't necessarily impress anyone. Also, be sure you can do whatever it is the moment they ask. If you list "Belch the Pledge of Allegiance" as a skill, you'd better be able to do it right there. Special Skills can help you get the job, but it's also part of your presentation. If you get too cutesy, casting people are less likely to treat you as a professional.

Chances are, most of these errors or oddities aren't going to make or break your chances at getting the part, but your resumé introduces you and it should introduce you as a professional actor. If you've done that, you're one step closer to convincing a director you should be seriously considered for the part.

The Killer Resumé

Your resumé is often the most important piece of material a casting director or agent will receive from you. Present yourself in the best light possible. Highlight your strengths. Be sure that it's easy to read. And don't forget to include:

1. Your name

This should be at the top and in the largest font.

2. Your stats

Height, weight, hair and eye color are all standard. Don't include your age or age range. They'll figure that out themselves.

3. Your beeper or contact number

Obviously you want to be reachable. Don't include your address unless they specifically ask for it. You never know who'll get their hands on your resumé. Some agencies won't want your number on the resumé. They want all bookings to go through them. If you do have your number on a resumé and you get a call that should go through your agent, refer it to your agent. Work leads to work.

4. Room for an agency stamp or sticker

Once you get representation, you don't want to have to completely redesign your resumé!

5. For theatre, film, etc.

a. List production name to the left,

b. Your role in the middle,

c. Theatre, studio or production company to the right.

6. For film, also indicate type of work

(i.e. "Day Player" or "Principal")

You may have been brilliant in that independent film, but the agent/director may never have seen it. Listing "Queen Anne" on your resumé doesn't tell them anything, but indicating it was a principal does.

Commercials

Write "Commercial list available upon request"

This keeps you from getting into the sensitive and confusing issue of product conflict until you have to.

7. Training

Either list:

Areas of training

Corresponding teachers

Or

Schools or studios

Classes taken

Use whichever method shows you off best. If you've had impressive teachers, be sure to mention their names. If you've trained at schools that are recognizable, mention them.

8. University degrees

9. Special skills

a. Dialects

b. Sports (Indicate level of skill)

c. Languages spoken (Indicate fluency)

d. Odd skills or talents (Be sure you can do it!!)

Anything that doesn't fit into the above categories can go here. A lot of actors get cute in this section. That's fine, but if you list "Choking dog impressions," you'd better be able to impersonate a choking dog on a moment's notice.

10. Prioritize your Resumé

If your after theatre work, list that first. If film/commercials are more your game then throw that on top.

.esumé Services

Act I Bookstore
2540 N. Lincoln
Chicago, IL 60614
773/348-6757 • 773/348-5561 - fax
www.act1books.com

Act I Bookstore serves everyone from Chicago to Sao Paolo to Istanbul for its theatre and film book needs. You can find thousands of plays, acting books, screenplays, agent listings, monologues, musicals, audition notices, reading copies of shows currently auditioning, a professional resumé service, theatre games, and many other books for actors, directors, writers, producers, designers, teachers and filmmakers. Open Mon-Wed 10-8 and Thur-Sun 10-6. The best online bookstore for theatre and film is www.act1books.com.

Bob Behr
Resumés by Mac
4738 N. LaPorte
Chicago, IL 60630
773/685-7721 • 773/283-9839 - fax

Chicago Actor Help
Trent
5045 N. Damen, #1E
Chicago, IL 60625
773/334-1709
www.cah.freeservers.com

We provide specialized services for the beginning or professional actor. Like designing and printing resumés, cover letters, and agent or theatre mailing labels. Your resumé can be printed on the back of your headshot for a very professional look. We can even mail your headshot and cover letter to all the agents or theatres!

Ink Well
112 W. Illinois
Chicago, IL 60610
312/644-4700
312/644-4703 - fax

Trade Papers

Act One Reports
640 N. LaSalle #535
Chicago, IL 60610
312/787-9384
312/787-3234 - fax
www.actone.com

Updated listings of agencies, casting directors, photographers, and industry related information.

American Theatre
355 Lexington Ave.
New York, NY 10017
212/697-5230
212/557-5817 - fax
www.tcg.org

National theatre periodical containing news, features, and articles.

Audition News
P.O. Box 250
Bloomingdale, IL 60108
630/894-2278
630/894-8364 - fax
Audition notices for the greater Midwest.

Backstage
770 Broadway - 6th floor
New York, NY 10003
646/654-5700
www.backstage.com
The theatrical trade paper for the east coast.

Backstage West
5055 Wilshire Blvd. - 5th floor
Los Angeles, CA 90036
323/525-2356
323/525-2354 - fax
www.backstagewest.com
The theatrical trade paper for the west coast.

Breakdown Services, Ltd.
1120 S. Robertson Blvd. - 3rd floor
Los Angeles, CA 90035
310/276-9166
310/276-8829 - fax
www.breakdownservices.com
Creates cast breakdowns for film, TV, theatre and commercials.

Callboard
870 Market St. #375
San Francisco, CA 94102
415/430-1140
415/430-1145 - fax
www.theatrebayarea.org
The theatrical trade paper for the San Francisco area.

Casting News
P.O. Box 201
Boston, MA 02134
617/787-2991
The theatre and film trade paper for Boston and Eastern Massachusettes.

Equity News
Actor's Equity Association
165 W. 46th
New York, NY 10036
212/719-9570 • 212/921-8454 - fax
Union news and updates for members.

Hollywood Reporter
5055 Wilshire Blvd.
Los Angeles, CA 90036-4396
323/525-2150
www.hollywoodreporter.com

PerformInk
3223 N. Sheffield - 3rd floor
Chicago, IL 60657
773/296-4600 • 773/296-4621 - fax
www.performink.com
Chicago's Entertainment Trade Paper. The art, the business, the industry.

Ross Reports Television and Film
770 Broadway
New York, NY 10003-9595
646/654-5863
www.backstage.com/rossreports
Updates on production and casting in feature film and television.

Screen and Stage Directory
The National Casting Guide
888/332-6700
www.pgdirect.com
Resource directory for the acting industry on a national basis.

Screen Magazine
16 W. Erie
Chicago, IL 60610
312/664-5236
312/664-8425 - fax
www.screenmag.com
Chicago's film trade paper.

Show Music Magazine
Goodspeed Opera House
Box 466 - Goodspeed Landing
East Haddam, CT 06423-0466
860/873-8664
860/873-2329 - fax
www.goodspeed.org

Side Splitters
P.O. Box 5353
Wheaton, IL 60189
630/942-9710

The Chicago Creative Directory
333 N. Michigan #810
Chicago, IL 60601
312/236-7337
312/236-6078 - fax
www.creativedir.com

Theatre Directories
P.O. Box 510
Dorset, VT 05251
802/867-2223
802/867-0144 - fax
www.theatredirectories.com
Publishes Summer Theatre Directory, Regional Theatre Directory and more.

Variety
P.O. Box 15878
North Hollywood, CA 91615
800/552-3632 - subscriptions
www.variety.com

Answering Services

Burke Communications
P.O. Box 4152
Oak Park, IL 60303-4152
708/383-8580
708/386-1336 - fax
www.burkecommsystems.com

Beepers

Comm One Wireless
1437 W. Taylor
Chicago, IL 60607
312/850-9400
312/850-9442 - fax

MCI Worldcom
800/571-6682

Electronic Beepers Inc.
61 E. Washington
Chicago, IL 60602
312/332-6024

PortaCom
427 S. Dearborn
Chicago, IL 60605
312/939-PAGE
312/356-8804 - fax

Skytel
800/456-3333

SmartBeep
800/BEEP-199

Weblink Wireless
800/864-4357
888/304-9899 - fax
www.pagemart.com

Verizon Wireless
800/MOBILE-1

Cell Phones

Verizon Wireless
800/MOBILE-1

AT&T
888/344-3332

Cellular One
800/CELLONE

Comm One Wireless
1437 W. Taylor
Chicago, IL 60607
312/850-9400
312/850-9442 - fax

MCI Worldcom
800/571-6682
312/781-6030

Prime Co.
800/774-6326

The Sound Advantage
2911 N. Clark
Chicago, IL 60657
773/404-1288
773/404-1291 - fax

Supplies

ystery Tour
npster
ove, IL 60053
-5090
847/966-7280 - fax

All Dressed Up Costumes
150 S. Water
Batavia, IL 60510
630/879-5130
630/879-3374 - fax
www.alldressedupcostumes.com

Broadway Costumes, Inc. •
1100 W. Cermak
Chicago, IL 60608
312/829-6400
312/829-8621 - fax
www.broadwaycostumes.com

Center Stage
497 Rt. 59
Aurora, IL 60504
630/851-9191

Che Sguardo Makeup Studio •
500 N. Wells
Chicago, IL 60610
312/527-0821

Chicago Hair Group •
734 N. LaSalle
Chicago, IL 60610
312/337-4247
Focusing primarily on wigs.

Fantasy Costumes • Headquarters
4065 N. Milwaukee
Chicago, IL 60641
773/777-0222
773/777-4228 - fax
www.fantasycostumes.com

Grand Stage Lighting Company •
630 W. Lake
Chicago, IL 60661
312/332-5611
312/258-0056 - fax
www.grandstage.com

Josie O'Kain Costume & Theatre Shop
2419B W. Jefferson St.
Joliet, IL 60435
815/741-9303
815/741-9316 - fax
www.josieokain.com

Razzle Dazzle Costumes
1038 Lake St.
Oak Park, IL 60301
708/383-5962
708/383-0069 - fax
www.razzledazzlecostumes.com

Riley's Trick & Novelty Shop
6442 W. 111th
Worth, IL 60482
708/448-0075
708/448-0999 - fax
www.rileystrickshop.com

Syd Simons Cosmetics, Inc.
6601 W. North Ave.
Oak Park, IL 60302
877/943-2333
www.sydsimons.com

Stage Weapons

Arms and Armor
1101 Stinson Blvd. NE
Minneapolis, MN 55413
612/331-6473
www.armor.com

Center Firearms Co.
10 W. 37th St.
New York, NY 10018
212/244-4040 • 212/947-1233 - fax

The Armoury American Fencers Supply
1180 Folsom St.
San Francisco, CA 94103
415/863-7911
415/431-4931 - fax
www.amfence.com

Sheet Music

Act I Bookstore
2540 N. Lincoln
Chicago, IL 60614
773/348-6757
773/348-5561 - fax
www.act1books.com

Act I Bookstore serves everyone from Chicago to Sao Paolo to Istanbul for its theatre and film book needs. You can find thousands of plays, acting books, screenplays, agent listings, monologues, musicals, audition notices, reading copies of shows currently auditioning, a professional resumé service, theatre games, and many other books for actors, directors, writers, producers, designers, teachers and filmmakers. Open Mon-Wed 10-8 and Thur-Sun 10-6. The best online bookstore for theatre and film is www.act1books.com.

Carl Fisher Music
333 S. State
Chicago, IL 60604
312/427-6652
312/427-6653 - fax

Lighting Rental

Chicago Spotlight, Inc.
1658 W. Carroll
Chicago, IL 60612
312/455-1171
312/455-1744 - fax
www.chicagospotlight.com

Designlab
328 N. Albany
Chicago, IL 60612
773/265-1100
773/265-0800 - fax
www.designlab-chicago.com

Grand Stage Lighting Company
630 W. Lake
Chicago, IL 60661
312/332-5611
312/258-0056 - fax
www.grandstage.com

Dance Supplies

American Dance Center Ballet Co.
10464 W. 163rd Pl.
Orland Park, IL 60462
708/747-4969
708/747-0424 - fax
Ballet, Point, Jazz, Hip-Hop, Modern, Tap, Swing

Big N Little Shoes
3142 W. 111th
Chicago, IL 60655
773/239-6066

Dance & Mime Shop
643 W. Grand
Chicago, IL 60610
312/666-4406
www.danceandmimeshop.com

Illinois Theatrical
P.O. Box 34284
Chicago, IL 60634
773/745-7777
800/877-6027 - fax

Leo's Dancewear
1900 N. Narragansett
Chicago, IL 60639
773/745-5600
773/889-7593 - fax
www.leosdancewear.com

Motion Unlimited
218 S. Wabash - 8th floor
Chicago, IL 60604
312/922-3330
312/922-7770 - fax

Costume Shops

A Lost Eras Costumes & Props
Charlotte Walters
1511 W. Howard
Chicago, IL 60626
773/764-7400
773/764-7433 - fax
www.alostera.com

A Magical Mystery Tour
6010 W. Dempster
Morton Grove, IL 60053
847/966-5090
847/966-7280 - fax

Action Fabrics
214 E. Chicago Ave.
Westmont, IL 60559
630/323-1962

All Dressed Up Costumes
150 S. Water
Batavia, IL 60510
630/879-5130
630/879-3374 - fax
www.alldressedupcostumes.com

Beatnix
3400 N. Halsted
Chicago, IL 60657
773/281-6933
773/281-0929 - fax

Beverly Costume Shop
11628 S. Western
Chicago, IL 60643
773/779-0068
773/779-2434 - fax
www.beverlycostume.com

Broadway Costumes, Inc.
1100 W. Cermak
Chicago, IL 60608
312/829-6400
312/829-8621 - fax
www.broadwaycostumes.com

Center Stage
497 Rt. 59
Aurora, IL 60504
630/851-9191

Chicago Costume Company
1120 W. Fullerton
Chicago, IL 60614
773/528-1264
773/935-4197 - fax
www.chicagocostume.com

Dance & Mime Shop
643 W. Grand
Chicago, IL 60610
312/666-4406
www.danceandmimeshop.com

Facemakers, Inc.
140 Fifth St.
Savannah, IL 61074
815/273-3944
815/273-3966 - fax
www.facemakersinc.com

Fantasy Costumes Headquarters
4065 N. Milwaukee
Chicago, IL 60641
773/777-0222
773/777-4228 - fax
www.fantasycostumes.com

Flashy Trash
3524 N. Halsted
Chicago, IL 60657
773/327-6900
773/327-9736 - fax
www.flashytrash.com

Josie O'Kain Costume & Theatre Shop
2419B W. Jefferson St.
Joliet, IL 60435
815/741-9303
815/741-9316 - fax
www.josieokain.com

Leo's Dancewear
1900 N. Narragansett
Chicago, IL 60639
773/745-5600
773/889-7593 - fax
www.leosdancewear.com

Razzle Dazzle Costumes
1038 Lake St.
Oak Park, IL 60301
708/383-5962
708/383-0069 - fax
www.razzledazzlecostumes.com

Show Off
1472 Elmhurst Rd.
Elk Grove Village, IL 60007
847/439-0206
847/439-0219 - fax
www.showoffinc.com

Task Force Military
2341 W. Belmont
Chicago, IL 60618
773/477-7096

Thrift Stores

Ark Thrift Shop
3345 N. Lincoln
Chicago, IL 60657
773/248-1117

Ark Thrift Shop
1302 N. Milwaukee
Chicago, IL 60622
773/862-5011

Brown Elephant Resale
3651 N. Halsted
Chicago, IL 60657
773/549-5943

Brown Elephant Resale
3939 N. Ashland
Chicago, IL 60657
773/244-2930

Chicago's Recycle Shop
5308 N. Clark
Chicago, IL 60640
773/878-8525

Disgraceland
3338 N. Clark
Chicago, IL 60657
773/281-5875

Kismet Vintage Clothing and Furniture
2923 N. Southport
Chicago, IL 60657
773/528-4497

Little City Resale Shop
1760 W. Algonquin
Palatine, IL 60067
847/221-7130
847/358-3291 - fax

Ragstock
812 W. Belmont - 2nd floor
Chicago, IL 60657
773/868-9263 • 773/868-6819 - fax
www.ragstock.com

Right Place
5219 N. Clark
Chicago, IL 60640
773/561-7757

Sale Barn Square
971 N. Milwaukee
Wheeling, IL 60090
847/537-9886
www.salebarnsquare.com

Salvation Army Thrift Store
General Number
773/477-1771
www.salvationarmy.org

Threads
2327 N. Milwaukee
Chicago, IL 60622
773/276-6411

Time Well
Consignment Furniture
2780 N. Lincoln
Chicago, IL 60614
773/549-2113
www.chicago-antiques.com/timewell.htm

Unique Thrift Store
3224 S. Halsted
Chicago, IL 60608
312/842-8123

White Elephant Shop
Children's Memorial Hospital
2380 N. Lincoln
Chicago, IL 60614
773/883-6184

Libraries

Harold Washington Public Library
Chicago Public Libraries
400 S. State
Chicago, IL 60610
312/747-4300
www.chipublib.org

Newberry Library
60 W. Walton
Chicago, IL 60610
312/943-9090

North Suburban Library System
847/459-1300
www.nslsilus.org

Stock Montage
104 N. Halsted #200
Chicago, IL 60661
312/733-3239
312/733-2844 - fax
Library of stock stills

Actor's Tools

Bookstores

Act I Bookstore
2540 N. Lincoln
Chicago, IL 60614
773/348-6757
773/348-5561 - fax
www.act1books.com

Act I Bookstore serves everyone from Chicago to Sao Paolo to Istanbul for its theatre and film book needs. You can find thousands of plays, acting books, screenplays, agent listings, monologues, musicals, audition notices, reading copies of shows currently auditioning, a professional, theatre games, and many other books for actors, directors, writers, producers, designers, teachers and filmmakers. Open Mon-Wed 10-8 and Thur-Sun 10-6. The best online bookstore for theatre and film is www.act1books.com.

Afterwords Bookstore
23 E. Illinois
Chicago, IL 60611
312/464-1110
www.abebooks.com/home/afterwords

Barbara's Bookstore
1350 N. Wells
Chicago, IL 60610
312/642-5044
312/642-0522 - fax

Barbara's Bookstore
700 E. Grand
Chicago, IL 60611
312/222-0890

Barnes and Noble Bookstore
659 W. Diversey
Chicago, IL 60614
773/871-9004
773/871-5893 - fax
www.bn.com

Borders Books & Music
2817 N. Clark
Chicago, IL 60657
773/935-3909
www.borders.com

ks, Music & Cafe
an
610
4
www.borders.com

Feedback Theatrebooks
P.O. Box 220
Brooklin, ME 04616
207/359-2781
207/359-5532 - fax
Publishes books dealing with theatre.

Showfax
800/886-8716
www.showfax.com

Unabridged Books
3251 N. Broadway
Chicago, IL 60657
773/883-9119
773/883-9559 - fax

Casting Hotlines

Audition Hotline
312/409-9900

Illinois Filmboard Hotline
312/427-FILM

Chapter 4

Agencies

Defiant Theatre, "Cleansed"

Thou wouldst be great,
Art not without ambition, but without
The illness should attend it.

By Ben Winters

If you think being a performer is a tough gig, try being a talent agent for a day or two. For one thing, an agent is a person who spends all day interacting with advertising executives and actors, two professional classes not known for their equanimity. But the real tricky part is the business itself; as actors well know, entertainment is as stormy and variable an industry as they come.

"It's like a roller coaster, this business," testifies Elizabeth Geddes of the stalwart Geddes Agency, which first opened its door as a modeling agency back in 1967. "There's some really good years and some really awful years, and there's no way to tell what the next year is going to bring."

In 1970, the City of Chicago Yellow Pages included dozens upon dozens of listings for modeling agents (including the Playboy Agency, which lasted until the late 1980s) and a mere handful for screen and stage talent. By 1980 "theatrical agents"—as they are still, mostly inaccurately, classified—were on the upswing, with 30 or more in the business of finding performers for industrial films, television and radio commercials, and the odd TV show. (Plus the significant fraction of these who existed to represent performers in "belly dancing, strip tease and the exotic arts.")

What's interesting as one charts the ebb and flow of the agencies over the years is that the progression has never been a steady upward curve, with each subsequent year bringing more and more agents. The 1988

Sourcebook, an advertising industry bible that lists who's who in town, names fewer talent agents than were extant 10 years earlier. By 2000, over a decade later, that number had remained about steady—until three agencies got out of the game late in the year.

The quantity and quality of talent agencies (like the quantity and quality of work available) is controlled by a zillion more or less knowable factors, from who's in the mayor's office to what advertising theories are currently in fashion to the country and city's overall economic health. Agents, like the actors they seek to represent, are constantly at the mercy of an ever-changing marketplace.

This much is undeniable: Chicago's rise as a theatre town, accomplished in the later decades of the 20th century, coupled with the tremendous importance of the local advertising business (with many of the world's most famous ad-game players located up and down Michigan Avenue) have created a singular atmosphere. With the possible exception of New York, there's nowhere else in the world where so many actors are in such close proximity to the people who need them to move product.

"I think Steppenwolf and some of the Remains [Theatre] guys brought that here," says Geddes on how Chicago's explosion as a theatre scene helped court the attention of the commercial industry. "There's that reputation that just precedes the actor: If you have Steppenwolf or Remains or the Goodman on your resumé, people want to meet you, absolutely."

Nor is it just the actors who've been lucky enough to trod the boards at Steppenwolf who get in on that good fortune; with the rise to prominence of not only Steppenwolf and Goodman, but of Second City and other Chicago-based theatrical heavy hitters, the entire acting community developed a desirable sheen. And it was an acting community that was ever-growing: Actors in search of roles were (and are) drawn to the same well-reputed theatres as advertisers in search of talent.

Chicago became known as a place not only with a lot of actors, but with a lot of very good actors.

"People come here because they know they're going to get really good, really honest actors," Geddes explains. "I think you bring this thread through in your work, and it's true, it's real, you're in the moment, it's really honest work."

It's a reputation that has only strengthened over the years.

"We're definitely known for it," says one local agent with several years of on-camera experience. "Especially in L.A. and New York, people look at Chicago actors as real people, really strong actors with not only industry experience, but really great theatre experience. We've also got some amazing schools, like Northwestern and DePaul, where a huge pool of…talent has come from."

"With our theatrical people and our Second City people who go out to L.A. [who] are repped by our L.A. office, I know [the L.A. office has] said how thrilled they are with how well our actors are trained," reports Debby Kotzen, formerly of CED and now president of her own voice-over agency, Naked Voices. "The actors who are trained in Chicago are generally of a higher caliber than those coming from L.A."

Predating the solidification of Chicago as a center for acting talent (and arguably contributing to it) was the town's earlier establishment as a pillar of the advertising business. In the postwar ad boom of the 1950s, Chicago rose to prominence of the back of innovators like Leo Burnett (father of the so-called Chicago School of advertising) and Fairfax Cone of Foote, Cone and Belding. Such agencies remained relevant by holding on to their key customers as television became the key advertising mode. Local advertisers point to the famous "Where's the Beef?" spot of the early 1980s as pure Chicago: quirky, mildly bizarre, and incredibly catchy.

The talent agencies that sprang up over the 1970s, those that managed to survive, found their niche brokering between a growing talent pool and a growing pool of advertisers. Though the advertising business is overwhelmingly concentrated in New York, huge amounts of casting and shooting are done here in Chicago.

"The main [acting] industries in Chicago are commercial work and theatre, as opposed to industrials and film," says one local on-camera agent with several years in the business. "Commercials are the largest amount of work that we get here in Chicago, whereas in Los Angeles it's clearly film and TV, and in New York it's film, TV, and theatre. In Chicago, it's commercials, then industrials as well, and then theatre."

Within this general state of affairs there are the constant shifts and sea changes, inevitable in a business driven by the ever-changing needs of the advertising industry. Talent Agencies like ETA, Inc. and Salazar & Navas, which respectively specialize in representing African-American and Hispanic/Latin "types," found their place in the ad world as it gained respect for the non-white demographics.

Similarly, a late-80s to early-90s call in the market for non-traditional voice-over talent (meaning voices other than the game show/talk show booming male archetype) has meant a corresponding leap in interest from local performers who can fit the bill, and a need for agencies and agents to represent them. This has held particularly true for female voices, as it sank in to the advertising business that there was a new class of working wives with discretionary income, and who better to pitch to that market than women?

Kotzen notes another recent development in the voice-over demimonde: "I know [in past years] the ad agencies did all of their auditions in-house, and they are not doing as many in-house any more," she explains. "They're all going to agents…they've cut back on their people. In New York they still have a fair amount of auditions that are done in the ad agencies, but here and in L.A. they don't."

Meanwhile, agents have responded to their client's desire to bring in more and more people for each potential gig—which means more work for the agent, and, not incidentally, a more frustrating situation for actors.

"It's a fiercely competitive market at every level," says Lisa Lewis, a local actress and voice-over veteran. "There's a lot of competition...You used to go to an audition where there would be 30 people, and now there's a hundred. Everything is a cattle call."

Another, more painful example of the fickle nature of the agency game is the SAG/AFTRA strike that halted all union production for over six months in 2000. Union-franchised agencies had no choice but to wait it out until work could resume, and at least three—Harrise Davidson, Sa-Rah, and the local branch of CED, a national powerhouse—didn't make it.

Even without the strike, business has gotten tighter in recent years, thanks to a variety of unsettling trends summarized by longtime local standby Davidson, who closed her agency midway through 2000, in a farewell letter to PERFORMINK: "I'd become increasingly frustrated by the eroding commercial, voice-over and industrial market here and the stagnated pay-scale for what little film and TV work we do get," wrote Davidson in a personal address to actors and her fellow agents. "[And] the talent drain to L.A.; and watching good agents burn out and leave the business."

Davidson isn't the only one with doubts about the business's future: "I'm definitely not 100 percent enthusiastically optimistic about it," says one agent, who asked not to be named, about the possibilities of recovering from the strike. "I'm going to be wary about what's going on."

Others are exhibiting a cautious optimism in the wake of the strike.

"I don't think we'll ever recover what we've lost; there's no way to recover [from] six months of not shooting commercials and voice-overs. It's a major part of this town's business," says Geddes. "Three companies went out business, and that's a sad thing for the city…[but] we'll continue on absolutely. It's Chicago: That's what you do."

Of, course, commercials aren't all you do: If you're a lucky agent, or a lucky actor, you occasionally dip your toes into the slightly more glamorous worlds of film and television. But in this arena, even more so than with commercials and industrials, fate can be cruel to agents and actors alike.

When movies and television were young they never came to Chicago at all: Their cameras were too big and unwieldy to go traipsing around, especially when they could toss up a vaguely-Chicagoesque skyline on a Hollywood backlot. By the mid-70s things have started to open up, and occasional movies and episodic series were being shot in the real Chicago, creating a whole new field in which talent agents could operate.

"When Jane Byrne took over as mayor, that opened up the city for films" says Geddes, recalling the 1979-1983 mayor's welcoming attitude towards outside production, which precipitated the opening of the Chicago Film Office in 1980. "Prior to that, there was not much film happening."

Films started to crop up, including landmark cultural pieces like *The Untouchables* and *Ferris Bueller's Day Off*. Of course such films showed off the glorious skyline; more importantly, they required the casting of hundreds of extras and cameos, which meant a boon for local agents and actors. (A famous example is the appearance of improv legend Del Close as a grafting city councilman in *The Untouchables.*)

Once again, Chicago's reputation as a theatre town translated into a readiness on the part of producers to use local faces. The situation got even sunnier during the mid-nineties, when three weekly TV series—

"Turks," "Early Edition," and "Cupid"—were briefly all working here at once. The success of Chicago agencies at landing actors on those shows (all of which were tragically short-lived) is evident in the number of resumés that now include spots on one or more.

"The reason for using Chicago talent is two-fold," says Rick Moskal of the Film Office. "One is that [Chicago talent] has a great reputation, and two is that if it's going to be filmed in Chicago it doesn't make sense in terms of cost to audition people elsewhere and bring them in."

Local talent agencies were suddenly busy sending people to movie and film auditions—and not just for Chicago shoots.

"Chicago talent gets cast for shoots that don't even shoot here," says Moskal. "Chicago's reputation, built on its theatre, Second City and the like, has made Chicago that much more of an attractive place to film, and to cast out of for things being shot in other places."

Nowadays TV and film production is facing some of the same challenges as the commercial side, notably "runaway production" as more and more productions head to Canada, where filming is cheaper. Agents are weighing the pros and cons of the situation, developing strategies. Just as the commercial side of the industry must now recover from a six-month full-stop, the film and TV side must reshape itself to deal with new realities. Luckily, they're used to it.

Agencies

Agents Among Us

Dealing with your agent(s) is a full-time job, but if you do it well, it can be lucrative. Keep these steps in mind when seeking an agent:

1. Mailing

Materials

Your mailing should include a headshot and resumé, a cover letter and a self-addressed, stamped envelope. Refer to the checklists on headshots and resumés for more info.

Research

Different agencies do different things. Some focus on minority talent. Some are union, some aren't. Some handle theatrical bookings. Some have offices both here and in LA. Check them out before you start submitting.

2. Audition

I Should Bring...

Have at least 25 headshots and resumés with you and ready to go. If they want to represent you, you should be ready.

My Pieces

Have two or three pieces ready, even if they only want one. They'll probably put you on tape, so choose pieces that are suited to film. All these pieces should be contemporary; few agents care whether or not you can handle Shakespeare.

3. Relationship

Multi-Listing vs. Exclusivity

Most agents will not want to sign you exclusively at first. They'll wait until they've worked with you and decided that you're worth the commitment. In the meantime, you can sign with as many agents as you want. This is very different from LA or New York, where all talent is signed exclusively.

Checking In

Every agency has different policies for checking in. Follow them. You want to remind your agents that you exist without irritating them. To this end, call with specific questions, not general chit-chat (e.g., "I was just calling to make sure you had enough pictures and resumés" is much more palatable than "Hey! How ya' doin'?"). Don't drop by, unless that's the specific preference of the agent. Remember, they're busy trying to get you work. There's a fine line to follow here between keeping your face in their head and making them want to issue a restraining order. Use common sense.

Communicate

Let them know how an audition went. Keep them posted on the shows you do, the classes you take and the projects you're working on. Most importantly, let them know when you're going out of town (otherwise known as "booking out"). Nothing irritates an agent more than calling an actor and finding out they're on tour for the next month.

Union Status

It's up to you to keep track of your union status. If your next union job means you have to join, let your agent know.

Commission

An agent can only take 10 percent on a union job. They can take 20 percent for print work. If the gig is non-union, the agency can take more than 10 percent, and many do. Pay attention to the percentage your agent takes, particularly if you notice it changing. Incidentally, if an agent takes over 10 percent on a union job, they're breaking the law.

4. Booking

Be Available

Keep your pager or cell phone with you. If your agent wants to send you out, they may want to send you out right now.

Get the Info

Be sure you know where the audition is, when they're expecting you, whether there's copy, what you should wear, when it shoots, etc. Your agent may be in a hurry to get off the phone, but if you don't know these things you're going to look bad at the audition.

5. Exclusivity

Benefits

Being exclusive is more prestigious, and you usually get more attention. The agency has invested in you, so they're more likely to try to get you work.

Problems

Be sure you like your agency and the people you're dealing with before you go exclusive. You're stuck with them. Also, inform other agencies that represent you of your decision promptly.

6. Collecting

It's your responsibility to collect from your agent. Keep track of what they owe you. This can be a difficult game to play, as many actors don't want to anger their agent by bugging them for money. However, they do have a responsibility to pay you. If you need to know what your legal rights are, you can start by calling the Illinois Department of Labor. Also check out "Actors Don't Have to Be Victims" in the Unions chapter.

7. Scams

No agent should ever insist that you get headshots with a particular photographer or that you take classes from a particular studio. They can recommend, but they can't insist. Similarly, they shouldn't charge you a fee to sign with their agency. These are all scams designed to take advantage of inexperienced actors. If this happens, or if you're placed in any other situation that makes you uncomfortable, find another agent.

Talent Agencies- Union Franchised

Ambassador Talent
312/641-3491
333 N. Michigan, Suite 910
Chicago, IL 60601

Send headshot and resumé. Agency will call, if interested. All ages.

SAG/AFTRA/AFM franchised.

Aria Model and Talent Management
312/243-9400
1017 W. Washington, Suite 2C
Chicago, IL 60607

Mary Boncher, Marie Anderson and David Kronfeld, co-owners.

Actors/models must submit resumé headshot/composite by mail. Agency will contact you, if interested. No voice-over.

SAG/AFTRA/Equity franchised.

Georgia Mindell - on-camera beauty, TV, film

Vicki Fellner - commercial print
Annette Navarro - men's print

Jennifer Kramer - new faces

Sebastian McWilliams - men's fashion, fashion director

Emily Bartolime - women's fashion

Susanne Johnson-runway

Robert Schroeder - on-camera

Katherine Tenerowicz - women's fashion, print

Nancy Tennicott - runway

Baker & Rowley
312/850-4700
1347 W. Washington, Suite 1B
Chicago, IL 60607

Diane Rowley, Director

Send five headshot/resumés and two voice demos with a S.A.S.E. Agents will contact you if interested. Multi-cultural representation. Open registration Tuesdays 12-2pm. No other drop-ins.

AFTRA/SAG/Equity franchised.

Diane Rowley - on-camera, print, tradeshow

Corissa McCottry - children

Roberta Kablach - office manager

Big Mouth Talent
312/421-4400
935 W. Chestnut, Suite 415
Chicago, IL 60622

Send headshot and resumé with a S.A.S.E. Agency will call if interested. All ages. Attn: Brooke Tonneman.

SAG/AFTRA/Equity franchised.

ETA, Inc.
773/752-3955
7558 S. South Chicago Ave.
Chicago, IL 60619
Joan P. Brown, President

Mail composites and resumés to Joan P. Brown, who will contact you, if interested.

SAG/AFTRA Franchised.

Agency Finder

Most Agencies are located just north and west of the loop (At right). A few agencies can be found in selected suburbs (Below).

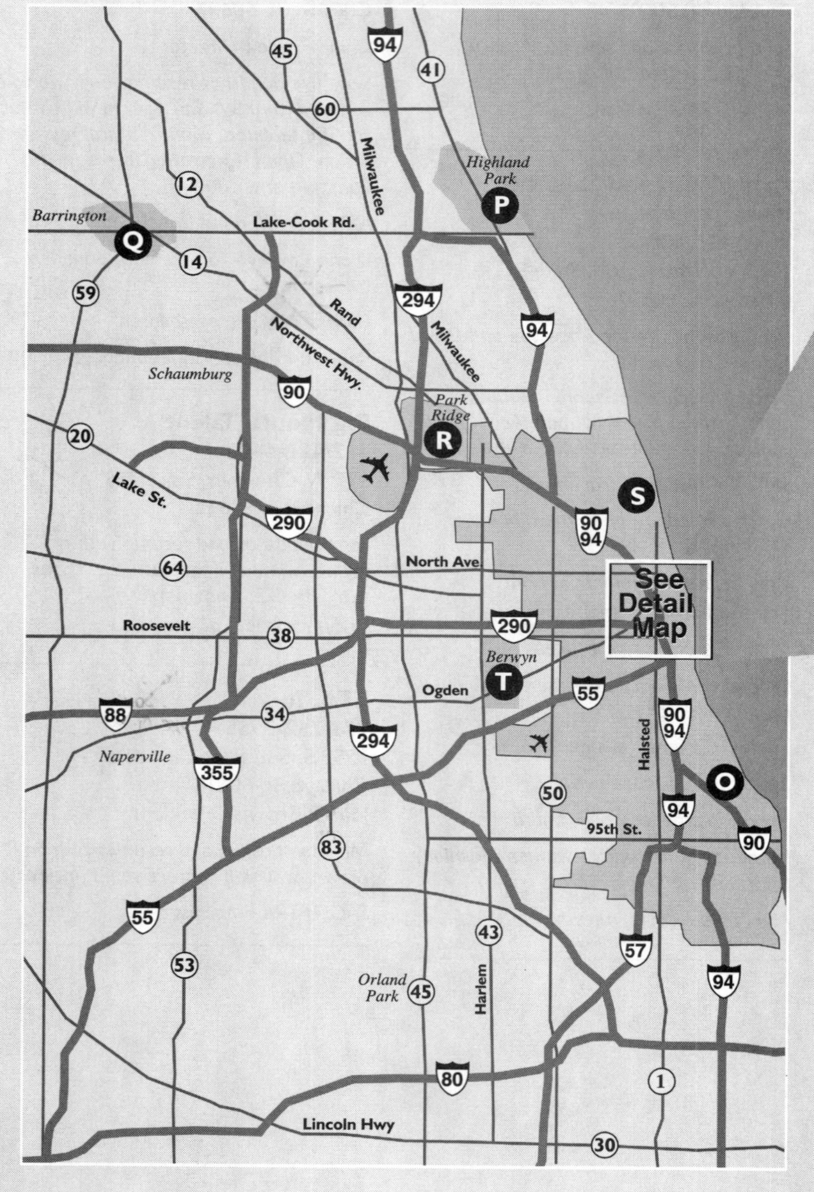

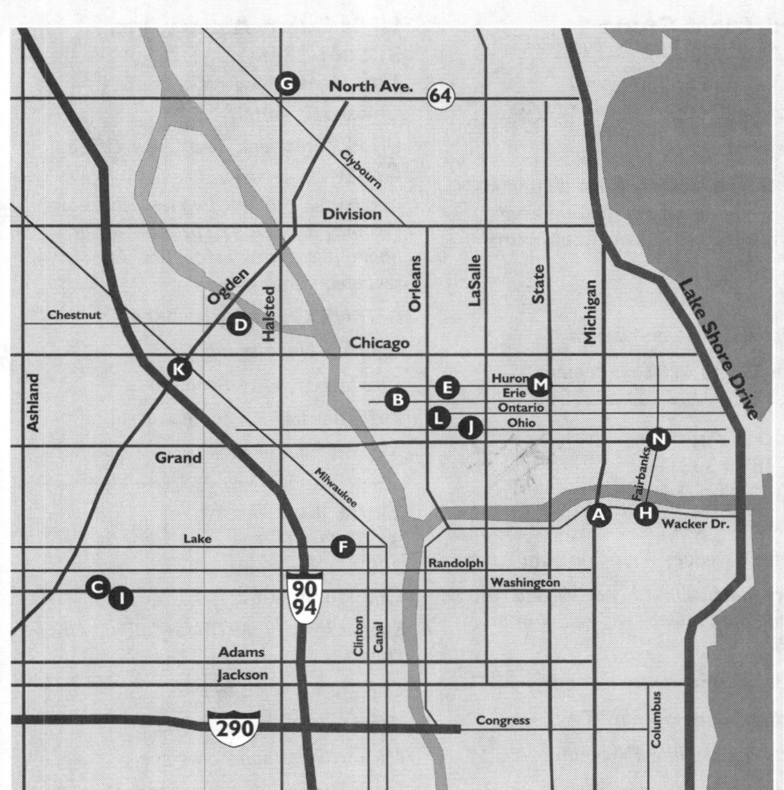

A- ***Ambassador Talent***
333 N. Michigan

A- ***Aria Model and Talent Management***
333 N. Michigan

B- ***Arlene Wilson Models***
430 W. Erie

C- ***Baker & Rowley***
1347 W. Washington

D- ***Big Mouth Talent***
935 W. Chestnut

E- ***Emilia Lorence Agency***
325 W. Huron

F- ***Ford Talent Group***
641 W. Lake

G- ***Geddes Agency***
1633 N. Halsted

H- ***Karen Stavins Enterprises, Inc.***
303 E. Wacker

I- ***Lily's Talent Agency***
1301 W. Washington

J- ***Linda Jack Talent***
230 E. Ohio

K- ***Salazar & Navas***
760 N. Ogden

L- ***Shirley Hamilton Inc.***
333 E. Ontario

M- ***Stewart Talent***
58 W. Huron

N- ***Voices Unlimited***
541 N. Fairbanks

O- ***ETA, Inc.***
7758 S. South Chicago Ave.

P- ***Norman Schucart Enterprises***
1417 Green Bay Rd.
Highland Park, IL

Q- ***Concept Model Management, Inc.***
1301 S. Grove Ave.
Barrington, IL

R- ***McBlaine & Associates***
805 Touhy Ave.
Park Ridge, IL

S- ***Talent Group, Inc.***
1228 W. Wilson

T- ***Talented Kids, Inc.***
6950 W. Windsor Ave.
Berwyn, IL

Agencies

Ford Talent Group 4
312/707-8700
641 W. Lake St., Suite 402
Chicago, IL 60661

Katie Ford, President

Noreen Threlkeld, Chicago area director
Actors, please submit pictures and resumés to Ford Talent Group, attn: new talent.

AFTRA/SAG franchised.

Davia Lipscher - on-camera

Linise Belford - kids on-camera

Geddes Agency
312/787-8333
1633 N. Halsted, Suite 300
Chicago, IL 60614

Elizabeth Geddes, Vice-President

Actors must submit headshot and resumé by mail only. Agency will call, if interested.

AFTRA/SAG/Equity franchised.

Elizabeth Geddes - film, TV, theatre

Paula Muzik - film, TV, theatre

Kathleen Collins - voice-over

Erica Wilde - agent assistant

Shirley Hamilton, Inc.
312/787-4700
333 E. Ontario, Suite 302B
Chicago, IL 60611

Shirley Hamilton, President

Lynn Hamilton, Vice President

Registration by mail only with S.A.S.E. Actors must submit headshot and resumé. Agency will contact by mail, if interested.

AFTRA/SAG/Equity franchised.

Lynn Hamilton - on-camera, trade show, voice-over

Monica Campbell - TV, film

Laurie Hamilton - print, TV, film

Lily's Talent Agency, Inc.
312/601-2345
1301 W. Washington, Suite B
Chicago, IL 60607

Lily Ho, President; Tom Colby, Office Director

Actors must submit two headshots and resumés and S.A.S.E. by mail. Include phone number and statistics. Agency will respond, if interested.

AFTRA/SAG/Equity franchised.

Lily Ho - Head agent

Sara Strzepek - on-camera

Heidi Bauers - on-camera, print

Melissa Fullen - print

Linda Jack Talent
312/587-1155
230 E. Ohio, Suite 200
Chicago, IL 60611

Submit by mail. AFTRA/SAG/Equity franchised.

Linda Jack - voice-over

Vanessa Lanier - voice-over

Mickey Grossman - on-camera

Stacy Shafer - on-camera, new talent submissions

Amie Richardson - kids

Emilia Lorence Agency
312/787-2033
325 W. Huron St., Suite 404
Chicago, IL 60610

Fred Kasner, owner. Judy Kasner, president

Mail registration only. Actors should send 3 headshots and resumés with phone numbers. Children also send S.A.S.E.. Voice-over talent should submit a tape. Agency will call for reading at a later date, if interested.

AFTRA/SAG/Equity franchised.

Jackie Grimes - on-camera, voice-over

Judy Kasner - on-camera, industrial, feature film, TV

Vicki Karagianis - convention, trade-show

Salazar & Navas, Inc.
312/666-1677
760 N. Ogden, Suite 2200
Chicago, IL 60622

Myrna Salazar, President

Trina Navas, Vice President

Hispanic/Latin types preferred, but all types considered and represented. New talent seen on Tuesdays, 12-4pm.

AFTRA/SAG franchised.

Myrna Salazar - on-camera, voice-over, film, commercial print, children, print adults

Trina Navas - on-camera, voice-over, film, commercial print

Norma Martinez - children

Norman Schucart Enterprises
847/433-1113
1417 Green Bay Rd.
Highland Park, IL 60035

Norman Schucart, President

New talent should first submit headshot/composite and resumé with phone number by mail (include S.A.S.E. postcard). If interested, the agency will arrange to interview you in Chicago.

AFTRA/SAG franchised.

Norman Schucart - TV, industrial film, print, live shows

Nancy Elliott - TV, industrial film, print, live shows

Stewart Talent
312/943-3131
58 W. Huron
Chicago, IL 60610

Jane Stewart, President

Actors: mail or drop-off two pictures and resumés. The appropriate agent will contact you within six to eight weeks, if interested. No walk-ins.

AFTRA/SAG/Equity franchised.

Maureen Brookman - TV, stage, film

Maryann Drake - TV, stage, film

Todd Turina - TV, stage, film

Nancy Kidder - industrial film

Joan Sparks - voice-over

Wade Childress - commercial print

Kathy Gardner - children, print

Sheila Dougherty - children, commercials

April Sheik - Jr. kids

Voices Unlimited
312/832-1113
541 N. Fairbanks Ct.
Chicago, IL 60611

Sharon Wottrich - President

Voice-over talent should submit commercial and/or narrative tape, two min. or less with resumé. An agent will contact you if interested.

AFTRA/SAG franchised

Linda Bracilano - voice-over

Arlene Wilson Models
312/573-0200
430 W. Erie #210
Chicago, IL 60610

Michael Stothard, President

Submit headshot and resumé by mail first. The agency will contact you, if interested.

AFTRA/SAG/Equity franchised.

Dan Deely - agency director

Peter Forster - acting division

Sarah Wilson - women's fashion

Laura Alexander - children, on-camera, commercial print

Anna Jordan - on-camera, voice-over, commercial print

Lisa Goren - children

Amanda Lorenzen - men's division

Talent Agencies- Non-Union

Concept Model Management, Inc.
630/686-6410
1301 S. Grove Ave., Suite 160
Barrington, IL 60010

www.conceptmodels.com, email mark@conceptmodels.com

Models only please. Exclusive and non-exclusive talent. 17-24 years in age. No walk-ins. Send photo & resumé/composite card. Agency will call if interested.

Karen Stavins Enterprises, Inc.
312/938-1140
303 E. Wacker Dr., Concourse Level
Chicago, IL 60601

Submit picture and resumé, composites or voice tapes. Attn: New Talent. Agency will contact you, if interested. Non-union talent booked for commercials, industrials, TV/film, voice-over, trade shows, live shows. 17 years and older.

McBlaine & Associates, Inc.
(See our on next page)
847/823-3877
805 Touhy Ave.
Park Ridge, IL 60068

Mary Poplawski, President

No drop-ins. Send a headshot and resumé with a S.A.S.E.

Kristin Runfeldt, Paige Ehlman, Brett Ehlman—print, voice-over, industrial, commercial, film, children, new faces, music video.

Nouvelle Talent
312/944-1133
P.O. Box 578100
Chicago, IL 60657

Ann Toni Sipka, President

Send picture and resumé. Agency will contact you, if interested.

Ann Toni Sipka—(New York)television, film, trade show

Carlotta Young—trade show

Talent Group, Inc.
773/561-8814
1228 W. Wilson
Chicago, IL 60640
talentgrp@aol.com

No drop-ins. Send a headshot and resumé or voice-over tape addressed to Juliet Wilson. Ages 18 and older.

Talented Kids, Inc.
708/795-1788
6950 W. Windsor Ave.
Berwyn, IL 60402
www.talentedkidsagency.com

Representing children, infants to 16 years old. Please send photo and resumé. Agency will call if interested. Auditions held periodically throughout the year.

Talent Agencies- Milwaukee

Jennifer's Talent Unlimited, Inc.
414/277-9440
740 N. Plankinton, Suite 300
Milwaukee, WI 53203

Jennifer L. Berg, President

Actors must submit a headshot and resumé Attn: Marna. Agency will contact you, if interested.

AFTRA franchised.

Lori Lins, Ltd.
414/282-3500
7611 W. Holmes Ave.
Milwaukee, WI 53220

Lori Lins, President

Actors must submit headshot,resumé and cover letter. Agency will respond, if interested.

AFTRA/SAG franchised and non-union.

Lori Lins—booker

Jenny Siedenburg—booker

Betty Antholine—booker

Arlene Wilson Talent, Inc.
414/283-5600
807 N. Jefferson, Suite 200
Milwaukee, WI 53202

Michael Stothard, President

Catherine Hagen, Agency Director

Open call for actors Wed. 1:30-3pm. Must have current headshots and resumés or voice demo. May also send materials.

AFTRA franchised.

Carol Rathe—voice-over, on-camera, broadcast dir.

Tradeshow Agencies

Best Faces
312/944-3009
1152 N. Lasalle, #F
Chicago, IL 60610

www.bestfacesofchicago.com
email: bestfaceschicago@aol.com

Send materials attn: Judy Mudd. Agency will contact you, if interested.

Corporate Presenters
(A division of Karen Stavins Enterprises)
312/938-1140
303 E. Wacker Dr., Concourse Level
Chicago, IL 60601

Attn: New Talent

Submit composite or headshot. Agency will contact, if interested. Narrators, hosts/hostesses and models booked for trade shows, conventions, special promotions and variety acts. 17 years and older.

The Group, Ltd
702/895-8926
10120 S. Eastern, Suite 355
Henderson, NV 89052

Mail materials. No drop-ins. No talent under 21. Agency represents females (21-40)/males (21-50). Trade show talent only. Interested in all talent including narration, foreign languages and prefer audio prompter. Contact: Mary Troxel, Talent Coordinator.

Casting Directors

Actors are generally welcome to submit one headshot and resumé and keep in touch with post cards. Never call a casting director; it will only hurt your chances of ever getting work through that individual.

Jane Alderman Casting
312/397-1182
Mailing address only
c/o Act One Studios
640 N. LaSalle, Suite 535
Chicago, IL 60610

Attn: Jane Alderman—casting director

All City Casting
(union,non-union)
773/588-6062
P.O. Box 577640
Chicago, IL 60657-7640

Attn: June Pyskacek

Chicago Casting Center
312/327-1904
777 N. Green Street
Chicago, IL 60622
Attn: Janet Louer, Tina O'Brien, Siobhan Sullivan

HollyRik & Heitz Casting
312/664-0601
920 N. Franklin #205
Chicago, IL 60610
Attn: Rik Kristinat or Hal Watkins

JAZ Casting
(union, non-union)
312/343-8111
3617 N. Kedvale
Chicago, IL 60641
Attn: Jennifer Rudnicke, Cathy Kulnig

K.T.'s
773/525-1126
P.O. Box 577039
Chicago, IL 60657-7039
See listing under Extra Casting for info.

David O'Connor Casting
312/226-9112
1017 W. Washington, Suite 2A
Chicago, IL 60607
Attn: David O'Connor

Beth Rabedeau Casting
312/664-0601
920 N. Franklin, #205
Chicago, IL 60610
Attn: Jason Rabedeau

Reginacast
312/409-5521 Talent Hotline
8491 Sunset Blvd., Suite 372
West Hollywood, CA 90069
Chicago address - P.O. Box 585
Willow Springs, IL 60480

Segal Studio
312/563-9368
1040 W. Huron
Chicago, IL 60622
Attn: Jeffery Lyle Segal

Simon Casting
312/202-0124
1512 N. Fremont, #202
Chicago, IL 60622
Attn: Claire Simon

Tenner, Paskal Casting
312/527-0665
20 W. Hubbard, #2E
Chicago, IL 60610
Rachel Tenner, Casting Director; Mickie Paskal, Casting Director

Trapdoor Casting
773/384-0494
1655 W. Cortland
Chicago, IL 60622
www.trapdoortheater.com
Attn: Beata Pilch & Nicole Wiesner

Extras Casting

Casting by McLean/For Extras
P.O. Box #10569
Chicago, IL 60610

Send headshots and resumés by mail. Include phone number, social security number and all sizes on resumé.

Holzer & Ridge Casting
773/549-3169

K.T.'s
P.O. Box 577039
Chicago, IL 60657-7039

Send 6 pictures or composites and resumés. Include phone number, address, social security number, height, weight, hair and eye color, age (or age range), car color and make.

Reginacast
312/409-5521 Talent Hotline
8491 Sunset Blvd., Suite 372
West Hollywood, CA 90069
Chicago address - P.O. Box 585
Willow Springs, IL 60480
reginacast@aol.com
www.reginacast.com

Send a current photo with your age and height, phone numbers and email address to both locations. If possible, please email and call hotline number for specific requirements before mailing.

Literary Agents

Austin Wahl Agency
1820 N. 76th Ct
Elmwood Park, IL 60070
708/456-2301
Submission Policy: Write letter of interest, describing material. Include synopsis, publication history, and sample of writing.

International Leonards Corporation
3612 N. Washington Blvd
Indianapolis, IN 46205
317/926-7566
Submission Policy: Write letter of interest, include queries and S.A.S.E. Agency will contact, if interested. Accepting submissions for TV, Film. NO BOOKS.

Stewart Talent
58 W. Huron
Chicago, IL 60610
312/943-3131
Literary Submissions: Send 2 page synopsis/summary and letter of inquiry with S.A.S.E. to Stewart Talent, attn: Literary Division. Agency will contact you, if interested.

Chapter 5

Film, TV and Industrials

Stage Left, "Chagrin Falls"

Auditioning for Film

Life's but a walking
shadow, a poor player
That struts and frets
his hour upon the stage
And then is heard no more.

By Rachael Patterson

Your first film audition…yikes! What should you expect? Well, first of all, if you have been called in for an audition, someone thinks that you—not your version of somebody else—are a real possibility for the role. With that in mind, how should you proceed? You need to keep your power in the process and understand your job as an actor and the questions you should ask. Chicago casting director Jane Alderman says that many actors don't feel worthy enough to ask for all of the information from their agents. She reminds actors that "You are trying to get a job…you can ask questions."

The Nuts & Bolts

When you get a call from your agent, you should be prepared. Alderman suggests that you keep a pad of paper and a checklist by the phone. You should get the following information: where and when the audition will take place, when the callbacks and shoot dates are, and also ask who is directing/producing the project. Knowing about the players will help you do your homework. You can research their film credits and get a sense of the kind of projects they have worked on in the past. (Hint: Check out the Internet Movie Database at imdb.com) Are you auditioning for Michael Mann, Ron Howard, John Hughes or David Lynch? Knowing that alone begins to give you a sense of the potential world of the film. If you have an audition for a television film or an episodic, knowing what the network is can also help. For example, the WB tends to be hip and trendy with an emphasis on sex appeal, whereas HBO is often darker, edgier and you get to talk dirty.

It is also important to ask if there is a full script available to read. (Hint: It's a SAG rule that a script is available to actors 24 hours prior to the audition.) Reading the full script is especially helpful if you are auditioning for a functionary role, such as a nurse or bartender. It aids your preparation to know if you are working in a hip café in Greenwich Village or in an Oklahoma truck stop. "Preparation is key," says Mickie Paskal of Tenner Paskal Casting. "You need to understand your role in the world of the film, where you fit. If you are auditioning for Cop #1, make sure you are believable as a cop, as well as making an interesting choice."

You can also ask who will be at the audition and whether it's a table read with the casting director, or if you will be taped. And when you get your script, read the scene carefully. Don't assume that pages have been faxed or stapled in the correct order. If the scene doesn't make sense, then call and ask your agent if the pages seem out of order.

The Main Adjustment

Now that you know what to expect in the room, it's time to trust your instincts and begin to prepare your scene and make choices. It's vital that "you don't worry about camera rules that don't exist," says Alderman. The primary difference between stage and screen is an adjustment of focus. On camera, you no longer have an obligation to an audience. You now have only one eyeball looking at you, not an audience of 700. And that one eyeball, the camera, picks up what you think. Remember, on camera you are most interesting when you are seen listening and thinking. A good screen actor is one who is always thinking (inner monologue) and processing what they are receiving.

This adjustment, however, doesn't mean that you can not move. Phrases such as "Less is more," "Bring it down" or "You're too big for the camera" tend to paralyze actors. You must have a physical life and "fill the frame."

You can turn away from the camera, touch your face, bring your hands into the frame, you can move, you can physicalize your intentions. If the script says that you slap your partner or kiss them, you can raise your hand as though to slap or you can respond as though you have just been kissed.

A good question to ask prior to being taped is "What is my frame?" The size of the frame (usually a medium shot, waist up) will indicate the size of your read and how physical you can be. If you are framed chest up, it "looks" as though your partner is just an arm's length away from you—as though you are sitting across the kitchen table, even though the reader is standing behind the camera, half way across the room.

With all this in mind, Patrick Tucker advises in his book, "The Secrets of Screen Acting," that if you are told in an audition to "bring it down," do nothing but lower your volume and the auditor will almost always be pleased. Don't make the mistake of decreasing your physicality or sense of importance in the scene.

Lack of importance and personalization tend to be the most consistent acting problems for theatre trained performers. Actors are often surprised when they see an audition tape. They say that "it felt like I was doing so much, and on the tape I'm not doing nearly enough." Mickie Paskal urges the actor to "go further, personalize more deeply, and find more specific images."

She also says that it is vital to "be alive and involved in the scene, before the camera is rolling. It seems false when we see an actor 'get ready' on film."

Preparing your Scene: Reading the Script

The following is a distillation of the guideposts discussed in Michael Shurtleff's book, "Audition."

1. Don't start to read from the point of innocence. Instead, start to read—FOR THE FIRST TIME—having the following foreknowledge: This is a film about me in a love relationship. What is my problem with the other person? What am I going to do today in order to solve that problem?
2. "This is a film about me." This means you must personalize. When talking about the scene, say "I" rather than he or she. You must use yourself—the BIG YOU—in the given circumstances of the scene. Look at the facts of the scene. If in the scene you have left your lover, ask what might make you leave your lover. If in the scene you have had three drinks prior to the scene, ask what makes you lose control. If in the scene the role you are playing seems to be confused, this doesn't mean you are playing a stupid or confused person. Rather, ask what makes you feel confused. Don't play beneath your intelligence.
3. "In a love relationship." This means you must explore the need that exists in every relationship, Love means need, not necessarily

"romantic" love. Think about what you love/admire/envy/desire about the other person. This is what keeps you in the scene. The scene is sometimes about the terms of the love. My mother is overbearing and critical, and I want her to love me as a warm and fuzzy, Girl Scout leader, cookie baking, affectionate mommy. The love in the scene may be the lack of love, or the inability to love.

4. "What is my problem with the other person (find the conflict)." The script exists on two levels: the script (the text/the lines/the plot/the situation) and the subtext, what's beneath the script. Relationship is what the actor should play, not the situation. The relationship is defined by your history with the other person and the conflict. You should always search for the essential problem in the relationship—the ongoing problem, the personality problem, the deep, grave and constant problem—the problem that is always the problem with the other person (i.e. too judgmental, immature, control freaks, or dreamers). Remember that sometimes what draws you to someone is also what drives you crazy about them. The solution to the problem is what's worth "the fighting for." For example: "If you loved me, you would [find the solution to the problem]."
5. "Today." This is what makes the scene important. Today is the day I stay and fight. Ask yourself, "Why must I get what I am fighting for today?" Lastly, consider the actions you will play in order to get what you are fighting for. An action is an undeniable communication with your partner that you do in order to get what you are fighting for. Think of verbs. Think of transitive verbs. Don't think, "I will be angry with her." Think, I will "threaten her," "flirt with her," "guilt her," "beg her," "plead with her," "belittle her," "needle her," or "light a fire under her butt."

If you have actions to play, then you have something to do. And suddenly the scene becomes interesting.

And remember, the folks you are auditioning for are people who are on your side and really want to cast their project. So take risks and have fun.

For more information on auditioning, visit www.theauditionstudio.com or www.performink.com.

Demo Tapes

Audio One, Inc.
325 W. Huron #512
Chicago, IL 60610
312/337-5111 • 312/337-5125 - fax

Sherri Berger
(Director of Voice Over U)
773/774-9886
www.sherriberger.voicedemo.com

Bosco Productions
(See our ad on previous page)
160 E. Grand - 6th floor
Chicago, IL 60611
312/644-8300

Dress Rehearsals Studios, Ltd.
312/829-2213
312/829-4085 - fax
www.chicagostudios.com

Hathaway Studios
510 W. Belmont Ave., Ste. 1810
Chicago, IL 60657-4600
773/755-0612 • 773/755-0612 - fax
www.matthathawaymusic.com

Quality New York City professionals now in Chicago. CD, Tape Demo Recording. Voice-Over Coaching & Script Consultation. Also Video Reel editing.

Music Workshop
Bob Kalal
4900 W. 28th Pl.
Cicero, IL 60804
708/652-4040
members.xoom.com\musicwkshop

Rainbow Bridge Recording
117 W. Rockland Rd.
Libertyville, IL 60048
847/362-4060
847/362-4653 - fax

Renaissance Video
130 S. Jefferson
Chicago, IL 60661
312/930-5000 • 312/930-9030 - fax
www.whateverwerks.com

Bobby Schiff Music Productions
363 Longcommon Rd.
Riverside, IL 60546
708/442-3168 • 708/447-3719 - fax

Sound Advice
Kate McClanaghan, Gina Mazza,
Tyrone Dockery
2028 W. Potomac #2 & 3
Chicago, IL 60622
773/772-9539
www.voiceoverdemos.com

Get trained by two of Chicago's top former agents. Gina Mazza (CED) and Tyrone Dockery (Stewart) and Kate McClanaghan, Producer at top Ad Agency (DDB Worldwide). Training includes the following:

Commercial technique

Cold reading

Vocal Technique

Audition technique

In studio voice-over workshop

Mastering the business of being a working talent

Sound Advice is the most complete, start-to-finish voiceover demo production service. We maintain no one does what you do. The copy is written/selected specifically fo you by Professional Producers. Our mailing list and marketing plan is unparalleled. We coach, direct and produce you to get you completely poised to work. Get trained and produced by two of Chicago's top former Talent Agents, Gina Mazza (CED) and Tyrone Dockery (Stewart) and Kate McClanaghan, Producer at top Ad Agency (DDB Worldwide).

Sound/Video Impressions
110 S. River Rd.
Des Plaines, IL 60016
847/297-4360
847/297-6870 - fax

VoiceOver 101
Ray Van Steen
325 W. Huron #512
Chicago, IL 60610
312/587-1010 • 312/337-5125 - fax

Private, individual coaching sessions in voicing TV/Radio commercials, narrations. Employs record/playback method in recording studio environment. Basics through production of voice-over demo. Van Steen is a published writer on the subject, and has voiced thousands of commercials. Phone for free, no-obligation brochure.

Reels

Absolute Video Services, Inc.
715 S. Euclid
Oak Park, IL 60302
708/386-7550
708/386-2322 - fax
www.absolutevideoservices.com

Allied Vaughn
1200 Thorndale Ave.
Elk Grove Village, IL 60007
847/595-2900
847/595-8677 - fax
www.alliedvaughn.com

Argonne Electronics
7432 N. Milwaukee
Niles, IL 60714
847/647-8877

Cinema Video Center
211 E. Grand
Chicago, IL 60611
312/644-0861
312/644-2096 - fax
www.networkcentury.com

ELB's Entertainment, Inc.
Eugene Barksdale
2501 N. Lincoln Avenue #198
Chicago, IL 60614-2313
800/656-1585
800/957-3527 - fax
www.elbsentertainment.com

Film to Video Labs
5100 N. Ravenswood #200
Chicago, IL 60640
773/275-9500
773/275-0300 - fax
www.ftvlabs.com

Golan Productions
1501 N. Magnolia
Chicago, IL 60622
773/274-3456
312/642-7441 - fax
www.atomicimaging.com

Hathaway Studios
510 W. Belmont, Ste. 1810
Chicago, IL 60657-4600
773/755-0612
773/155-0612 - fax
www.matthathawaymusic.com

Quality New York City professionals now in Chicago. Video Reel editing. Also CD, Tape Voice-Over Demo Recording.

Intervideo Duplication Services
3533 S. Archer
Chicago, IL 60609
773/927-9091
773/927-9211 - fax
www.historicvideo.com

Master Images Video Duplication
112 Carpenter Ave.
Wheeling, IL 60090
847/541-4440

Northwest Teleproductions
142 E. Ontario
Chicago, IL 60611
312/337-6000
312/337-0500 - fax
www.nwtele.com

Nxtrm (pronounced Nextroom)
230 E. Ontario #302
Chicago, IL 60611
312/335-3620
312/9335-3622 - fax
www.nxtrm.com

Rainbow Bridge
117 W. Rockland Rd
Libertyville, IL 60048
847/362-4060
847/362-4653 - fax

Renaissance Video
130 S. Jefferson
Chicago, IL 60661
312/930-5000
312/930-9030 - fax
www.whateverwerks.com

Sound/Video Impressions
110 S. River Rd.
Des Plaines, IL 60016
847/297-4360
847/297-6870 - fax

Video Replay, Inc.
118 W. Grand
Chicago, IL 60610
312/467-0425
312/467-1045 - fax
www.videoreplaychicago.com

Ear Prompters

Credible Communication, Inc.
Instant Memory™ Ear Prompting Systems
155 Little John Trail NE
Atlanta, GA 30309
404/892-0660
www.ear-prompter.com

Sargon Yonan
67 E. Madison #1415
Chicago, IL 60603
312/782-7007
312/782-7529 - fax

Thou art so far before
That swiftest wing of recompense is slow
To overtake thee. Would thou hadst less deserv'd,
That the proportion both of thanks and payment
Might have been mine! Only I have left to say,
More is thy due than more than all can pay.

By Ben Winters

If you're an actor who wants to make a living, there's plenty of reasons a Screen Actors Guild (SAG) card can be worth more in your wallet than a Visa Platinum. The vast majority of paying gigs in Chicago aren't in theatre, they're in commercials and industrials. For folks doing that kind of work, the union offers a certain set of protections: a guaranteed pay scale and working conditions, not to mention the peace of mind that comes from the protection of union muscle.

Alas, it takes time and toil (and that pesky entrance fee) to gain entry into SAG (or the Association of Film, Television and Radio Artists, SAG's oft-overlooked sister union). In the meantime, there's plenty of paying non-union work to be had, from industrial videos to local commercials to passing out detergent samples at your local Jewel-Osco. While some local agencies work exclusively with union clients, many specialize in non-union gigs. Even SAG-franchised agencies can do non-union work—provided they don't send union actors to non-union jobs.

But there's a major pitfall: A non-union actor is a one-man or one-woman show. You've got to be ready to hustle, not only to get your headshots in the mail, nail the audition and nail the gig, but to collect your payment afterwards. As any non-union actor who's been around the block a time or two can tell you, sometimes the hardest part of the job isn't memorizing the lines, it's getting the fee.

Here's how it works when all goes smoothly: The client hires the agency and the agency hires the talent (that's you). Talent and agent have a contract, signed in advance, affording the agency a certain percentage of the fee; after the work is completed the client sends along two checks, one for your share and one for the agency. (Under a SAG contract, the agency gets 10 percent from the actor's cut and another 10 percent from the client; non-union fees are higher, ranging from fifteen/fifteen upwards.)

It is the agent's responsibility to forward your payment to you, and any agent will say they always do so immediately upon receiving it. And yet the city is full of actors with horror stories to tell of waiting anywhere from "months and months" to "over a year" to "forever" to get their cash from a gig.

Without the union behind you, keeping yourself from the ranks of the unpaid is your own responsibility, and it can be a daunting task. But with a little savvy and a little patience, it's not impossible.

The first steps to ensuring timely payment are taken before the job even starts, indeed before the audition even takes place.

The city is full of agencies, and most are fully licensed, reputable operations. But though clip joints are getting rarer (knock on wood), the talent agent business, like any industry with a lot of cash sloshing around, will always have its share of fly-by-night operations and rip-off artists ready to prey on starry-eyed would-be actors. Part of your responsibility when pursuing the work is to be smart. By staying alert for certain tell-tale signs of the scam artists, you can avoid trouble when it comes time to get paid.

If an agency starts giving you a long list of charges, for example, you know you're in the wrong place. State law dictates that under no circumstances can a talent agency insist an actor use a particular photographer for their headshots, or demand you sign up for some sort of audition newsletter (for a nominal fee, of course…). No mandatory classes, no asking you to come in and answer the phones. An agent is licensed to send you out on potential employment as a performer; any of the extras are not only against the law, they're a sure tip-off that this particular agent is in the game to make as much dough as possible at your expense.

If you're unsure about a particular agency, trust your instincts and do a little background work. Ask your fellow actors if they've heard anything. Or call the Department of Labor. Any non-sketchy agency will have their license (along with a $5,000 bond) on file with the DOL.

Illinois Department of Labor
160 N. LaSalle - 13th floor
Chicago, IL 60601
312/793-1817

But what if all goes well—it's a seemingly decent agency, you have a good audition, and you do the work—and you end up sitting around waiting for that precious check? Here's a few pointers on what to do next:

1. Wait

The Private Employment Agency Act of the State of Illinois Compiled Statutes (that's 225 ILCS 515/0.01, available online at www.legis.state.il.us/ilcs) dictates no maximum or minimum time by which a client must pay an agent. In other words, under the law, an advertiser or other employer of actors has no particular obligation to get your money to your agent within any duration of time whatsoever.

Where there is no law, however, there is common practice. As a rule of thumb, an actor on a non-union job can expect to wait from two weeks to a month for a check to be issued and sent along.

So don't call your agent the day after the shoot and demand your cash. Jumping the gun isn't just rude—it's potentially deadly to your career. Pestering an agent about money prematurely is like sending a letter telling them in no uncertain terms that you're irresponsible and unprofessional, and they'll be less and less inclined to send you out on further auditions.

Hard as it may be, the first step is to hang tight. Borrow a little more scratch from mom and dad and wait at least a few weeks before getting worried.

2. Wait Some More

The truth is, agents are exceptionally busy people, and they don't need cash-poor actors banging the door before there's any good reason. The most likely cause for any delay in your payment is that the agency hasn't yet been paid by the client. The hard truth is that—again according to the Private Employment Agency Act—the agent doesn't owe you a cent until they've gotten the checks from the client.

(That PEA Act is a treasure trove of fascinating information, by the way—did you know that agents can't send female performers to "any questionable place, or place of bad repute, house of ill-fame or assignation house, or to any house or place of amusement kept for immoral purposes, or place resorted to for the purpose of prostitution or gambling"? Also, those known to be "questionable characters, prostitutes, gamblers, intoxicated persons, or procurers" aren't even allowed inside an agency.)

Give your agent the benefit of the doubt. But when more than a month has elapsed and you're still looking down the barrel of an empty mailbox, it's time to take action.

3. Call your Agent or Pay Them a Visit

"The check was always sitting up there, and it's just that nobody knew it was there," says one non-union actor of an elusive payment. "I went up there and I said, 'I did work for you all on such and such date, on such and such contract, now where's my money?'"

Lo and behold, the money was indeed there, waiting patiently to be retrieved.

"Apparently it just wouldn't happen over the phone," he says. "I had tried like three times...when I went up there, they looked and found it. It was in their files."

A local voice-over agent suggests that, if after 30 days a check is still not forthcoming, it's perfectly reasonable to call and inquire as to its whereabouts—it's always possible that (as in the above case) the check has arrived and been mislaid or overlooked.

"Thirty days after the job is an industry standard," says this agent. "It's completely appropriate for the actor to give their agent a call and say, 'I just want to give you a head's up.' Trust me: We want to get [checks] out as quickly as possible."

Sometimes a quick phone call is all it takes to get things straightened out, whether the problem is at the agency or (as is more common) with the client. "Usually the actor will call you and say, 'Where's my money, this project happened a while ago?' That's when I would call the client and say, 'This actor worked on this day, when can we expect payment?' And then [the client] is usually really nice about it. Either they're behind in their paperwork, or the actor is jumping the gun and it felt like a month but it's only been two weeks."

Make sure of your dates, and then call. Try to be polite, but not timid. Remember that as intimidating as it can be to talk with someone who can control your destiny (in whatever way), the truth is that agents work for you, not the other way around. Part of their job is making sure that you get paid.

If you start to sense you're being blown off, be persistent and find out what's going on…hey, it's your money.

4. Drastic Measures

If your series of phone calls to the agent proves fruitless, it may be time for the big guns.

One possibility is to call up the client directly and ask what's going on—a rare, but not unheard of action, according to Markmann. (Here's another reason to check your contract before doing the job: Some agreements specifically stipulate that an actor may not contact the client in these circumstances.) If they tell you they sent out checks to the agency a month ago, you know something is fishy.

At the very least, you remind them of your existence, something your agent may have been too busy to get to, and hopefully hurry the check along.

Another, less palatable option is to sue the agent in small claims court for non-payment, either by hiring a lawyer or by going after them by yourself ("prose" is the technical term, Latin for…"by yourself"). If you've always wanted to play Clarence Darrow, this might be fun, but more likely it would be an aggravating, expensive waste of time.

The smart move is to call the Department of Labor and chat with Markmann, who handles these kinds of things for a living. An agent late on payment will be much more affected by a call from Markmann, who comes with all the weight of the State of Illinois, than from you and your non-union.

Markmann most likely has a relationship with the agency, probably with your specific agent, and is in a position to find out exactly what's going on with your money. If she's not satisfied with their answers, she can take steps not only to recover your fee but to land the agency in hot water for their delinquency.

6. Learn… Move On… Join the Union

If there's no other lesson to be learned from being jerked around by an agent, or simply from suffering through the occasional unavoidable delays, it's that SAG/AFTRA membership is to be coveted and strived for. Union membership is more than a feather in your cap; it means minimizing exactly this sort of aggravation.

Chapter 6

Unions & Organizations

Union representatives preparing to enter negotiations.

Neo-Futurists, "Missing Parts"

The time approaches
That will with due decision make us know
What we shall say we have and what we owe.
Thoughts speculative their unsure hopes relate,
But certain issue strokes must arbitrate.

By Carrie L. Kaufman

Let's face it, Chicago is a non-Equity town. Joining Actors Equity Association (AEA) is a step you have to think through carefully. Sure, you will get paid a decent wage (though by no means a living one) for the run of an Equity show, but after that show closes, there are fewer opportunities to get cast in another Equity show. In general, Equity actors can't work in non-Equity theatre. But non-Equity actors can work alongside union actors at the Goodman or Steppenwolf.

There are, at any given time, over 200 theatres in this city and only 40 or so are Equity. Of those, over 40 percent are Tier N; this basically means the stage between Equity and non-Equity.

This is not to say that actors can't, or shouldn't, join Actors Equity Association. But you must be wise about where your career is going and if you are ready to make the commitment.

If you are Equity already, AEA in Chicago has made it easier to work in what used to be non-Equity theatre. The Chicago Area Theatre (CAT) contract has seven tiers with different salary structures. The two lower ones (Tier N and Tier 1) make it possible for previously non-Equity theatres to hire at least one Equity actor on a low budget.

If you are faced with the decision of whether or not to join Equity, remember that if a company thinks you're good enough to turn Equity, they'll probably think you're good enough to cast in the future.

Membership

There are three ways to join Actors Equity Association:

1) Get cast in an Equity show and sign an Equity contract.

2) Be a member in good standing of one of the six other unions that make up the 4-A's (Associated Actors and Artists of America). The sister unions are: AFTRA (the American Federation of Television and Radio Artists), SAG (the Screen Actors Guild), AGMA (the American Guild of Musical Artists), AGVA (the American Guild of Variety Artists), HAU (the Hebrew Actors Union), and IAU (Italian Actors Union). You have to pay the initiation fee and dues for Equity if you want to join.

3) Join the Equity Membership Candidate Program.

The first avenue is possible, but rare.

The second is up to the other unions.

The Equity Membership Candidate Program (EMC) gives non-Equity actors the chance to work in Equity theatres and earn points toward Equity membership. The first step is getting cast for a non-Equity role by an Equity theatre that participates in the program. That's where summer theatre comes in.

Once you enroll and pay your $100 fee (which will go toward your initiation fee once you join the union), you earn points for each week you work in an Equity show until you reach 50 weeks, when you can join the union. At that point, you cannot be hired by an Equity theatre unless they sign you to an Equity contract. It is not unusual for a non-Equity actor to reach 50 weeks and then drop out of the EMC program so they don't have to join Equity. At that point you can rejoin EMC, but you have to pay another $100 and start again from scratch.

The initiation fee for joining Actors Equity Association is $800. Members also must pay semi-annual dues totaling $78 and pay two percent of their gross salary for each Equity contract they sign.

Benefits

Equity members have access to a health plan, a vision care plan and dental plan. Equity actors can be eligible for one year of health benefits if they complete 10 Equity work weeks in a 12 month period. They have to keep working 10 weeks or more each following year to maintain health benefits.

Other benefits are a bit less tangible but make up the backbone of Equity's existence. All producers must post a bond, for instance, for each show so Equity members can get paid if the show closes early. The union also administers a pension plan and provides workers' compensation. Actors under Equity contracts must be given certain breaks at certain periods of time, and the work space must be of a certain standard. Actors also can't work more than so many hours in a day or week. If you supply a costume piece you must, under Equity rules, be paid rental for that costume by the theatre.

I could go on. It's a union.

Contracts

Equity theatres in the Chicago area work under four basic types of contracts: CAT (Chicago Area Theatre), LORT (League of Resident Theatres), Dinner Theatre and Children's Theatre.

CAT

The Chicago Area Theatre contract came to being in the mid-1980s as a more flexible alternative to other Equity contracts. It is divided into seven tiers that specify, among other things, different salary arrangements and shows per week. Each tier has a standard minimum salary and benefits, but often theatres negotiate their own. Every tier but Tier N requires at least one Equity actor and an Equity stage manager. Tier N requires the stage manager be an Equity Membership Candidate. Tiers 2-6 require understudies, though the understudies do not have to be Equity members. An Equity understudy who is required to be there all the time would be paid the same as an Equity actor. An understudy who is hired on a "stand-by" basis would be paid a salary equivalent to three tiers down from the tier the show is working under. For instance, a stand-by understudy for a Tier 6 theatre would be paid a Tier 3 salary, which would go up when the understudy went on.

CAT theatres can be for-profit or non-profit.

Here is a brief rundown of the CAT tiers and their weekly salaries:

Tier 6: up to eight performances a week with a minimum salary of $627.75 for actors and $750.75 for stage managers.

Tier 5: up to eight performances a week with a minimum salary of $523 for actors and $612 for stage managers.

Tier 4: up to seven performances a week with a minimum salary of $442.50 for actors and $507.75 for stage managers.

Tier 3: up to six performances a week with a minimum salary of $307.25 for actors and $357 for stage managers.

Tier 2: up to five performances a week with a minimum salary of $224 for actors and $258.25 for stage managers.

Tier 1: up to four performances a week with a minimum salary of $146 for actors and $178.75 for stage managers.

Tier N: up to four performances a week with a minimum salary of $145 for actors, with no requirement to hire understudies or contribute to the health insurance fund. An Equity stage manager isn't required either unless the show has three or more Equity actors. If a stage manager is hired under Tier N, it will cost $177.75 a week. In addition, Tier N theatres must do 50 percent of their season as Equity shows. Tier N work weeks do not count towards an actor's eligibility for health care benefits.

In addition, each Tier except N has to contribute to the health insurance and pension funds. For Tier 1 through 3, the health cost is $92.25 per Equity actor per week. For Tiers 4 through 6, it's $100.25 per actor per week.

All tiers and categories must pay 8 percent of their total Equity salary each week to the pension fund.

In addition, CAT contracts offer a "More Remunerative Employment" (MRE) clause. Essentially, if an actor gets a higher paying job—say a national commercial—then the theatre is required to let the actor do the commercial and put on an understudy in his stead until the job ends. This was a recognition that actors in Chicago earn their bread and butter from on-camera work and that if theatres wanted to attract actors who might earn more, they needed to promise them time off when opportunities came up. The MRE is applicable to all CAT contracts, including CAT N. It is not applicable to many other Equity contracts. LORT and Dinner Theatre contracts, for instance, don't have MREs.

LORT

The League of Resident Theatres is a membership organization of non-profit regional theatres around the U.S. Guthrie is LORT. Arena Stage is LORT. Basically, the anchor regional theatre in any city is probably a member of LORT and therefore under a LORT Equity contract. LORT contracts with Equity permit touring and cover musical and non-musical theatre. Salary and contract requirements are based on the theatre's budget and box office grosses. There are five levels: A, B+, B, C & D. Theatres may employ a resident company but are not required to do so. Chicago has three LORT contract theatres: Goodman, Northlight and Court. They pay health and pension.

Dinner Theatre

There are six tier structures under the Dinner Theatre contract. Salary is based on seating capacity. Actors Equity must approve any dinner theatre in Chicago (and New York City, Los Angeles County or San Francisco). Dinner does not have to be served in the same room as the show. This puts theatres such as Marriott Theatre at Lincolnshire—which often sells restaurant/theatre packages—under this contract. Health and pension is covered under this contract.

Theatre for Young Audiences

TYA is the contract for professional children's theatre in Chicago. Actors can be hired on a weekly contract or a per performance contract. Performances generally don't begin after 7 p.m. and may not exceed 90 minutes in length. The contract allows for "associated artist activity," such as classes and workshops with students. Both local and overnight touring are permitted. This contract is used both for resident companies who have an outreach program and for companies that make their livings touring schools. Actors can make decent supplementary income doing children's theatre in Chicago. And actors get health and pension.

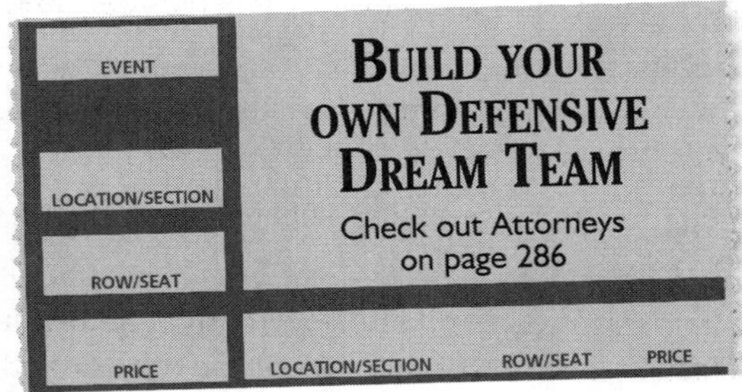

By Carrie L. Kaufman

In Chicago, actors can get pretty steady work in commercials, industrials, voice-overs and film. And almost all of that work is union.

The American Federation of Television and Radio Artists (AFTRA) and the Screen Actors Guild (SAG) are the two non-stage performer unions. They are closely related. In fact, in Chicago AFTRA and SAG are run out of the same office under one executive director. They are, like all unions, run by an elected board of members.

Whether or not a production is covered by AFTRA or SAG is quite complicated. The two unions have always worked out an agreement meting out jurisdiction. A few years ago they were set to merge, but the merger vote was narrowly defeated.

Currently, SAG and AFTRA have no national agreement as to what is supposed to be the jurisdiction of which union. SAG simply refuses to talk to AFTRA, whom they see as their pesky little brother. So while the two unions are in limbo, they're holding on to the traditional jurisdictions.

SAG covers all movies and most animation and prime time television, regardless of the medium. If a movie is shot on film, it's SAG. If it's shot on digital video, it's still SAG. It's SAG even if it is only released on TV.

SAG used to cover all animation, but AFTRA has made some in-roads. The federation has recently signed some television animation shows and even a couple of sitcoms—long the purview of SAG.

AFTRA covers all daytime television, plus specials like awards shows. AFTRA also covers radio.

Union jurisdiction gets murky when it comes to commercials, industrials (workplace videos), basic cable and non-prime time programming or syndicated programming. Officially, it's up to the producer to decide which contract to use. Producers usually just use the contract they're most familiar with.

In cities where AFTRA and SAG are administered out of the same office, the staff figures out some sort of equitable solution. In Chicago, for instance, jurisdiction over television commercials and industrials is determined by the medium used. Commercials and industrials in Chicago, for instance, are SAG if they are shot on film and AFTRA if they are shot on video. This is all rather arbitrary. Other jointly run offices might operate differently on this decision.

The real battle on the horizon between AFTRA and SAG is basic cable and the Internet. Original movies, dramas or sit-coms made for cable outlets like Lifetime, Fox Family or A&E are up for grabs and important for both unions. So, too, is Internet jurisdiction. We'll see in the next few years how it plays out.

Membership

Joining AFTRA and SAG is fairly easy, though not cheap. You can join AFTRA at any time by simply paying the initiation fee and half a year's dues. For SAG, you first have to get cast under a SAG contract. That means you land your first big commercial (for convenience, let's say it's shot on film and is SAG), or even a local SAG commercial, or you get the role of the young doctor who comes into the hospital room and says, "It's late. Everybody out," in the latest Bruce Willis flick. Once you get that contract, you are eligible to join SAG. But you don't have to join right away.

As you're signing that contract, you will likely hear—from your agent or the casting director, or even the production coordinator—two words: Taft-Hartley. "You're Taft-Hartley now, so you'd better call the union," the production coordinator will say as she bumps you up from an extra to a speaking role.

The Taft-Hartley Act is one of the laws that covers unions and is also known as the National Labor Relations Act. Essentially, it says that a union can't require somebody to join until 30 days after their first day of employment. For a steel worker, that's a month after they're hired. For an actor, that could be years after they get their first job.

Once you get that first SAG job, you have 30 days to take as much union work as you can land without joining the union. If you land a union job 31 days after your first, though, you immediately have to join the union.

This is when actors get in trouble. The initiation fee for SAG is currently $1,272. That number is just a bit more than two session fees for a commercial. Minimum yearly dues are $100, to be paid in twice yearly installments—the first in addition to the initiation fee when you join.

The initiation fee for AFTRA is currently $1,000. Minimum yearly dues are $116, to be paid in twice yearly installments. Dues for both unions are based on an actor's earnings.

So, you've spent all the money you made two years ago doing SAG jobs under the Taft-Hartley 30-day protection. Now you have to fork over $1,272 to the union before you even step on the set. Don't have it? Too bad. You should have put it away two years ago in anticipation of having to join. You either come up with the money or lose the job and possibly your agent's good will. SAG and AFTRA do offer payment plans, but you have to be ready to fork over something.

Contracts

There are multiple SAG and AFTRA contracts for various aspects of the business. Since most SAG and AFTRA work in Chicago is for commercials, we'll focus on that.

If you make a commercial for radio or TV, you will be paid a $500 session fee. Above that, if your commercial runs on network TV—ABC, NBC, CBS, FOX—then you will get paid every time that commercial runs. If the commercial runs on cable, you will get paid a flat rate above the session fee for 13-weeks of use. Most commercials will have a combination of cable and network runs.

Tracking those ads is a bit of a problem. SAG and AFTRA assert that they are being underpaid because some commercials that run aren't counted when residuals checks are totaled up. Under the 2000 commercials contract, the unions and the industry are going to study electronic monitoring (like the V-Chip concept) on TV commercials.

Tracking Internet ads is a bit easier, and SAG and AFTRA have limited jurisdiction on Internet commercials. Commercials made for broadcast and moved to the Internet will earn actors $1,500, or three session fees, for each 13-week period of use. Ads made directly for the Internet are subject to negotiation by the actor and his agent and the ad agency.

For more comprehensive information on the SAG/AFTRA commercials contract, head to www.performink.com. You will also find updates there on the TV and movies contracts that were negotiated in June of 2001.

Product Conflict

If the ad agency stops running a commercial, they still might have to pay you. Under rules governing product conflict, an actor under contract to do a commercial for one type of product—such as a Nissan Sentra—cannot turn around and do a commercial for a competitive product—

such as the Ford F150. Remember, image is everything, and neither ad agencies nor their clients want that cuddly, yet enigmatic man the public is so identifying with to show up selling a competitive product.

This is only true while the contract is in effect. Once the contract expires, the actor is free to do whatever commercial he or she gets.

If the advertiser wants to retire a campaign and use new actors, but doesn't want that well-identified actor to show up shilling for a competitor, the advertiser must pay the actor a holding fee to keep him or her from being in a competitive commercial. The holding fee, paid every 13 weeks, is equivalent to the session fee. For national campaigns with a lot of exposure, the agency and client might pay the fee for a few years.

This does not apply for non-union commercials, and that can be problematic. If you do a non-union commercial for your local used car lot and sign a contract with no expiration date, then that car lot can use your commercial anytime.

Years later, when you land that national Ford account and your face is plastered all over the place, the used card dealership could drag out that old commercial and ride on Ford's coat tails. Ford won't like that very much and you could be in big trouble. If you're lucky, you'll just have to forfeit all your earnings (which you hopefully haven't spent yet). Worst case, Ford may decide to pull the entire commercial and you could be liable for all of the expenses incurred to put that commercial together. Everything. The entire production—hundreds of thousands of dollars—could be charged to you.

Similar consequences can ensue if you did a union commercial for McDonald's in 1999 and have simply "forgotten" about those checks McDonald's is still paying you in holding fees.

But remember, if you do a union commercial for McDonald's and they stop paying you holding fees, they cannot run that commercial again without hiring you again. Then you are free to do the Burger King commercial.

Benefits

AFTRA and SAG are unions and give their members the same benefits as any union, including pension, retirement and health plans.

Currently, in both unions, actors must earn at least $7,500 in a 12-month period to be eligible for health insurance. For AFTRA, that's going to remain the same. For SAG, that's going to go up to $9,000 per year beginning in Jan. 2003. Minimum earnings will then increase each year until 2007, when an actor will have to make at least $11,000 to be eligible for health insurance.

So far, AFTRA is still keeping its minimum earnings for eligibility at $7,500.

On a set, AFTRA and SAG negotiate everything from meals and bathroom breaks to overtime. There are myriad rules, and it would behoove any actor to call the AFTRA/SAG office to find out what they are.

If an actor is on a shoot and something comes up that is questionable—say the production manager says everybody is working overtime and not getting paid overtime rates—it's not a union actor's responsibility to argue. Tell the production manager that it's all right with you if it's all right with your union and your agent, then get on the horn and call either one. Let them do the arguing for you.

Joining a union is never an easy process. There are rules and regulations galore. Sometimes it might seem as if they get in the way. But all the rules are there to protect the members, and actors need all the protection they can get.

Unions

Actors Equity Association
203 N. Wabash #1700
Chicago, IL 60601
312/641-0393
312/641-6365 - fax
www.actorsequity.org

American Federation of Television & Radio Artists
(AFTRA)
1 E. Erie #650
Chicago, IL 60611
312/573-8081
312/573-0318 - fax
www.aftra.org

Directors Guild of America
400 N. Michigan #307
Chicago, IL 60611
312/644-5050
312/644-5776 - fax
www.dga.org

Screen Actors Guild (SAG)
1 E. Erie St., #650
Chicago, IL 60611
312/573-8081
312/573-0318 - fax
www.sag.org

As actors, we are often left to fend for ourselves, particularly if we are not in a union. Fortunately, the government provides a number of agencies that will help you deal with disputes of hiring or payment. Following is a list of the main ones.

Employment Issues

Illinois Department of Labor
160 N. LaSalle - 13th floor
Chicago, IL 60601
Wage Claim Division (for employment compensation)
312/793-2808

If your dispute is directly with an employer and it deals with your pay, call the **Wage Claim Division** of the Department of Labor. They step in when an actor is paid less than they were hired for or when an actor is not paid at all (if, in fact the theatre or production company has agreed to pay in the first place).

If you feel you've been wronged in your pay, file a complaint with the Wage Claim Division. They will send a letter to the employer. When they get the employer's response, they will compare your claim to their response and either dismiss it or send it to the next level—a hearing. If the employer is found liable in the hearing, he or she has a certain amount of time to pay. If the employer still doesn't pay, Wage Claim then sends it to the Attorney General's office, where legal proceedings are begun. For this last phase to take place, actors need to stay in touch with the Department of Labor after an employer is found liable. The department has no way of knowing if the employer has fulfilled his or her obligations unless you tell them.

The Equal Opportunity Employment Commission

National Office
1801 L Street, N.W.
Washington, D.C. 20507
202/663-4900
TDD: 202/663-4494
www.eeoc.gov

Chicago District Office
500 West Madison #2800
Chicago, IL 60661
312/353-2713
TDD: 312/353-2421

The **EEOC** protects against discrimination in the workplace. If you feel you've been sexually harassed, call the EEOC and make a complaint. If you feel you've been dismissed because of your race, call the EEOC. There are laws that protect you and the commission will check out your story. Chances are, you aren't the only one who has complained.

In cases of sexual discrimination—including harassment and pregnancy—you can also call the **Women's Bureau,** which has regional offices all over the country. The Chicago office of the Women's Bureau is at 312/353-6985. They cover the Illinois, Indiana, Michigan, Minnesota, Ohio and Wisconsin areas.

The Women's Bureau is not an enforcing agency. They are a resource for information and statistics on women in the workplace. But they can give you advice or point you in the right direction if you feel you've been wronged.

Department of Human Rights
100 W. Randolph #10-100
Chicago, IL 60601
312/814-6200
www.state.il.us.dhr

The Illinois Department of Human Rights deals with any sort of discrimination in the work force. They are essentially the state alternative to the EEOC. If you've been fired because you're pregnant, call them. If you've been fired because you're over 40, they can help. If you've been fired or not hired because you're African-American or Hispanic or have an unfavorable military discharge or an arrest record, call them. They are also the place to call if you've been the victim of sexual harassment.

Consumer Issues

Illinois Attorney General
100 W. Randolph
Chicago, IL 60601
312/814-3000
(Check the white pages for specific departments.)

The Office of the Attorney General deals with consumer issues. If you pay to get your headshots reproduced and the company goes bankrupt after it's cashed your check, call the Attorney General's office.

Better Business Bureau
Chicago Office
330 N. Wabash
Chicago, IL 60611
312/832-0500

The Better Business Bureau deals with contracts and obligations. If you paid a photographer to take your headshot but the film came out totally black, and he won't give you your money back, call the Better Business Bureau as well as the Attorney General's office).

If, however, that same photographer asks you to pose nude or if an agent starts yelling and screaming obscenities at you, the Better Business Bureau will be of no help. They may be sympathetic, but they do not deal with matters of behavior.

Similar Organizations

The Actors' Fund
203 N. Wabash #2104
Chicago, IL 60601
312/372-0989
312/372-0272 - fax
www.actorsfund.org

Chicago Access Corporation
322 S. Green #100
Chicago, IL 60607
312/738-1400
312/738-2519 - fax
www.cantv.org

Chicago Dance Coalition
410 S. Michigan #819
Chicago, IL 60605
312/419-8384

Chicago Federation of Musicians
Local 10 208 AFM
175 W. Washington
Chicago, IL 60602
312/782-0063
312/782-7880 - fax
www.livemusichicago.com

Chicago Film Office
1 N. LaSalle #2165
Chicago, IL 60602
312/744-6415
312/744-1378 - fax
www.ci.chi.il.us/wm/specialevents/filmoffice/

Chicago National Association of Dance Masters
5411 E. State St. #202
Rockford, IL 61108
815/397-6052
815/397-6799 - fax
www.cnadm.com
Workshops only; no ongoing classes

Illinois Film Office
100 W. Randolph - 3rd Floor
Chicago, IL 60601
312/814-3600
312/814-8874 - fax
www.commerce.state.il.us

National Dinner Theatre Association
P.O. Box 726
Marshall, MI 49068
616/781-7859
616/781-4880 - fax
www.ndta.com

Society of Stage Directors & Choreographers (SSDC)
1501 Broadway #1701
New York, NY 10036
212/302-6195
212/391-1070 - fax

University/Resident Theatre Association (U/RTA)
1560 Broadway #414
New York, NY 10036
212/221-1130
212/869-2752 - fax
www.urta.com

Women in the Director's Chair
941 W. Lawrence #500
Chicago, IL 60640
773/907-0610
773/907-0381 - fax
www.widc.org

Women's Theatre Alliance
P.O. Box 64446
Chicago, IL 60664-0446
312/408-9910
http://wtachicago.org

Chapter 7

Theatres

Northlight, "The Gamester"

Audition, Audition!

The audition is the one constant of an actor's life. We're always looking for new work, and no one's come up with a better way to hire actors. It's unfair and inaccurate, but it's a fact of life for an actor. All we can do is give the best audition we can at all times. Here's some advice on how.

1. Finding a Piece

Monologue Books

These have their ups and downs. On the up: The monologue is cut and ready to go. On the down: The monologue is convenient, so someone else has probably already used it.

Plays

Many fantastic writers have monologues to be found in their lesser-known works. That means you need to read those obscure works. Of course you should be reading plays all the time anyway, right? Right.

Other Sources

There are monologues to be found in literature, poetry, movies, biographies, soup cans, etc. Some directors prefer pieces from traditional sources, but, generally speaking, if it's a good piece it doesn't matter where it's from.

Write Your Own

This is a controversial possibility. Most directors seem to be opposed to this route because generally, actors aren't strong writers. If it's a good monologue, you might get away with it, but you probably shouldn't admit the pieces are original.

Cross-Gender Pieces

If you're going to do a piece intended for the opposite gender, make sure it's good. Auditors sometimes find these pieces distracting, so if you go for it, it had better be strong enough to overcome that possible reaction.

2. Preparing a Piece

Choosing a Piece

A good piece shows your strengths. If you're a physical actor, choose a piece that allows you to be physical. If you have great emotional range, find an emotionally charged piece.

Practice, Practice, Practice

Try the piece out for your friends; don't let your first performance of a piece count.

3. What Should I Wear?

Suggestions
You don't want to wear a costume. This would be bad. However, if your a woman, wearing a long skirt when you audition for a period piece can be worthwhile.

Don't Limit
Tight clothing, uncomfortable shoes or anything that limits your movement should be avoided.

4. Getting There

Leave Time
When you make the appointment, be sure you know how to get to the audition location. Be sure to leave more than enough time for travel. If you're late, the auditors won't care that the eL was running slowly or your car had a flat. They only care that you've upset their schedule, and they won't be sympathetic.

Call Ahead
If you can't make an audition, CALL. Nothing will anger an agent or director more than a missing actor. What's more, many of them have long memories.

5. On Site

Arrival
Be kind to everyone. The audition monitor isn't necessarily a mere peon for you to abuse. They can, and often do, let directors know about abusive or rude actors, and those people won't get work. Your audition begins the moment you enter the building.

The Walls Have Ears
Before and after your audition, be wary of voicing loud opinions. The walls are thin, and you never know who's listening.

Conflicts
Be honest in listing your conflicts. If you try to introduce them after being cast, you'll only anger the director/producer/whomever. If you have to be out of town for a wedding, let them know. If a conflict is negotiable, let them know that. Keep communicating, though, or you'll alienate someone.

6. The Audition

Choose a Focal Point
Be sure you're going to be performing at least three-quarters front. No profiles. Most auditors seem to prefer you not act to furniture. Above all, don't focus on the person for whom you're auditioning. They want to watch your piece, not be a part of it.

Make Strong Choices

Strong choices are key—both in monologues and cold readings.
The auditors see dozens of auditions; don't let yours blend in with the rest.

Take Direction

If the director asks for a new take on a piece, do it. This is a good thing. It means the director is interested and wants to see if you can take direction. Take it.

Get In, Get Out

Enter with confidence, perform with confidence, leave with confidence.

Don't Apologize!

Never, ever, ever. The audition you feel was poor may have seemed fine to the director. Let them decide how you did.

7. Musical Auditions

Make Your Music Friendly

Put it in a three-ring binder on sturdy paper that's easy to handle. The accompanist is sight reading and turning pages, so make seeing and handling the music easy.

Keep It Playable

Don't expect your accompanist to transpose for you. You'll just piss them off. Also, choose songs with easy accompaniments. You don't want your audition destroyed because the accompanist can't play your song.

Set a Tempo

Let them know how you like it.

Don't Shoot the Piano Player

Your accompanist is doing his/her best. Don't blame the accompanist when they screw up. Even if it's awful, keep the beat, keep singing and let the accompanist follow you. The auditors know when the accompaniment is a mess, but they won't appreciate you pointing it out in word or gesture. Keep a smile on your face.

8. Afterwards

Send a Card

Particularly after a call back or after being called in from a general, send a postcard saying thanks. Don't ask about the decision; just say "Hi."

Don't Be Rude

If you're offered a part you don't want or can't take, call back and let them know. Someone else is waiting on your decision, so make it and make the call.

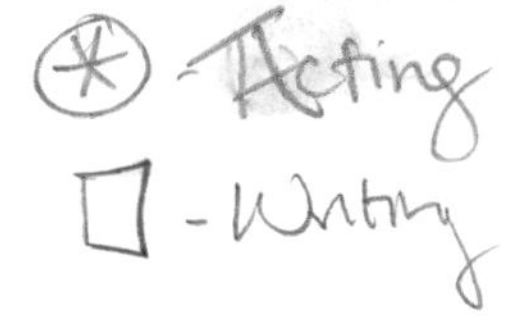

Theatres– Equity

About Face Theatre
Eric Rosen – Artistic Director
Verna Bond-Broderick – Managing Director
1222 W. Wilson, 2nd Floor West
Chicago, IL 60640
773/784-8565
773/549-3290 – box office
faceline1@aboutfacetheatre.com
www.aboutfacetheatre.com

Equity — CAT N — Resident

Founded in 1995. Starting non-Equity pay is $100/week plus rehearsal pay. Nearest eL stop is Belmont on the red and brown lines.

About Face Theatre is dedicated to the creation of performances that examine and participate in the development of the gay, lesbian, and bisexual communities. They received two Jeff Award nominations for Bash and The Terrible Girls.

They accept unsolicited synopses from playwrights, but do not accept director proposals.

Actors Workshop Theatre
Michael Colucci – Artistic Director
Thomas Jamroz – Managing Director
1350 N. Wells, Suite F521
Chicago, IL 60610
312/337-6603
colucci@actorsworkshop.org
www.actorsworkshop.org

Equity — CAT N — Non-resident

Founded in 1994. Starting non-Equity pay is a percentage of box office. They hold non-Equity generals.

Actor's Workshop Theatre explores the entire body of work of a single playwright.

They do not accept unsolicited synopses, but they do accept director proposals

---

American Theater Company
Brian Russell – Producing Artistic Director
Gregory Werstler – Managing Director
1909 W. Byron
Chicago, IL 60613
773/929-5009
773/929-1031 – box office
atcfolk@aol.com
www.atcweb.org

Equity — CAT II — Resident

Founded in 1985. Starting non-Equity pay is $75/week. The nearest eL stop is Irving Park on the Brown line.

American Theatre Company is an ensemble of actors that tells great stories about real people in an honest way.

Their 2000-2001 season included:
- Endgame
- Working
- Vick's Boy
- Catch-22
- American Buffalo.

They won a 2001 Jeff Award for Endgame.

They accept synopses and director proposals.

The Artistic Home
Kathy Scambiatterra – Artistic Director
Amy Rising – Managing Director
1420 W. Irving Park
Chicago, IL 60613
773/404-1100
theartistichome@aol.com

Resident company founded in 1998. They hold auditions in the spring.

The Artistic Home Acting Ensemble exists to create relationship driven theatre and film and to tell stories that provoke thought and change through a cohesive approach to craft.

They accept script submissions and director proposals.

Apple Tree Theatre
Eileen Boevers, Ross Lehman – Artistic Directors
Cecilie Keenan – Managing Director
595 Elm Place #210
Highland Park, IL 60035
847/432-8223
847/432-4335 – box office
www.appletreetheatre.com

Equity — CAT III — Resident

Founded in 1983, they hold Equity generals in the summer and attend non-Equity Unifieds. The nearest Metra stop is the Highland Park stop.

Apple Tree is committed to producing a diverse and challenging selection of both dramas and musicals, from new works to classics, all of which illuminate the human condition.

Their 2000-2001 season included:
- Syncopation
- Big River
- Fuddy Meers
- M. Butterfly
- 2 1/2 Jews

Their season earned them four Jeff Award nominations.

They accept synopses and director proposals.

Auditorium Theatre Council
50 E. Congress
Chicago, IL 60605
312/922-2110 x0
www.auditoriumtheatre.org

Equity — Production

Black Ensemble Theater
Jackie Taylor – Artistic Director
Lephate Cunningham Jr. – Managing Director
4520 N. Beacon
Chicago, IL 60640
773/769-5516
773/769-4451 – box office
blackensemble@aol.com
www.blackensembletheater.org

Equity — CAT I — Resident

Founded in 1976. Starting non-Equity pay is $35/show. The nearest eL stop is Wilson on the Red line.

Black Ensemble Theater produces Black plays designed to reach an interracial audience. They won a 2001 Jeff Award for actor in The Nat King Cole Story.

They accept synopses and director proposals.

Chicago Dramatists
Russ Tutterow – Artistic Director
Ann Filmer – Managing Director
1105 W. Chicago
Chicago, IL 60622-5702
312/633-0630
312/633-0630 – box office
NewPlays@aol.com

www.chicagodramatists.org

Equity — CAT I — Resident

Founded in 1979. Starting non-Equity pay is $50/week. They hold non-Equity generals in the summer. The nearest eL stop is Chicago Ave. on the Blue line.

Chicago Dramatists, the playwrights' theatre, is dedicated to the development, production, and advancement of playwrights and new plays.

They do not accept synopses or director proposals.

Chicago Shakespeare Theater
Barbara Gaines – Artistic Director
Criss Henderson – Executive Director
800 E. Grand
Chicago, IL 60611
312/595-5656
312/595-5600 – box office
www.chicagoshakes.com

Equity — CAT V — Resident

Founded in 1986, starting non-Equity pay is $325 a week. They hold non-Equity generals in September.

The 2000-2001 season included: Two Gentleman of Verona, The School for Scandal, King Lear. Two Gents and King Lear each received a 2001 Jeff Award.

They do not accept synopses or director proposals.

Chicago Theatre Company
Douglas Alan-Mann – Artistic Director
Luther Goins – Managing Director
500 E. 67th
Chicago, IL 60637
773/274-1370
773/493-5360 – box office
luther goins@aol.com
www.chicagotheatrecompany.com

Equity — CAT I — Resident

Founded in 1984. Starting non-Equity pay is $75 a week. Nearest eL stop is 69th Street on the Red line.

The Chicago Theatre Company takes a unique African-American approach to their craft.

Their 2000-2001 season included:
- Morning, Noon, and Night
- Billy
- Being Beautiful

Their co-production (with Live Bait Theatre) of Love Child won a 2001 non-Equity Jeff Citation. Being Beautiful won a 2001 Equity Jeff Award for supporting actor in a musical.

They accept synopses and director proposals.

Court Theatre
Charles Newell – Artistic Director
Diane Claussen – Managing Director
5535 S. Ellis
Chicago, IL 60637
773/702-7005
773/753-4472 – box office
info@courttheatre.org
www.courttheatre.org

Equity — LORT D — Resident

Founded in 1955, starting non-Equity pay is $225/week. They hold general auditions in mid-April. Public Transportation: #55 Garfield bus stop at 55th St. and Ellis Ave.

Court Theatre exists to celebrate the immutable power and relevance of classical theatre.

Their 2000-2001 season included:
- The Invention of Love
- In the Penal Colony
- Hay Fever
- Twelfth Night
- Piano

Invention of Love and Hay Fever garnered four Equity Jeff nominations.

They accept synopses and director proposals.

Theatres

Division 13
Joanna Settle – Artistic Director
Katie Taber – Managing Director
28 E. Jackson, 10th floor T-463
Chicago, IL 60604
773/252-2510
info@division13,org
www.division13.org

Equity — CAT N — Non-resident

Founded in 1996. Starting non-Equity pay is a $400-600 stipend for the run.

Division 13 Productions' mission is to produce vital, distinctive works.

Their 2000-2001 season included:
How to be Sawed in Half
Macbett

Macbett won a 2001 Jeff Award for sound design.

They do not accept synopses or director proposals.

Drury Lane Theatre Evergreen Park
2500 W. 95th St.
Evergreen Park, IL 60805
708/422-0404
www.drurylane.com

Equity – Dinner Theatre, Tier 4

They received three Jeff nominations for their production of And the World Goes 'Round.

Drury Lane Theatre Oakbrook
Ray Frewen – Artistic Director
Diane Van Lente – Managing Director
100 Drury Ln.
Oakbrook Terrace, IL 60181
630/530-8300
630/530-0111 – box office
www.drurylaneoakbrook.com

Equity — Dinner Theatre — Resident
Founded in 1984.

Drury Lane Oakbrook is a self producing dinner theatre in the western suburbs. They won two Jeff Awards for 2000/2001 season for Big the Musical.

They do not accept synopses or director proposals.

Equity Library Theatre Chicago
773/743-0266.
franktfarrell@juno.com

Equity — Special Agreement

European Repertory Company
Yasen Peyankov, Dale Goulding – Artistic Directors
Rick Frederick – Managing Director
2936 N. Southport, 3rd floor
Chicago, IL 60657
773/248-0577
EuropeanRep@aol.com

Equity — CAT N — Non-resident

Founded in 1992. They attend the League Unifieds.

European Rep produces European plays and adaptations.

They accept synopses and director proposals.

Famous Door Theatre Co.
Karen Kessler – Artistic Director
Amanda LaFollette – Managing Director
P.O. Box 57029
Chicago, IL 60657
773/404-8283
773/327-5252 – box office
theatre@famousdoortheatre.org
www.famousdoortheatre.org

Equity — CAT I — Non-resident

Founded in 1987. Starting non-Equity pay is $15 - $20 per show. They hold non-Equity generals in May.

Famous Door is a working ensemble of theatre artists who present evocative and challenging premieres and seldom produced works.

Their 2000-2001 season included:
Early and Often
Pride's Crossing
A Going Concern

Early and Often won a 2001 Jeff Award.

They accept synopses and director proposals.

Festival Theatre
Dale Calandra – Artistic Director
Sandy Wiedegreen – Managing Director
P.O. Box 4114
Oak Park, IL 60303
708/524-2050
festival_op@yahoo.com
www.oprf.com/festival

Equity — CAT III — Resident

Founded in 1974. Pay ranges from $600 to $1,200 for the summer. They hold generals in February or March. Nearest eL stop is Harlem on the Green line.

Festival Theatre performs classics in Austin Gardens.

Their 2001 season included:
Taming of the Shrew

They do not accept synopses or director proposals.

First Folio Shakespeare Festival
Alison C. Vesely - Artistic Director
David M. Rice - Managing Director
146 Juliet Ct.
Clarendon Hills, IL 60514
630/986-8067
firstfolio@firstfolio.org
www.firstfolio.org

Equity — CAT III — Resident

Founded in 1996. Starting non-Equity pay is $75-$100/week. They hold generals in January. First Folio specializes in outdoor Shakespeare using the Folio technique to approach the text.

Their 2001 season included:
Macbeth
As You Like It

They do not accept synopses but do accept director proposals.

Goodman Theatre
Robert Falls – Artistic Director
Roche Schulfer – Executive Director
170 N. Dearborn
Chicago, IL 60601
312/443-3811
312/443-3800 – box office
www.goodman-theatre.org

Equity — LORT B — Resident

Founded in 1925. They hold general auditions in the summer. They are in the Loop, accessible by multiple eL train lines.

Their 2000-2001 season included:
King Hedley II
House
The Amen Corner
Wit
Blue Surge
Garden
Among the Thugs
A Christmas Carol

House (scenic design) and Wit (best actress) received two Jeff Awards.

They accept synopses but do not accept director proposals.

Theatres

greasy joan & co.

P.O. Box 13077
Chicago, IL 60613
www.greasyjoan.org

Equity — CAT N

greasy joan was founded in 1995 by a diverse group of actors, directors and dramaturgs dedicated to the exploration of classical theatre and the re-discovery of its contemporary energy.

Illinois Theatre Center

Etel Billig – Artistic Director
P.O. Box 397
Park Forest, IL 60466
708/481-3510
ilthctr@bigplanet.com
www.ilthctr.org

Equity — CAT III — Resident

Founded in 1976. Starting non-Equity pay is $200 per week. They hold generals in July. Nearest Metra stop is Richton Park.

ITC is the only resident, professional, Equity theatre presenting year-round productions in the south suburbs.

Their 2000-2001 season included:

- All My Sons
- Shmulnik's Waltz
- Stars in Your Eyes
- Traveler in the Dark
- Flyin' West
- The Princess of President Street
- As Thousands Cheer

They accept synopses but do not accept director proposals.

Irish Repertory of Chicago

4013 N. Milwaukee #452
Chicago, IL 60641
773/275-2600
773/871-3000 – box office

irishrep@ameritech.net
www.irishrep.com

Equity — CAT III

They accept synopses but do not accept director proposals.

Journeymen Theater Company

Frank Pullen – Artistic Director
3915 N. Janssen
Chicago, IL 60613
773/857-5395
thejourneymen@hotmail.com
www.thejourneymen.org

Equity — CAT I — Resident

Founded in 1995. They hold generals in the fall. The nearest eL stop is Diversey on the Brown line.

The Journeymen seek to draw upon humanities in a way that helps the general public understand a topic of public concern.

Their 2000-2001 season included:

- Master Harold and the Boys
- The Eight Reindeer Monologues
- Lilies

Master Harold was nominated for a 2001 Jeff Award.

They accept synopses and director proposals.

Light Opera Works

Lara Teeter – Artistic Director
Bridget McDonough – Managing Director
927 Noyes St.
Chicago, IL 60614
847/869-7930
847/869-6300 – box office
postmaster@light-opera-works.org
www.light-opera-works.org

Equity — Guest Artist — Resident

Founded in 1980. Starting non-Equity pay is $275 for a chorus role. They hold generals in January.

Light Opera Works produces music from a variety of world traditions.

Their 2000-2001 season included:
- The Gondoliers
- Man of La Mancha
- Tintypes
- The Great Waltz

They do not accept synopses or director proposals.

Lookingglass Theatre Company

Laura Eason – Artistic Director
Jacqui Russell – Managing Director
2936 N. Southport - 3rd floor
Chicago, IL 60657
773/477-9257
773/477-8088 – box office
www.lookingglasstheatre.org

Equity — CAT III — Non-resident

Founded in 1988. Starting non-Equity pay is $325 per week. They hold generals in the summer.

Lookingglass is an ensemble based company that produces primarily original work (new plays and adaptations) that combines a highly physical, visual style with strong narrative.

Their 2000-2001 season included:
- Metamorphosis
- Nelson Algren for Keeps and a Single Day
- Hard Times

Hard Times won them five 2001 Jeff Awards, including production, adaptation and director.

They do not accept synopses or director proposals.

Madison Repertory Theatre

D. Scott Glasser – Artistic Director
Tony Forman – Managing Director
122 State St. #201
Madison, WI 53703
608/256-0029
608/266-9055 – box office
postmaster@madisonrep.org
www.madisonrep.org

Equity — SPT — Resident

Founded in 1968. They hold generals in the spring.

The mission of Madison Repertory Theatre is to produce, in an intimate setting, a wide range of professional theatre work that illuminates the human condition.

Their 2000-2001 season included:
- I Love You, You're Perfect, Now Change
- Wit
- Side Man
- Noises Off
- Full Gallop
- The House of Bernarda Alba
- Art

They accept synopses but they do not accept director proposals

---

The Moving Dock Theatre Company

Dawn Arnold – Artistic Director
2970 N. Sheridan Rd. #1021
Chicago, IL 60657
773/327-1572
dawndock@aol.com

An itinerant company founded in 1998. Pay varies.

The Moving Dock Theatre Company is dedicated to the actor's creative process and to developing theatre that moves. An ensemble, movement-based approach for both developed pieces and scripted works, The Moving Dock explores the essence of the experience of theatre.

They accept script submissions and director proposals.

Marriott Theatre
Rick Boynton – Artistic Director
Terry James – Managing Director
10 Marriott Dr.
Lincolnshire, IL 60069
847/634-0204
847/634-0200 – box office
producer@marriotttheatre.com
www.MarriottTheatre.com

Equity — Dinner Theatre — Resident

Founded in 1979, they hold generals in the spring and fall. They won four 2001 Jeff Awards for The King and I and Mame, including best musical for the former.

They do not accept synopses or director proposals.

Metropolis Performing Arts Center
Alan Salzenstein – Executive Director
111 W. Campbell St. #203
Arlington Heights, IL 60005
847/577-5982
847/577-2121 – box office
info@metroploisarts.com
www.metropolisarts.com

Equity – Various Contracts — Resident

Metropolis Performing Arts Centre presents a complete performing arts experience with professional live theatre, music, dance, comedy, cabaret, children's shows, and educational programs.

They do not accept synopses or director proposals.

Naked Eye Theatre Company
Jeremy Cohen – Artistic Director
1454 W. Hollywood
Chicago, IL 60660
312/409-9800
773/327-5252 – box office
jcohen@rcnchicago.com

www.nakedeyetheatre.org

Equity — CAT N — Non-resident

Founded in 1998.

Naked Eye develops, nurtures, and produces writers who are speaking with an original, clear, theatrical voice.

Their 2000-2001 season included:
- Stopkiss
- Closetland
- Cannibals

They accept synopses and director proposals.

Next Theatre
Kate Buckley – Artistic Director
Robert Scogin – Managing Director
Noyes Cultural Arts Center
927 Noyes St.
Evanston, IL 60201
847/475-6763
847/475-1875 – box office
kateshakes@aol.com
www.nexttheatre.org

Equity — CAT N — Resident

Founded in 1981. They hold generals in August. Nearest eL stop is Noyes on the Purple line.

Next produces cutting edge productions of new plays, Midwest premieres, and radical interpretations of classics.

Their 2000-2001 season included:
- A Doll's House
- The Incident

The Incident got five Jeff Award nominations.

They do not accept synopses or director proposals.

Northlight Theatre
B.J. Jones – Artistic Director
Richard Friedman – Managing Director
9501 Skokie Blvd.
Skokie, IL 60076
847/679-9501
847/673-6300 – box office
ntheatre@aol.com
www.northlight.org

Equity — LORT D — Resident

Founded in 1974. Starting non-Equity pay is $150. They hold generals in June. Nearest eL stop is Dempster on the Yellow line.

Northlight is a leading regional theatre in Chicago.

Their 2000-2001 season included:
- An Experiment with an Airpump
- bee-luther-hatchee
- Enter the Gaurdsmen
- The Gamester
- The Last Five Years

Their 2000-2001 season earned them 13 Jeff Award nominations.

They accept synopses but do not accept director proposals.

Organic Theater Company
Ina Marlowe – Artistic Director
Katie Klemme – Managing Director
1420 Maple Ave.
Evanston, IL 60201
847/475-0600
847/475-2800 – box office
organictheater@aol.com
www.organictheater.com

Equity — CAT II — Resident

Founded in 1972. Starting non-Equity pay includes a rehearsal stipend and $100/week. They hold generals in August. Nearest eL stop is Davis on the Purple line.

The Organic Theater Company is committed to theatre with depth of character and literary strength.

Their 2000-2001 season included:
- An American Daughter
- Boss Grady's Boys
- The Gift
- Romeo and Juliet
- The Little Prince
- Of Mice and Men
- Things We Do For Love
- Amy's View, which was nominated for a 2001 Jeff for supporting actress.

They accept synopses but do not accept director proposals.

Peninsula Players
Greg Vinkler – Artistic Director
Todd Schmidt – Managing Director
W4351 Peninsula Players
Fish Creek, WI 54212
920/868-3287
www.peninsulaplayers.com

Equity — Special Agreement — Resident

Founded in 1937. Starting non-Equity pay is $400/week. They hold generals in March. Peninsula Players is America's oldest professional resident summer theatre.

Their 2001 season included:
- The Cherry Orchard
- Bob Almighty
- Radio Gals

They do not accept synopses or director proposals.

Phoenix Theatre
Bryan Fonseca – Artistic Director
Sharon Gamble – Managing Director
749 N. Park Ave.
Indianapolis, IN 46202
317/635-2381
317/635-7529 – box office
info@phoenixtheatre.org
www.phoenixtheatre.org

Equity — CAT I — Resident

Founded in 1983. Starting non-Equity pay is $125/week.

They do not accept synopses or director proposals.

Piven Theatre Workshop
Byrne and Joyce Piven – Artistic Directors
Diane Leavitt – Managing Director
927 Noyes St.
Evanston, IL 60201
847/866-6597
847/866-8049 – box office
PivenTW@aol.com
www.piventheatreworkshop.com

Equity — CAT N — Resident

Founded in 1971. They pay a $150 stipend. They hold generals in July or August. The nearest eL stop is Noyes on the Purple line.

Their 2000-2001 season included:
- Burn This
- Three Sisters
- American Voiles
- King Lear

They do not accept synopses but they do accept director proposals.

Red Hen Productions
Elayne LeTraunik – Artistic Director
Brian LeTraunik- Managing Director
5123 N. Clark
Chicago, IL 60640
773/728-0599
RedHenProd@aol.com
www.redhenproductions.com

Equity — CAT I — Resident

Founded in 1997. Starting non-Equity pay is $100/run. The nearest eL stop is Argyle or Berwyn on the Red line.

Red Hen Productions does new work and rarely done established works.

Their 2000-2001 season included:
- Class Enemy
- A Dybbuk

They accept synopses but do not accept director proposals.

A Red Orchid Theatre
Guy Van Swearingen – Artistic Director
Jody Van Swearingen – Managing Director
1531 N. Wells
Chicago, IL 60610
312/943-8722
arot@a-red-orchid.com
www.a-red-orchid.com

Equity — CAT N — Resident

Founded in 1993. Nearest eL stop is Clark/Division on the Red line and Sedgewick on the Brown line.

A Red Orchid Theatre likes to work, play, work, play, work, play, work, play.

Their 2000-2001 season included:
- George Dandin

They accept synopses and director proposals.

Remy Bumppo
James Bohnen – Artistic Director
Stephanie McCanles – Managing Director
3717 N. Ravenswood #245
Chicago, IL 60613
773/528-8762
773/871-3000 – box office
remybumppo@eathlink.net

Equity — CAT III — Non-resident

Founded in 1996.

Remy Bumppo Theatre Company is dedicated to producing contemporary and classical language-driven plays.

They do not accept synopses or director proposals.

Roadworks
Geoffrey M. Curley- Artistic Director
Jennifer Avery – Managing Director
1144 W. Fulton Market #105
Chicago, IL 60607
312/492-7150
info@roadworks.org
www.roadworks.org

Equity — CAT I — Non-resident

Founded in 1992. Starting non-Equity pay is $75 per week. The nearest eL stop is Ashland on the Green line or take the Halsted bus.

Roadworks' mission is to cultivate the next generation of theatre patrons.

Their 2000-2001 season included:
- Some Explicit Polaroids
- The Santaland Diaries
- Betty's Summer Vacation
- Serenading Louie
- Life Under 30

Serenading Louie earned them a Jeff Award nomination.

They accept synopses but do not accept director proposals.

Running With Scissors
P.O. Box 408438
Chicago, IL 60640
773.353.7582
www.rwscissors.org
timidh@mindspring.com

Equity, Tier Cat N

Founded in 1999. Starting non-Equity pay: varies with show, but RWS is committed to paying all performers.

They do not hold general auditions. They accept scripts, synopses and outside directors.

RWS is a collective of multi-disciplinary artists committed to rigorous artistic invention. It is our mission to create work that provokes us and our audience to examine our ideals, the world around us, and our place in it.

Seanachai Theatre Company
Michael Grant – Artistic Director
Joel Moorman – Managing Director
2206 N. Tripp
Chicago, IL 60639
773/878-3727
info@seanachai.org
www.seanachai.org

Equity — CAT N — Non-resident

Founded in 1995. Starting non-Equity pay is $30 a week. They hold generals in September or October.

The mission of Seanachai Theatre Company is to create compelling productions and programs that focus the energy of artists toward a common goal of exceptional storytelling. They received a non-Equity Jeff Citation nomination for actor for A Night in November and an Equity Jeff Award for New Work for The Pagans.

They accept synopses and director proposals.

Theatres

Second City
1616 N. Wells
Chicago, IL 60614
312/664-4032
312/337-3992 – box office
sc1616@secondcity.com
www.secondcity.com

Equity - Special Agreement

Second City has been an institution in Chicago theatre and improv-based sketch comedy since 1959. The nearest eL stop is Sedgewick on the Brown line.

They do not accept script submissions or directors proposals. All work is written by the cast.

Shakespeare on the Green
Karla Koskinen – Artistic Director
Steve Carmichael – Managing Director
700 E. Westleigh Rd.
Lake Forest, IL 60045
847/604-6344
847/604-6342 – box office
drakethe@mail.barat.edu
www.barat.edu/shakespeare

Equity — CAT I — Resident

Founded in 1992. Starting non-Equity pay is $400. They hold generals in April. Nearest Metra stop is Fort Sheridan.

Professional Equity Company, high production values, performing outdoors in a stunning location. Free to the public.

They do not accept synopses or director proposals.

Shakespeare Project of Chicago
Mara Polster
2529 W. Carmen
Chicago, IL 60626
773/334-TSP1

tspchicago@aol.com

Equity – Staged Reading

The Project started in 1995 to serve a community of Equity actors who had expertise in Shakespeare. They have worked under numerous Equity contracts, as is needed for each production.

ShawChicago
Robert Scogin – Artistic Director
Deborah Davis – Managing Director
442 W. Webster Ave.
Chicago, IL 60614
312/409-5605
info@shawchicago.org
www.shawchicago.org

Equity — Staged Reading — Non-resident

Founded in 1994. They hold generals in September. Nearest eL stop is Randolph on the Brown line (when producing at the Cultural Center).

Following its tradition of entertaining and, at the same time, illuminating its audiences through gales of laughter, and the occasional tear, ShawChicago's goal is to set the intelligent people talking and to strike the stupid people dumb.

Their 2000-2001 season included:
- Man and Superman
- Don Juan in Hell
- Arms and the Man

They do not accept synopses or director proposals.

Steppenwolf Theatre Company
Martha Lavey – Artistic Director
Michael Gennaro – Executive Director
758 W. North - 4th floor
Chicago, IL 60614
312/335-1888
312/335-1650 – box office
theatre@steppenwolf.org
www.steppenwolf.org

Equity — CAT VI, III & I (mainstage, studio & garage) — Resident

Founded in 1974. Nearest eL stop is North/Clybourn on the Red line.

Steppenwolf Theatre Company is a Chicago based international performing arts institution committed to ensemble collaboration and artistic risk through work with its permanent ensemble, guest artists, partner institutions, and the community.

Their 2000-2001 season included:
- The Weir
- The Drawer Boy
- Uncle Vanya
- Hedda Gabler

The Ballad of Little Jo

The latter won two Jeff Awards. The season garnered them 16 Jeff nominations.

They do not accept synopses or director proposals.

Strawdog Theatre Company
Jen Avery, Michael Dailey, Jess Hill – Artistic Directors
Tim Zingleman – Managing Director
3829 N. Broadway
Chicago, IL 60613
773/528-9889
773/528-9696 – box office
admin@strawdog.org
www.strawdog.org

Equity — CAT N — Resident

Founded in 1988. They hold generals in August/September. The nearest eL stop is Sheridan on the Red line.

Their 2000-2001 season included:
- Disco Pigs
- Our Country's Good
- Return to the Howard Bowl II: The Ball of Justice

They accept synopses and director proposals.

Terrapin Theatre
Brad Nelson Winters – Artistic Director
Susie Griffith – Managing Director
P.O. Box 138-356
Chicago, IL 60613
773/989-1006
terrapintheatre@hotmail.com

Equity — CAT N — Non-resident

Founded in1992.

Terrapin strives to inspire, delight, and challenge its audience.

Their 2000-2001 season included:
- The Sneeze
- The Government Inspector
- The Nina Variations

They accept synopses.

Theatres

Theatre at the Center
Michael Weber – Artistic Director
907 Ridge Rd.
Munster, IN 46321
219/836-0422
219/836-3255 – box office
mweber935@aol.com
www.theatreatthecenter.com

Equity — CAT III — Resident

Founded in 1991. They hold generals in February.

They do not accept synopses or director proposals.

Victory Gardens Theater
Dennis Zacek – Artistic Director
Marcelle McVay – Managing Director
2257 N. Lincoln
Chicago, IL 60614
773/549-5788
773/871-3000 – box office
VGTheater@aol.com
www.victorygardens.org

Equity — CAT IV — Resident

Founded in 1974. Starting non-Equity pay is half the Equity salary. They hold auditions in the summer. The nearest eL stop is Fullerton on the Red, Brown and Purple lines.

Victory Gardens is Chicago's leading producer of new work, with an emphasis on Chicago playwrights. They were nominated for a 2001 Jeff Citation for Hambone.

They accept synopses but do not accept director proposals.

Walkabout Theater Company
Kristan Schmidt – Artistic Director
Michael Karry – Managing Director
3241 N. Ravenswood
Chicago, IL 60657
773/248-9278
kschmidt@Winston.com

Equity — CAT N — Non-resident

Founded in 1999.

Walkabout produces original theatrical works .

Their 2000-2001 season included:
- Disciple
- Prelude: The Life and Times of Katherine Mansfield

They accept synopses but do not accept director proposals.

Writers' Theatre Chicago
Michael Halberstam – Artistic Director
John Adams – Managing Director
c/o Books on Vernon
664 Vernon Ave.
Glencoe, IL 60022
847/835-7366
847/835-5398 – box office
writerstheatre@aol.com
www.writerstheatre.org

Equity — CAT V — Resident

Founded in 1992. They hold Equity generals in late September. The nearest Metra stop is Glencoe.

The Writers' Theatre is a professional company dedicated to a theatre of language and passion. The word and the artist is our primary focus. In our intimate environment, we offer productions that bring our audiences face to face with literature's greatest creators and creations.

Their 2000-2001 season included:
- Spite for Spite
- Booth
- Butley
- The Father

They accept synopses but do not accept director proposals.

Non-Equity Theatres

Aguijon Theater Company
Rosario Vargas – Artistic Director
2707 N. Laramie Ave
Chicago, IL 60639
773/637-5899
773/279-1795 – box office
Aguijontheater@aol.com
Resident

Founded in 1989. Starting pay is $200.

Aguijon is commited to producing Spanish-language theatre.

Their 2000-2001 season included:
Las Tres Gracias
Un Robo y una Loteria
Ceviche en Pittsburgh

They accept synopses and director proposals.

AKA Rachel Productions
P.O. Box 477747
Chicago, IL 60647
312/902-1500
www.akarachel.com

Albright Theatre Company
103 S. Lincoln
Batavia, IL 60510
630/406-8838

Resident theatre founded in 1974

The Albright Theatre presents community theatre productions to Batavia and the surrounding areas.

They accept synopses and director proposals.

Alchymia Theatre
Scott Fielding – Artistic Director
4249 N. Lincoln
Chicago, IL 60614
773/755-6843
773/250-7262 – box office
alchymia@altavista.com
www.alchymia.org

Resident theatre founded in 1999. Pay varies. Nearest eL stop is Montrose, Damen, and Western on the Brown line.

Alchymia produces shows using the principles of Michael Chekhov.

Their 2000-2001 season included:
Rosmersholm
Flood

They accept synopses but do not accept director proposals.

Alphabet Soup Productions
Susan Holm – Artistic Director
Mark A. Pence – Managing Director
P.O. Box 85
Lombard, IL 60148
630/932-1555

Resident company founded in 1987. Starting pay runs $20-25/performance. They hold generals in Sept. and Feb.

Alphabet Soup Productions provides quality children's theatre within a fractured fairytale style.

Their 2000-2001 season included:
Beauty and the Beast
Little Red Riding Hood

They do not accept synopses or director proposals.

Theatres

American Girl Theater
111 E. Chicago
Chicago, IL 60611
877/AG PLACE
www.americangirl.com/agp/

Attic Playhouse
Kimberly Loughlin – Artistic Director
P.O. Box 10
Highland Park, IL 60040
847/433-2660
AtticPlay@aol.com
www.atticplayhouse.com

Resident theatre founded in 1998. They pay actors a modest stipend. They hold generals in July.

Attic Playhouse is proud to showcase a variety of theatrical productions.

Their 2000-2001 season included:
- Collected Stories
- Beau Jest
- A Christmas Carol
- The Foreigner
- Little Footsteps
- Cat on a Hot TIn Roof
- Murder at the Howard Johnson's

They accept synopses and director proposals.

Azusa Productions
Maggie Speer – Artistic Director
Stephen Dunn – Managing Director
312/409-4207

Founded in 1996. Pay runs from 0-$100.

They do not accept synopses or director proposals.

Backstage Theatre Company
Melissa Young – Artistic Director
Amy Monday – Managing Director
P.O. Box 118142
Chicago, IL 60611
312/683-5347

Founded in 2000.

Their 2000-2001 season included:
- Arsenic and Old Lace
- Montage a Trois
- The Misanthrope

They accept synopses and director proposals.

Bailiwick Repertory
David Zak – Artistic Director
Rusty Hernandez – Managing Director
1229 W. Belmont
Chicago, IL 60657-3205
773/883-1090
BailiwickR@aol.com
www.bailiwick.org

Resident company founded in1982. They pay $10-25/show. They hold generals in September. The nearest eL stop is on Belmont on the Red, Brown, and Purple lines.

Their 2000-2001 season included:
- Present Laughter
- The Christmas Schooner
- Mrs. Coney
- Gypsy
- Bonnie and Clyde
- Something Cloudy, Something Clear
- Mother Son
- Santa Claus is Coming Out
- Glory Box
- Go by Night
- Corpus Christi
- Emotional Monogamy
- Power Strokes
- Posing Strap Pirates
- Passing Ceremonies
- Prism
- Sappho in Love
- The Second Coming of Joan of Arc
- Strange Light
- The All Girl Review
- Directors Fest

They received Jeff nominations for Mother Son and Present Laughter.

They accept synopses and director proposals.

Barrel of Monkeys
Halena Kays – Artistic Director
Kristie Koehler – Managing Director
2936 N. Sourthport, Ste. 210
Chicago, IL 60657-4120
773/296-0218
312/409-1954 – box office
monkey@barrelofmonkeys.org
www.barrelofmonkeys.org

Resident company founded in 1997. They pay $50 per show. They hold generals in the fall.

Barrel of Monkeys is an ensemble of actors and teachers; we teach creative writing in Chicago Public Schools and adapt and perform the stories in the schools as well as in public performances.

Their 2000-2001 season included:
That's Weird, Grandma

8-10 performances/year at Chicago Public Schools

They do not accept synopses or director proposals.

Beverly Theatre Guild
Edward Fudacz – Artistic Director
773/925-8292
312/409-2705 – box office
www.beverlytheatreguild.org

They are a resident company founded in 1963. The nearest eL stop is the 95th/Dan Ryan on the Red line.

Their 2000-2001 season included:
Broadway Magic
Bad Seed
Phildelphia Story

They accept synopses and director proposals.

Borealis Theatre Company
Jeffrey Baumgartner – Artistic Director
347 S. Gladstone Ave.
Aurora, IL 60506-4892
630/844-4928
borealis@admin.aurora.edu
www.borealis-theatre.org

Bowen Park Theatre Company
Maggie Speer – Artistic Director
Rik Covalinski – Managing Director
39 Jack Benny Dr.
Waukegan, IL 60087
847/360-4741
wkarts@waukeganparks.org
www.waukeganparks.org/jbc

They are a resident compandy founded in 1986. Pay varies.

The purpose of Bowen Park Theatre Company is to bring high quality performances to Lake County and surrounding audiences.

They accept synopses and director proposals.

Theatres

Boxer Rebellion Theater

Steven Young – Artistic Director
Kern Wasan- Managing Director
1257 W. Loyola Ave.
Chicago, IL 60626
773/465-7325
Topkat74@yahoo.com
www.boxerrebellion.org

Resident company founded in 1998. The nearest eL stop is Loyola on the Red line.

Boxer Rebellion strives to ignite response and produce substantive, modern works.

Their 2000-2001 season included:
- Museum
- The Resurrectionists
- Pippin

They received two Jeff nominations for The Resurrectionists.

They accept synopses and director proposals.

Breadline Theatre Group

Paul Kampf – Artistic Director
Heather Carpenter – Managing Director
1802 W. Berenice
Chicago, IL 60613
773/327-6096
breadline@breadline.org
www.breadline.org

Resident company founded in 1993. The nearest eL stop is Irving Park on the Brown line.

Breadline is dedicated to producing exclusively World Premiere theatre and cultivating the full range of artistic skills involved in producing theatre art. They received a 2001 Jeff Citation nomination for new work for American Gothic.

They accept synopses but do not accept director proposals.

Broutil & Frothingham Productions

Brian Posen – Artistic Director
Mike Checuga – Managing Director
1415 W. Lill Ave
Chicago, IL 60614
773/665-8899
posini@aol.com

An itinerant company founded in 1997. They pay $500/run.

Broutil and Frothingham focuses on farce and high comedy.

They do not accept synopses but they do accept director proposals.

Cenacle Theatre Company

556 W. 18th
Chicago, IL 60616
312/491-8484

CenterLight Theatre

Patti Lahey – Artistic Director
3444 Dundee Rd.
Northbrook, IL 60062
847/559-0110 x237
ICODACenterLight@aol.com
www.icodaarts.org

A resident company founded in 1974. They pay $10-15/performance.

Center Light allows deaf, hard of hearing, and hearing artists to work together to create a unique and powerful theatrical experience for all audiences.

Their 2000-2001 season included:
- Joseph and the Amazing Technicolor Dreamcoat
- Scapino
- Mother Goose
- A Return to Broadway Visions
- The Vision Quest

They do not accept synopses but they do accept director proposals.

Chase Park Theatre

Karen Fort
4701 N. Ashland
Chicago, IL
312/742-4701
Karenfort@interaccess.com
www.chicagoparkdistrict.com

A resident company founded in 1974 [illegible] nearest eL stop is Lawrence on the Red line.

Community theatre for the theatre community that is designed to showcase new actors.

They accept synopses but do not accept director proposals.

Chicago Kids Company

Jesus Perez – Artistic Director
Paige Coffman – Managing Director
4050 N. Milwaukee
Chicago, IL 60641
773/205-9600
CKCPaige@aol.com
www.ChicagoKidsCompany.com

A resident company founded in1992.

They pay $25/show. They hold generals in September and January. The nearest eL stop is Irving Park on the Blue line.

Chciago Kids Company provides quality performances for children in Chicago ages 2 to 12.

They do not accept synopses or director proposals.

Circle Theatre

Alena Murguia, Todd Cornils,
Greg Kolak
7300 W. Madison
Forest Park, IL 60130
708/771-0700
708/771-0700 - fax
www.circle-theatre.org

A resident company founded in 1983. The nearest eL stop is Harlem on the Green line. They received Jeff Citations for Triumph of Love and The Life.

They accept synopses but do not accept director proposals.

City Lit Theater Company

1020 W. Bryn Mawr
Chicago, IL 60660-4627
773/293-3682
metapage@aol.com
www.citylit.org

---

cobalt ensemble theatre

Laura Bailey, Artistic Director
PMB 225
5313 N. Clark St.
Chicago, IL 60640
312/458-9182
www.cobaltensemble.org

Open Audition for each show, Call in Actors from generals, files or past knowledge. Cast from Ensemble.

Their 2000-2001 season included:
I Am Yours
Alarms & Excursions

Founded in 1997, cobalt ensemble is a passionate group of theatre professionals dedicated to creating daring and evocative work that engages both artists and audiences.

Collaboraction Theatre Company
Anthony Moseley – Artistic Director
Erin West – Managing Director
1945 W. Henderson
Chicago, IL 60657
312/409-2741
info@collaberaction.org
www.collaboraction.org

An itinerant company founded in 1997.

Collaberaction is devoted to producing dynamic, contemporary theatre on the stage and beyond.

Their 2000-2001 season included:
- Refuge
- Sketchbook One
- The Life and Times of Tulsa Lovechild: A Road Trip

Refuge won a 2001 Jeff Citation for supporting actor.

They accept synopses but do not accept director proposals.

ComedySportz
2851 N. Halsted
Chicago, IL 60657
773/549-8080
jed@comedysportzchicago.com
www.comedysportzchicago.com

A resident company founded in 1987. The nearest eL stop is Diversey on the Brown line.

They do not accept synopses or director proposals.

Common Air Theatre Company
1948 W. Berteau
Chicago, IL 60613-1837
773/209-7507
commonairtheatre@hotmail.com

Congo Square Theatre Company
1156 W. Grand #2R
Chicago, IL 60622
773/913-5808
dsanders@congosquaretheatre.org
www.congosquaretheatre.org

An itinerant company founded in 1999. Pay varies.

Congo Square produces multicultural theatre

Their 2000-2001 season included:
- The Piano Lesson
- Before It Hit Home
- The Island

They accept synopses and director proposals.

Corn Productions
2620 N. Lawndale
Chicago, IL 60647
312/409-6435
mediaminx@hotmail.com
www.cornservatory.org

Chronicles Theater Company
4312 N. Sheridan Rd
Chicago, IL 60613
773-327-4118
chronicles@att.net
Bobby Zaman – Executive Artistic Director
Rodrick Jean-Charles – Managing Director

Open Audition for each show. Calls in Actors from generals, files or past knowledge. Cast from Ensemble

2001 marked the inaugural season for Chronicles Theater Company.

Curious Theatre Branch
The Lunar Cabaret
2827 N. Lincoln Ave.
Chicago, IL 60654
773/327-6666
jemlunar@enteract.com

Deep Productions
7327 S. Evans
Chicago, IL 60619
312/682-6507
www.urbanscenze.com

Defiant Theatre
Jim Slonina – Artistic Director
Jennifer Gehr – Managing Director
3540 N. Southport #162
Chicago, IL 60657
312/409-0585
defianttheatre@defianttheatre.org
www.defianttheatre.org

An itinerant company founded in 1993. The nearest eL stop is Addison on the Brown line, or take the Addison bus #152.

Defiant Theatre productions juxtapose an unlimited vocabulary of performance and stagecraft styles with the aim of astonishing and provoking audiences rather than pacifying them, and whenever, possible, they do it without pants.

Their 2000-2001 season included:
- Godbaby
- Macbeth
- Cleansed

They accept synopses and director proposals.

Dolphinback Theatre Company
Matt McGaughey – Artistic Director
Susan Dietz – Managing Director
1321 W. Columbia #3A
Chicago, IL 60626
773/743-4332
dolphinback@juno.com

An itinerant company founded in 1993. They hold generals in the fall.

Dolphinback challenges Chicago audiences with original theatre.

They accept synopses and director proposals.

Dorothy Nickle Performing Arts Company
David-Matthew Barnes – Artistic Director
Nick A. Moreno – Managing Director
4227 N. Lincoln Ave.
Chicago, IL 60618
773/784-4530
info@dnpacproductions.com
www.dnpacproductions.com

A resident company founded in 2000. They hold auditions in August. The nearest eL stop is Montrose or Western on the Brown line.

The Dorothy Nickle Performing Arts Company is dedicated to producing theatre that celebrates women, minorities, and children from different backgrounds.

They accept script submissions and director proposals.

Dramatists Revolutionary Army
3257 W. Wrightwood #1D
Chicago, IL 60647
773/508-9307

Duncan YMCA Chernin Center for the Arts
Ifa Bayeza – Artistic Director
Pam Dickler – Managing Director
1001 W. Roosevelt
Chicago, IL 60608
312/738-7980
312/738-5999 – box office
YArtsChgo@aol.com

A resident company founded in 1997. They pay $25/show. The nearest eL stop is Halsted and UIC on the Blue line.

The first YMCA dedicated entirely to arts and education, Duncan has professional productions as well as youth productions.

They accept script submissions and director proposals.

Eclipse Theatre Company
P.O. Box 578960
Chicago, IL 60657-8960
312/409-1687
Eclipsetheatre@hotmail.com
www.eclipsetheatre.com

An itinerant company founded in 1992. They pay $100/run. They attend the League unifieds.

Eclipse Theatre Company is Chicago's only theatre company dedicated to producing the works of one single playwright in one single season.

Their season is within the calendar year.
Their 2001 season included:
2
Childe Byron
A Woman Without a Name

They won five Jeff Citations for their 2000 season, four for Another Part of the Forest (including best production, ensemble and director) and one for A Watch on the Rhine.

They do not accept synopses but they do accept director proposals.

Ego Productions
Tai Palmgren – Artistic Director
Lizz Leiser – Managing Director
3912 N. Clark
Chicago, IL 60613
773/281-5346
lizz@egoproductions.org
www.egoproductions.org

An itinerant company founded in 1999. Pay varies.

Ego productions is a playwright based company that focuses on producing progressive world premieres by Chicago playwrights.

Their 2000-2001 season included:
The Unspeechable Curse of Kaptain Kreepee
The Jack Slate Radio Show

They accept script submissions and director proposals.

Emerald City Theatre Company
Karen Cardarelli – Artistic Director
Beth Klein – Managing Director
2936 N. Southport
Chicago, IL 60657
773/529-2690
773/935-6100 – box office
emeraldcitytheatre@msn.com
www.emeraldcitytheatre.com

A resident company founded in 1996. They pay $10/performance plus rehearsal pay. They hold auditions in July and January. The nearest eL stop is Fullerton on the Red and Brown lines.

Emerald City Theatre is Chicago's only theatre solely dedicated to producing family theatre.

They do not accept synopses but they do accept director proposals.

ETA Creative Arts Foundation
Runako Jahi – Artistic Director
Abena Joan Brown – Executive Director
5212 S. Dorchester
Chicago, IL 60615
773/752-3955
www.etacreativearts.org

A resident company founded in 1971. They pay $30/show. The nearest eL stop is 69th St. on the Red line.

ETA is commited to telling the African story.

They accept script submissions and director proposals.

Excaliber Shakespeare Company
Darryl Maximilian Robinson
The Harrison Street Galleries Studio Theatre
208 W. Harrison St.
Oak Park, IL 60304
773/533-0285

Factory Theatre
Steve Walker – Artistic Director
P.O. Box 408679
Chicago, IL 60640
312/409-3247
nonthings@yahoo.com
www.factorytheater.com

An itinerant company founded in 1992.

Factory Theatre produces original, ensemble generated plays usually satirical or comedic in nature.

They accept script submissions and director proposals.

Fantasy Orchard Children's Theatre
Dana Low – Artistic Director
P.O. Box 25084
Chicago, IL 60625
773/539-4211
www.kidtheater.com

An itinerant company founded in 1989. They pay $20/show. The hold auditions in the fall.

Fantasy Orchard presents faerie and folk tales reflecting the cultural diversity of Chicago's children.

Their 2000-2001 season included:
The Witch's Face & Other Tales of Wonder

They accept synopses and director proposals.

Theatres

Fantod Theatre
Annie Joseph – Artistic Director
Heather Wesson – Managing Director
P.O. Box 7750
Chicago, IL 60647
773/203-3692

An itinerant company founded in 1998. They pay $50-$75.

Fantod Theater lets new playwrights cut their teeth by providing for them a workshop-to-full production process.

Their 2000-2001 season included:
The Major
Pond 7

They accept script submissions and director proposals.

Firstborn Productions
Gregory D. Gerhard – Artistic Director
Kirk A. Gillman – Managing Director
1618 W. Fargo #1
Chicago, IL 60626
773/728-2814
www.firstborn.org

An itinerant company founded in 1995.

Firstborn Productions strives to create compelling and dynamic theatre incorporating visual metaphor, intellectual material and emotional character interplay.

Their 2000-2001 season included:
Cyber:/womb by Vivienne Laxdal

They accept script submissions and director proposals.

Fleetwood-Jourdain Theatre
2100 Ridge Ave.
Evanston, IL 60201
847/328-5740

Fourth Wall Productions
Stephen A. Donart – Artistic Director
4300 N. Narragansett
Chicago, IL 60634
773/481-8535
sdonart2@aol.com

Free Associates
2936 N. Southport #210
Chicago, IL 60657
773/296-0541
312/988-9000 – box office
freeassociates@aol.com
www.thefreeassociates.com

A resident company founded in 1992. They perform at the Royal George. The nearest eL stop is North and Clybourn on the Red line.

The Free Associates is an improvisational theatre that celebrates the style and standards of great literature, film and television through parody.

Their 2000-2001 season included:
BS
Alfred Hitchcock Resents
My Cousin Rachel

They accept synopses and director proposals.

Free Street
Ron Biebanski – Artistic Director
David Schein – Managing Director
1419 W. Blackhawk
Chicago, IL 60622
773/772-7248
gogogo@freestreet.org
www.freestreet.org

A resident company founded in 1969. They pay $5.15/hour. They hold auditions in October. The nearest eL stop is Division/Milwaukee/Ashland on the Blue line.

Free Street opens the potential of youth through theatre and writing so they can be creative, active participants in their own destiny.

Their 2000-2001 season included:
CoTingle
Zeros

They do not accept synopses but they do accept director proposals.

Frump Tucker Theatre Company
Vincent P. Mahler – Artistic Director
Laura Wells – Managing Director
P.O. Box 118315
Chicago, IL 60611
312/409-2689
Mr.Tucker@FrumpTucker.org
www.frumptucker.org

An itinerant company founded in 1995.

Always drawn to language-driven, thematically challenging comedies, Frump Tucker invites Chicago to "play with your head" during its 2001-2002 season of Chicago premieres that will make you think while you laugh.

Their 2000-2001 season included:
How I Learned to Drive
Three Days of Rain

They accept synopses and director proposals.

Galileo Players
1850 N. Clark #202
Chicago, IL 60614
773/388-2943
galileoflan@yahoo.com
www.galileoplayers.com

GayCo Productions
1450 W. Winona
Chicago, IL 60640
773/531-5086
312/458-9400 - fax
eningeraa@earthlink.net
www.gayco.net

Great Beast Theater
6651 N. Greenview #3
Chicago, IL 60626
312/409-1887

Green Light Performing Company
Domenick Danza – Artistic Director
2014 W. Belle Plaine
Chicago, IL 60618
773/935-9380
gperform@aol.com
www.greenlightgo.org

An itinerant company founded in 1993. They pay $50/show. They hold auditions in July/August. The nearest eL stop is Irving Park on the Brown line.

Green Light Performing Company creates and tours original audience-participation, educational musical theater performances to schools, libraries, and museums throughout the state of Illinois.

They do not accept synopses or director proposals.

Theatres

Griffin Theatre
Richard Barletta – Artistic Director
Bill Massolia – Managing Director
5404 N. Clark
Chicago, IL 60640
773/769-2228
griffin@interaccess.com
www.griffintheatre.com

A resident company founded in 1988. The nearest eL stop is Berwyn on the Red line.

They do not accept synopses or director proposals.

Grounded Theatre
David Lightner – Artistic Director
Karen Elyse Rosenberg – Managing Director
810 Concord Ln.
Hoffman Estates, IL 60195
847/989-7927
dlightner@ameritech.net
www.groundedtheatre.org

An itinerant company founded in 2000. Pay varies.

It is the mission of the Grounded Theatre to challenge, test, and promote social conciousness through performance.

Their 2000-2001 season included:
- Animal Farm
- Spoon River Anthology
- Justice is Served

They accept script submissions and director proposals.

Half Cocked Productions
Arik Martin – Artistic Director
2148 W. Sunnyside, 2nd floor
Chicago, IL 60625
773/297-2745
Arikmartin@yahoo.com

A resident company founded in 1999. Pay varies. The nearest eL stop is Damen on the Brown line.

Half Cocked is an eager and raucous young ensemble dedicated to raw, visceral theatre.

Their 2000-2001 season included:
- Bad-ass & the Devil
- Serendipity
- Gelo to Oblivion
- Need

They accept synopses and director proposals.

HealthWorks Theatre
Peter Reynolds – Artistic Director
Stephen Rader – Managing Director
3171 N. Halsted, 2nd floor
Chicago, IL 60657
773/929-4260
HWT96@aol.com
www.healthworkstheatre.com

An itinerant company founded in 1988. They pay $40/show and $100 rehearsal pay. They hold auditions in August and December. The nearest eL stop is Belmont on the Red, Brown, and Purple lines.

HealthWorks Theatre Company is an educational theatre company dedicated to working with communities to address critical health and social issues.

They do not accept synopses or director proposals.

HyperWorld Theatre
Kathleen Collins – Artistic Director
4655 N. Campbell
Chicago, IL 60625
773/784-8100
hyperworldtheatre@hotmail.com
www.hyperworldtheatre.com

An itinerant company founded in 2001.

Hyperworld Theatre seeks out material relevant to today's world.

Their 2000-2001 season included:
Top of the Food Chain
The Death of Zukasky

They accept synopses and director proposals.

The Hypocrites
Sean Graney – Artistic Director
Mechelle Moe – Executive Director
P.O. Box 578542
Chicago, IL 60657
312/409-5578
the_hypocrites@yahoo.com
www.the-hypocrites.com

An itinerant company founded in 1997.

Their 2000-2001 season included:
The Cherry Orchard (remounted at Theatre on the Lake)
Lakeboat
AJAX
Arcadia

They do not accept synopses or director proposals.

ImprovOlympic
3541 N. Clark
Chicago, IL 60657
773/880-9993
improvolymp@enteract.com
www.improvolymp.com

The home of long-form improv.

The Infamous Commonwealth Theatre
773/248-7427 x3
1604 W. Cullom, 3WC
Chicago, Illinois 60613
Send Headshots to: Genevieve Hurst, Artistic Director

The Infamous Commonwealth Theatre's mission is to illuminate diverse perspectives around one centralized theme per year using contrasting theatrical voices; to raise consciousness to an art and art to a consciousness.

Janus Theatre
Terence Domschke
P.O. Box 1567
Chicago, IL 60193
847/931-7247
JanusThtre@aol.com

Katharsis Theatre Company
312/660-3701x2775
info@katharsistheatre.com
www.katharsistheatre.com

Founded in 2000. Pay varies.

Theatres

Keyhole Players
Frank Merle – Artistic Director
Matthew David – Managing Director
2003 W. Warner, Apt. 1
Chicago, IL 60618
773/517-2950
773/525-3683 – box office
keyholeplayers@excite.com
www.keyholeplayers.homestead.com

An itinerant company founded in 1999.

Keyhole Players produces shows to expose social issues.

They accept synopses and director proposals.

L'Opera Piccola
Sifra Werch – Artistic Director
Sasha Gerritson – Managing Director
5239 N. LaCrosse Ave.
Chicago, IL 60630
312/560-1072
www.loperapiccola.org

An itinerant company founded in 1996.

They pay $300 a run.

L'Opera Piccola aspires to bring traditional opera to the world by linking the singers of today with the success of tomorrow.

Their 2000-2001 season included:
- Don Pasquale
- Luccia di Lammermoor

They do not accept synopses but do accept director proposals.

Laboratory Theatre
Michele Gerard Good
151 W. Burton
Chicago, IL 60610
312/286-0552

Late Nite Catechism
Vicki Quade - Producer
773/528-2569
312/988-9000 – box office
www.latenitecatechism.com

Late Nite Catechism is a hilarious send-up of the Catholic ritual. It is based at the Royal George. Quade produces other shows as well.

Lifeline Theatre
Dorothy Milne – Artistic Director
Melissa Bareford – Managing Director
6912 N. Glenwood
Chicago, IL 60626
773/761-0667
773/761-4477 – box office
www.lifelinetheatre.com

A resident company founded in 1983. They pay $15-35/performance. The nearest eL stop is Morse on the Red line.

Lifeline theatre produces literary adaptations and original works.

Their 2000-2001 season included:
- Pistols for Two
- The Silver Chair
- Jane Eyre
- Cooking with Lard

KID SHOWS:
- The Story of Ferdinand
- Hen Lake
- The Emperor's Groovy New Clothes

They received Jeff citations for Pistols for Two and Jane Eyre.

They do not accept synopses or director proposals.

Limelight Theatre Guild of Bensenville
c/o Bensenville Public Library
200 S. Church Rd.
Bensenville, IL 60106
630/415-0894
limelight@clearnet.org
www.clearnet.org/limelight

Founded in 1994

Limelight Theatre Guild casts people with an enthusiasm and willingness to learn.

They accept synopses and director proposals.

Live Bait Theater
Sharon Evans – Artistic Director
Lotti Pharriss – Managing Director
3914 N. Clark
Chicago, IL 60613
773/871-1212
staff@livebaittheater.org
www.livebaittheater.org

A resident company founded in 1988.

They pay $20/show. The nearest eL stop is Sheridan or Addison on the Red line.

Live Bait Theater exclusively produces new work by Chicago area playwrights and solo performers. Their co-production (with the Chicago Theatre Company) of Love Child won the 2001 Jeff Citation for new work.

They accept script submissions and director proposals.

Low Sodium Entertainment
Aaron Daniel Haber – Artistic Director
Anna Stein – Managing Director
3741 N. Kenmore Ave., #2
Chicago, IL 60613
773/549-3250
Lowsodiume@aol.com
www.lowsodiumentertainment.com

An itinerant company founded in 1996. They pay a percentage of box office.

Low Sodium Entertainment is the Onion sponsored, underground improv comedy movement of Chicago and New York.

They do not accept synopses or director proposals.

The Mammals
Bob Fisher – Artistic Director
4625 N. Winchester
Chicago, IL 60640
773/293-0431
fisherbob@hotmail.com

A resident company founed in 1997. The nearest eL stop is Damen on the Brown line.

The Mammals explore new performance works, embracing the genres of science fiction, horror, and phantasmagoria. They also utilize techniques of these three genres in application to classical texts from the Western Cannon.

Their 2000-2001 season included:
- Horror Chamber of Perfection
- Dream Play
- Distorted
- Clay Continent

They accept synopses but do not accept director proposals.

Mary-Arrchie Theatre Co.
Rich Cotovsky
731 W. Sheridan
Chicago, IL 60613
773/871-0442

Theatres

MPAACT
P.O. Box 10039
Chicago, IL 60610
312/409-6724
312/409-6724 - fax
mpaact@aol.com
www.mpaact.org

An itinerant company founded in 1991.

Pay varies. They hold auditions in October.

MPAACT exists to develop, nurture, and sustain Afrikan Centered Theatre.

Their 2000-2001 season included:
Fascia
Chris T.

They accept script submissions and director proposals.

Murder Mystery Players
Oak Park, IL 60302
630/543-5151
RJBooch@aol.com
www.mysteryplayers.com

Murder Mystery Productions
60 Shore Dr.
Burr Ridge, IL 60521
info@murderme.com
www.murderme.com

Museum of Contemporary Art
Peter Taub – Artistic Director
Yolanda Cesta Cursach – Managing Director
312/397-3843
312/397-4010 – box office
ycursach@mcachicago.org
www.mcachicago.org

Founded in 1996. The nearest eL stop is Chicago on the Red line.

The MCA is a presenting organization that commissions new works from local, national and international artists.

They do not accept synopses but do accept director proposals.

Music Theatre Workshop
Meade Palidofsky – Artistic Director
5647 N. Ashland
Chicago, IL 60660
773/561-7100

Mystery Shop
Mary Heitent – Artistic Director
551 Sundance Ct.
Carol Stream, IL 60188
630/690-1105
TMS@themysteryshop.com
www.themysteryshop.com

An itinerant company founded in 1988.

They pay $30-45/show. They hold auditions in September.

The Mystery Shop is a travelling theatre company that specializes in adult and children's participatory mysteries and programs.

They accept script submissions but do not accept director proposals.

Neo-Futurists
Greg Allen – Artistic Director
Daniel Cress – Managing Director
5153 N. Ashland
Chicago, IL 60640
773/878-4557
773/275-5255 – box office
bizczar@neofuturists.org
www.neofuturists.org

A resident company founded in 1988. They pay $15/show. They hold auditions as needed. The nearest eL stop is Berwyn on the Red line.

The Neo-Futurists create their own audience interactive theatre dedicated to social, political and personal enlightenment.

They do not accept synopses or director proposals.

New Millennium Theatre Company
Chad Wise – Artistic Director
Zenna Gustafson – Managing Director
1040 W. Granville, Suite #308
Chicago , IL 60660
773/743-9681
artisticdirector@nmtchicago.org
www.nmtchicago.org

An itinerant company founded in1998.

Their 2000-2001 season included:
Scooby-Doo Mystery Theatre
Nuts & Mints
Getting Away With Murder
Scooby-Doo Mystery Theatre II
The Living Canvas

They accept script submissions and director proposals.

New Tuners
(See our ad on the next page)
John Sparks – Artistic Director
Joan Mazzonelli – Executive Director
1225 W. Belmont
Chicago, IL 60657
773/929-7367
773/327-5252 – box office
tbtuners@aol.com
www.newtuners.org

A resident company founded in 1969. They pay $25-$500/gig. The nearest eL stop is Belmont on the Red/Brown/Purple lines.

They do not accept synopses or director proposals.

The Noble Fool
Jimmy Binns – Artistic Director
Paul Botts – Managing Director
16 W. Randolph
Chicago, IL 60601
312/630-2633
312/630-2631 – box office
info@noblefool.com
www.noblefool.com

A resident company founded in 1994. Pay varies.

Noble Fool elevates the art of comedy in all its forms through performance, promotion, and education, drawing from improvisation and music to foster an active relationship between performers and audience.

They accept script submissions and director proposals.

North Shore Theater of Wilmette
1200 Wilmette Ave.
Wilmette, IL 60091
847/256-9787

Northbrook Theatre
3323 Walters Ave.
Northbrook, IL 60062
847/291-2367

Theatres

Open Eye Productions
Jon C. Sevigny – Artistic Director
Sara R. Sevigny – Managing Director
1460 W. Farragut
Chicago, IL 60640
773/293-1557
openeyeproductions@hotmail.com
www.openeyeproductions.com

An itinerant company founded in 1996. Pay varies. They hold auditions in the fall.

Open Eye vows to stay true to their ensemble by producing innovative, character driven works, regardless of their genre.

Their 2000-2001 season included:
- Better Living
- Tom Foolery

They accept script submissions and director proposals.

Opera Factory
1636 W. Summerdale
Chicago, IL 60640
847/673-6300

Ouijar
8033 N. Hamlin
Skokie, IL 60076
312/409-1011
janrk@aol.com

Pegasus Players
Arlene Crewsdon – Artistic Director
1145 W. Wilson
Chicago, IL 60640
773/878-9761
pegasusp@megsinet.net
www.pegasusplayers.com

Resident company founded in 1978. They pay $35/performance. The nearest eL stop is Wilson on the Red line.

Pegasus Players presents the highest quality artistic work and provides exemplary theatre, entertainment and arts education at no charge to people who have little or no access to the arts

Their 2000-2001 season included:
- Rum & Coke
- Ev'ry Time I Feel the Spirit
- 15th Annual Young Playwrights Festival
- John Callaway Tonight
- Muscle

They accept script submissions and director proposals.

Performing Arts Chicago
Susan Lipman – Executive Director
312/663-1628
733/722-5463 – box office
MAIL@PAChicago.org
www.PAChicago.org

Founded in 1959.

Performing Arts Chicago is a contemporary performing arts presenter, bringing music, dance, theatre, and puppet ensembles from around the nation and the world to Chicago.

Pendulum Theatre Company
Bill Redding – Artistic Director
Carolyn M. Lakar – Managing Director
2936 N. Southport
Chicago, IL 60657
773/-529-2692
PendulumT@aol.com
www.pendulumtheatre.org

They are an itinerant company founded in 1996. They pay $100/run.

Pendulum Theatre Company strives for artistic excellence in the production of lesser known plays of social signifigance.

Their 2000-2001 season included:
- A Hotel on Marvin Gardens
- A Cozy Evening with George Bernard Shaw

They accept script submissions and director proposals.

Pheasant Run Dinner Theatre
Diana L. Martinez
4051 E. Main St.
St. Charles, IL 60174
630/584-MEGA
www.pheasantrun.com

Phoenix Ascending Theatre
4227 N. Lincoln
Chicago, IL 60618
773/327-2134
www.phoenixascending.com

Plasticene
Dexter Bullard
2122 N. Winchester #1F
Chicago, IL 60614
312/409-0400
info@plasticene.com
www.plasticene.com

Iterant company founded in 1995. They pay $500/show. They hold auditions in July.

Plasticene Physical Theatre Company is a critically acclaimed theatre company that builds original non-text-based theatre works and teaches physical and experimental theatre as "The Plasticene Studio."

They do not accept script submissions or director proposals.

Playground Theatre
3341 N. Lincoln
Chicago, IL 60657
773/871-3793
312/905-9385
www.the-playground.com

A resident company founded in 1997.

The Playground is an improv co-op, consisting of member groups who would share in the responsibilities of running the theater.

Porchlight Theatre
L. Walter Stearns – Artistic Director
Jeannie Lukow – Managing Director
2936 N. Southport
Chicago, IL 60657
773/325-9884
www.porchlighttheatre.com

They are an itinerant company founded in 1995. They pay $150/run. They hold auditions in July/August.

Porchlight Theatre presents intimate and inventive musical theatre.

Their 2000-2001 season included:
- Into the Woods
- Passion

Both plays won Jeff Citations.

They accept script submissions and director proposals.

Profiles Theatre
Joe Jaharaus – Artistic Director
Darrell W. Cox – Managing Director
3761 N. Racine
Chicago, IL
773/549-1815
ProfilesCo@aol.com
www.profilestheatre.org

A resident company founded in 1988. They pay $10/show and hold auditions in August. The nearest eL stop is Sheridan on the Red line.

Profiles Theatre's primary goal is to bring new works to Chicago that illuminate the determination and resiliency of the human spirit.

They accept script submissions but do not accept director proposals.

Prologue Theatre Productions
2936 N. Southport #210
Chicago, IL 60657-4120
847/681-2025
prologuetheatre@home.com

An itinerant company founded in 1988. They pay $20/performance, $10/rehearsal.

Their 2000-2001 season included:
- The Melody Lingers On: The Songs of Irving Berlin

They accept script submissions but do not accept director proposals.

Prop Thtr
Scott Vehill – Artistic Director
Debra Hatchet – Managing Director
2621 N. Washtenaw
Chicago, IL 60647
773/486-7767
sviger@earthlink.net
www.propthtr.org

An itinerant company founded in 1981. They are mainly non-Equity, though they will hire Equity actors and work under a Guest Artist agreement. They pay non-Equity actors $200/run.

Prop produces only new plays and literary adaptations.

They accept script submissions and director proposals.

Push & Shove, Inc.
3802 N. Clark #2N
Chicago, IL 60613
773/477-8139
push_n_shove@hotmail.com

An itinerant company founded in 1998. Push & Shove is an ensemble of artists that produces cross-platform and multi-media shows.

They accept script submissions but do not accept director proposals.

Pyewacket
Kate Harris – Artistic Director
2322 W. Wilson
Chicago, IL 60625
773/275-2201

An itinerant company founded in 1997. They pay a percentage of the house.

They accept script submissions and director proposals.

Real Rain Productions
Rick Fonte – Artistic Director
Brian Wehrenberg – Managing Director
4939 N. Wolcott
Chicago, IL 60640
312/902-1500
www.realreain.org

An itinerant company founded in 2000. They pay $100/run.

Real Rain Productions is dedicated to new and imaginative work, an ensemble acting approach, and direct contact with the playwright.

They accept script submissions but do not accept director proposals.

Red Wolf Theatre Company
Susan Block – Artistic Director
David Tatosian – Managing Director
1609 W. Berteau
Chicago, IL 60613
773/248-9678
312/409-6024
redwolfthr@aol.com
www.redwolftheatre.com

An itinerant company. They pay actors a stipend.

Their 2000-2001 season included:
House of Blue Leaves
Betrayal
Death and the Maiden

Redmoon Theater
Jim Lasko – Artistic Director
Sandy Gerding – Managing Director
2936 N. Southport - 1st floor
Chicago, IL 60657
773/388-9031
information@redmoon.org
www.redmoon.org

An itinerant company founded in 1990.

Pay varies.

Redmoon Theatre is renowned for its unique style of spectacle theatre, using masks, physical performance and a range of puppetry styles. Their production of Hunchback won two Jeff Citations for 2000-2001.

They do not accept script submissions or director proposals.

Renaissance Theaterworks
Marie Kohler & Raeleen McMillion – Artistic Directors
342 N. Water St. #400
Milwaukee, WI 53202
414/273-0800
rtw@r-t-w.com
www.r-t-w.com

Rivendell Theatre Ensemble
1636 W. Summerdale
Chicago, IL 60640
773/472-1169
riv theatre@aol.com

Runamuck Productions
Heath Corson – Artistic Director
4655 N. Campbell
Chicago, IL 60657
773/784-8100
RunamuckP@aol.com

An itinerant company founded in 1995.

Runamuck Productions' mission is based on the idea that our adaptions create excitement about the source material while promoting literacy and encouraging positive reading habits.

Their 2000-2001 season included:
- Too Many Time Machines
- How Santa Got His Job
- Math Curse
- Bud & Lou

They accept synopses and director proposals.

S.T.A.R
Laurie Reyna – Artistic Director
3637 W. 51st
Chicago, IL 60632
312/802-8020
info@chicagostar.org
www.chicagostar.org

A resident company founded in 1988. They are on the Orange line.

S.T.A.R. is a not-for-profit community theatre.

Their 2000-2001 season included:
- Verdict
- Autumn Leaves
- Hard Candy
- Lone Star
- A Midsummer Night's Dream

They accept script submissions and director proposals.

Saint Sebastian Players
Jonathan Hagloch – Artistic Director
James Sobczak – Managing Director
St. Bonaventure Church
1621 W. Diversey
Chicago, IL 60614
773/404-7922
stsebplyrs@aol.com
members.aol.com/stsebplyrs

A resident company founded in1982. The nearest eL stop is Diversey on the Brown line.

Saint Sebastion Players produces plays, musicals, the annual monologue matchup competition, and original audience participation murder mysteries.

Their 2000-2001 season included:
- Much Ado About Nothing
- Holiday
- Elvicula

They accept synopses but do not accept director proposals.

Schadenfreude
Sandy Marshall – Artistic Director
Justin Kaufmann – Managing Director
c/o Heartland Studio Theater
7016 N. Glenwood
Chicago, IL 60626
773/293-0024
schadenmail@schadenfreude.net
www.schadenfreude.net

An itinerant company founded in 1997. Pay varies.

Schadenfreude features over the top political satire with music and a few surprises.

They do not accept script submissions or director proposals.

School Street Movement
Byron S. Stewart – Artistic Director
Angel Abcede – Managing Director
1511 W. Berwyn Ave.
Chicago, IL 60640-2109
773/784-6106
www.schoolstreetmovement.com

An itinerant company founded in1992. They pay $8/rehearsal, $50/performance. They hold auditions in the fall (Aug/Sept) and winter (Dec/Jan). The nearest eL stop is Berwyn on the Red line. They are also on the Clark Street bus route.

School Street Movement is a not-for-profit AIDS-awareness and educational organization that uses dance and theatre to get its message across. The organization is 10 years old and focused on communities of color.

They accept script submissions and director proposals.

Scrap Mettle SOUL
Richard Owen Geer – Artistic Director
Barbara Michelatti – Managing Director
4600 N. Magnolia, Suite C
Chicago, IL 60640
773/275-3999
scrapmettle@core.com
scrapmettlesoul.org

A resident company founded in 1994. They hold auditions in January or February. The nearest eL stop is Argyle on the Red line.

An intergenerational community performance ensemble that performs true stories from the Uptown-Edgewater community.

Their 2000-2001 season included:
Little Victories

They do not accept script submissions or director proposals

Sense of Urgency
Edwin A. Wilson – Artistic Director
905 S. Grove St.
Oak Park, IL 60304
708/386-6669
312/400-9298.
keitel@megsinet.net
www.senseofurgency.org

An itinerant company founded in 1995.

Sense of Urgency is an ensemble based theatre that produces literary and provocative theatre, as well as new works from a resident playwright.

Their 2000-2001 season included:
What the Butler Saw
All My Sons

Serendipity Theatre Company
1658 N. Milwaukee #242
Chicago, IL 60647
773/871-3000 – box office
contact@serendipitytheatre.com
www.serendipitytheatre.com

An itinerant company founded in 1999.

Serendipity's purpose is to expand the spectrum, maintain the integrity, and develop new visions of what is known as the American Theatre.

Their 2000-2001 season included:
The Day Maggie Blew Off Her Head

They accept script submissions and director proposals.

Shakespeare's Motley Crew
Laura Jones Macknin – Artistic Director
4926 N. Winchester
Chicago, IL 60640
773/878-3632
fuflans@attglobal.net

Itinerant company founded in 1991.

Shakespeare's Motley Crew tries to have fun with the classics.

Their 2000-2001 season included:
The Skull Beneath the Skin

They do not accept script submissions but they do accept director proposals.

Shapeshifters Theatre Company
4626 N. Knox
Chicago, IL 60630
773/282-7035 x17
www.irishamhc.com

Shattered Globe Theatre
Steve Kay, Linda Reiter – Artistic Directors
Jeremy Wintroub – Managing Director
2856 N. Halsted
Chicago, IL 60657
773/404-1237
773/871-3000 – box office
jupitersgt@aol.com

An itinerant company founded in 1990.

Pay varies. The nearest eL stop is Wrightwood on the Purple and Brown lines.

Shattered Globe Theatre is driven by a fundamental commitment to the philosophy of ensemble. They received 2001 Jeff Citation for Coyote on a Fence and Invitation to a March.

They accept synopses and director proposals.

Sliced Bread Productions
1444 W. Chicago
Chicago, IL 60622
312/950-1444

They received a 2001 Jeff Citation nomination for actress in Private Eyes.

Slimtack Theatre Company
1142 W. Lawrence #202
Chicago, IL 60640
773/944-8225
info@slimtack.org
www.slimtack.org

Slimtack is committed to the idea that the most important commodity in the theatre is the individual.

The Space Theatre
4829 N. Damen
Chicago, IL 60625
773/293-0431
fisherbob@hotmail.com

Speaking Ring Theatre
Jennifer Leavitt – Artistic Director
Mercedes Rohlfs – Managing Director
773/327-0917
info@speakingringtheatre.org
speakingringtheatre.org

An itinerant company founded in 2001.

Speaking Ring aspires, through ensemble based theatre, to inspire community interaction.

Their 2000-2001 season included:
Golden Boy
Oscar Rememberred
The Woolgatherer

They do not accept script submissions but they do accept director proposals.

Stage Actors Ensemble
656 W. Barry - 3rd floor
Chicago, IL 60657
perfloft@aol.com
www.theperformanceloft.com

Stage Center Theatre
5500 N. St. Louis
Chicago, IL 60625
773/794-6652
r-higginbotham1@neiu.edu
www.neiu.edu/~stagectr

Stage Left Theatre
Jessi D. Hill & Kevin Heckman – Artistic Directors
3408 N. Sheffield
Chicago, IL 60657
773/883-8830
SLTChicago@aol.com
www.stagelefttheatre.com

Resident company founded in 1982. Pay is 1 percent of box office gross. The nearest eL stop is Belmont on the Red, Brown and Purple lines.

Stage Left is Chicago's only theatre dedicated to producing plays that raise the level of debate on social and political issues.

Their 2000-2001 season included:
Police Deaf Near Far
The Memorandum

They accept synopses and director proposals.

Stage Right Dinner Theatre
276 E. Irving Park Rd.
Woodale, IL 60191
630/595-2044
www.giorgiosbanq.com/stageright.htm

Stage Right is a self producing dinner theatre in the western suburbs.

Stage Two Theatre Company
P.O. Box 448
Libertyville, IL 60048-0448
847/432-7469
www.stagetwo.org

Stir-Friday Night
Jennifer Liu – Artistic Director
P.O. Box 268560
Chicago, IL 60626
773/973-4533
stirfridaynight@hotmail.com

An itinerant company founded 1995.

Stir-Friday Night! is Chicago's premier Asian American sketch comedy troupe producing all original works.

Their 2000-2001 season included:
- Woktoberfest
- Stir-Friday Night!
- FLAKES: Now Fortified with Indians!

They accept script submissions and director proposals.

Stockyards Theatre Project
Jill Elaine Hughes – Artistic Director
3941 N. Pine Grove #706
Chicago, IL 60613
773/377-5001 x6487
stockyardstheatre@mailcity.com
www.angelfire.com/il2/stockyards

Itinerant company founded in 1999.

The Stockyards Theatre Project is the only theatre company in Chicago dedicated exclusively to Feminist theatre.

Their 2000-2001 season included:
- Femme Fatalies: 4 Plays by Women
- Don't Promise
- First Annual Women's Performance Art Festival
- Damn the Torpedoes!

They do not accept script submissions or director proposals.

Summer Place Theatre
P.O. Box 128
Naperville, IL 60566
info@summerplacetheatre.com
www.summerplacetheatre.com

A resident theatre founded in 1966.

Summerplace Theatre presents community theatre for Naperville and surounding areas.

Their 2000-2001 season included:
- Run For Your Wife
- 1776
- The Foreigner
- Into the Woods

They do not accept script submissions but do accept director proposals.

Sweat Girls
4514 N. Lincoln #330
Chicago, IL 60625
773/868-4620
info@sweatgirls.org
www.sweatgirls.org

A group of woman monologuists who are best known for I'm Sweating Under My Breasts, Sweat Dreams and (The Sweat Girls Are) Pigs at the Trough of Attention.

Sweetback Productions
Kelly Anchors and David Cerda – Artistic Directors
Steve Hickson – Managing Director
1517 W. Rosemont Ave. #3E
Chicago, IL 60640
312/409-3925

Itinerant company founded in 1994.

Sweetback is unique due to their cross dressing, pop culture homage.

Their 2000-2001 season included:
- Touched
- Rudolph the Red Hosed Reindeer

They accept script submissions and director proposals.

Tellin' Tales Theatre
Tekki Lomnicki
366 E. Randolph, Suite 1006
Chicago, IL 60601
312/409-1025

Theater Oobleck
Mickle Maher
2059 W. Huron, Apt. 2
Chicago, IL 60612
773/761-2741
773/743-6652 – box office
www.geocities.com/Broadway/Alley/1483

An itinerant company founded in 1983. They pay $20/show.

Oobleck does all original work, without a director, that is always free.

They do not accept script submissions or director proposals.

Theatre Corps
Blake Montgomery
1932 S. Halsted #506
Chicago, IL 60608
312/409-6621
Montblake@hotmail.com

Theatre of Western Springs
Tony Vezner – Artistic Director
Jeff Arena – Managing Director
4384 Hampton Ave.
Western Springs, IL 60558
708/246-4043
708/246-3380 – box office
www.theatrewesternsprings.com

A resident company founded in 1929.

They are three blocks from Metra on the Burlington West line at the Western Springs station

Theatre of Western Springs is like a university theatre department, without the university.

They accept script submissions and director proposals.

Theatre-Hikes
Frank Farrell – Artistic Director
Ron Wachholtz – Managing Director
4829 N. Damen #211
Chicago, IL 60625
773/293-1358
FrankTFarrell@juno.com
www.theatre-hikes.com

Itinerant theatre founded in 2001. They pay $20 per show. They hold auditions in March.

Theatre-Hikes provides the public with theatrical performances combined with hiking, offering an event that travels to various locations.

Their 2000-2001 season included:
The Two Gentlemen of Verona

They accept synopses and director proposals.

Theo Ubique Theatre
Fred Anzevino, Artistic Director
1434 W. Jarvis #2F
Chicago, IL 60626
773/338-7258

Founded in 1996 Resident

They rent to other companies as well. Black Box space, 35-40 Seats.

Open Audition for each show. Call in Actors from generals, files or past knowledge. Cast from Ensemble

The company, through their style of work are attempting to place the actor and his/her talent at the forefront, reminding us that theatre can only succeed when it is a communal event.

Thirsty Theater
Mitch Newman – Artistic Director
556 W. 18th
Chicago, IL 60616
312/491-8484
tarpoon@sprintmail.com

Timber Lake Playhouse
Brad Lyons – Artistic Director
P.O. Box 29
Mt. Carroll, IL 61053
www.artsaxis.com/tlp

TimeLine Theatre Company
P.J. Powers – Artistic Director
Pat Tiedemann – Managing Director
615 W. Wellington
Chicago, IL 60657
773/281-8463
312/409-8463 – box office
timelineco@aol.com
www.TimeLineTheatre.com

A resident company founded in 1997. They attend the unified auditions. The nearest eL stop is Wellington on the Brown line.

Their 2000-2001 season included:
The Seagull
Streeterville
Not About Nightingales

They received six Jeff Citations for Nightingales (including best production, ensemble and director) and one Citation for Streeterville.

They accept synopses and director proposals.

Timestep Players
Allen McCoy – Artistic Director
Tracy McCoy – Managing Director
P.O. Box 16442
Chicago, IL 60616
773/736-7077
800/684-0091 – box office
Allen@timestepplayers.com
www.timestepplayers.com

An itinerant company founded in 1991. They pay $300/week plus travel stipend. They hold auditions in September, February and April. The closest eL stop is Irving Park on the Blue line.

Timestep is a touring educational theatre company that designs original scripts geared toward specific statewide themes to promote reading and literacy in the United States.

Their 2000-2001 season included:
2001 Reading Odyssey
Amazing Stories from Around the World
Just for the Fun of it
Frizby's Reading Road Trip

They accept script submissions and director proposals.

Tinfish Productions
Dejan Avramovich – Artistic Director
Laurie Kladis – Managing Director
4247 N. Lincoln
Chicago, IL 60618
773/546-1888
Tinfish@Tinfish.org
www.Tinfish.org

Resident company founded in 1994. They pay $50. They hold auditions in July.

Tinfish produces European based literary plays by or about authors who are not necessarily associated with the theatre.

They accept script submissions and director proposals.

Tommy Gun's Garage
Rob Rahn
Sandy Mangen
1239 S. State
Chicago, IL 60605
312/461-0102
sandygun@earthlink.net
www.tommygunsgarage.com

A resident company founded in 1987. They pay $3.55/hour plus tips. They are on the Red and Orange lines.

"An audience interactive 'speakeasy' which offers a musical comedy revue wit da gangsters."

They do not accept script submissions or director proposals.

Trap Door Theatre
Beata Pilch – Artistic Director
Nicole Wiesner – Managing Director
1655 W. Cortland
Chicago, IL 60647
773/384-0494
trapdoor@xnet.com
www.trapdoortheater.com

A resident company founded in1994. Pay is via the tip jar. The nearest eL stop is Damen on the Blue line.

Trap Door performs rarified works by European playwrights using a bold and innovative physical performance style.

Their 2000-2001 season included:
Ten Tiny Fingers, Nine TIny Toes
Baal
Nightcoil
Porcelain
Morocco
The Automobile Graveyard

They accept script submissions and director proposals.

Theatres

TriArts, Inc.
Troy Fujimura – Artistic Director
John W. Rogers – Managing Director
5315 N. Clark #142
Chicago, IL 60657
773/866-8082 x2
info@triarts.org
www.triarts.org

An itinerant company founded in 1998. They hold auditions Jan/Feb.

TriArts is a production and design company dedicated to a unification of artistic and technical facets of theatre production.

Their 2000-2001 season included:
TriArts New Noise Festival
Offending Shadows
Hfob-N-Tempest

They accept script submissions and director proposals.

Tripaway Theatre
Karin Shook – Artistic Director
Anita Evans – Managing Director
2714 W. Leland, Garden
Chicago, IL 60625
773/878-7785
karin@tripaway.org
www.tripaway.org

An itinerant company founded in 1994.

They pay a small stipend per run.

Tripaway Theatre produces original works and adaptations with an immediacy that inspires action.

Their 2000-2001 season included:
The Acharnians

They accept synopses and director proposals.

Ulysses Theatre Company
Jennifer Byers – Artistic Director
Patrick Rybarczyk – Managing Director
4951 N. St. Louis Ave. #1
Chicago, IL 60625
773/478-1061
ulysses@ulyssestheatre.org
ulyssestheatre.org

An itinerant company founded in1997. Pay varies.

Ulysses Theatre Company explores those concerns which seem to jump out of the jumbled stream of social events and demand reflection.

Their 2000-2001 season included:
Corpus Christi
The Secret Fall of Constance Wilde

They accept script submissions and director proposals.

Village Players
Diane Fisher Post – Artistic Director
1006 Madison St.
Oak Park, IL 60302
708/524-1892
708/222-0369 – box office
office@village-players.org
www.village-players.org

Founded in 1961.

Village Players presents Mainstage and Family Series selections as Oak Park's oldest professional theatre.

They do not accept script submissions or director proposals

Village Theatre Guild
P.O. Box 184
Glen Ellyn, IL 60138-0184
630/469-8230
www.glen-ellyn.com/vtg

Vittum Theater
Colby Beserra – Artistic Director
Carissa Johnson – Managing Director
1012 N. Noble St.
Chicago, IL 60622
773/278-7471 x172
vittumtheater@yahoo.com

A resident company. The closest eL stop is Division on the Blue line.

The Vittum Theatre is commited to providing Chicago's students, educators, and families the opportunity to engage in an affordable educational experience that is rooted in the art of performance.

They do not accept script submissions but do accept director proposals.

VORTEX
Gary Charles Metz – Artistic Director
920 Barnsdale Rd.
LaGrange, IL 60526
708/352-9120
garycharlesmetz@aol.com
www.northstarnet.org/lpshome/VORTEX

A resident company founded in 1996.

Vortex is a group of artists that enjoys producing lesser known works.

Their 2000-2001 season included:
- Art
- Love Letters
- Mugsy's Merry Christmas
- Goodbye Charlie

They do not accept script submissions but do accept director proposals.

Wheaton Drama, Inc.
Randy Knott – Artistic Director
Mary Engle – Managing Director
111 N. Hale - P.O. Box 4
Wheaton, IL 60189
630/668-1928
630/668-1820 – box office

A resident company founded in 1931.

Wheaton drama is the community theatre for Wheaton and surrounding areas.

They do not accept script submissions or director proposals.

Wing & Groove Theatre Company
Megan Powell, Amy Tourne – Artistic Directors
1935-1/2 W. North
The Flat Iron Arts Building
Chicago, IL 60622
773/782-9416 x2
wingandgroove@yahoo.com
www.wingandgroove.com

A resident company founded in 1997.

They hold auditions in Oct./Nov. The nearest eL stop is Damen on the Blue line.

Wing & Groove Theatre Company is Just Theatre.

Their 2000-2001 season included:
- The Misanthrope
- Absurd Person Singular
- Our Town, Person or Persons Unknown

They accept synopses and director proposals.

Winnetka Theatre
Nancy Flaster – Artistic Director
620 Lincoln Ave.
Winnetka, IL 60093
847/604-0275
winnetkatheatre.homestead.com

Resident company founded in 1972.

Winnetka Theatre is a community theatre for the North suburbs

Their 2000-2001 season included:
- You're a Good Man Charlie Brown
- Amadeus
- Joseph and the Amazing Technicolor Dreamcoat

They do not accept script submissions but do accept director proposals.

WNEP Theater Foundation
Jen Ellison – Artistic Director
Mark Dahl – Managing Director
3210 N. Halsted - 3rd floor
Chicago, IL 60657
773/755/1693
igotgwat@aol.com
www.wneptheater.org

A resident company founded in 1993. The nearest eL stop is Belmont on the Red, Brown and Purple lines.

WNEP Theater creates highly imaginative and aggressively confrontational original theatrical events.

Their 2000-2001 season included:
- Phobia!
- Statuette: A Hollywood Musical
- When We Were Superstars

They accept script submissions and director proposals.

Chapter 8

Improv

Steppenwolf, "One Flew Over the Cuckoo's Nest"

Art thou afeared
To be the same in thine
own act and valor
As thou art in desire?

By Dr. Amy Seham

Chicago is a mecca for young performers who travel from all over the world to study improv comedy at its source. At the same time, Chicago improv techniques have infiltrated classrooms, workshops, rehearsals and comedy clubs across North and South America, Europe, Australia and Japan. The Second City, which creates comedy revues through improvisation, has earned recognition as the center of improv training and the incubator of such comic talents as John Belushi, Gilda Radner, and Mike Myers. The theatre is widely seen as a stepping stone to "Saturday Night Live" and other opportunities in television and film. But there is far more to the theory and practice of improv than the sketches of "Saturday Night Live" or the games on "Whose Line is it Anyway?" might suggest.

Improv's birthplace has become a laboratory where players experiment with rules and structures in a never-ending search for the freedom and connection this genre seems to promise. For a number of its idealistic proponents, improv is a serious art form, a mission, even a way of life.

Defining Three Historical Waves of Improv

In my recent book, "Whose Improv Is It Anyway? Beyond Second City," I divide the history of Chicago improv into three "waves" of development. The first wave of Chicago-style improv comedy consists of The Second City and its progenitor, The Compass Players, where the specific genre of Chicago-style improv comedy was created and developed beginning in the mid 1950s. Second City's influential Training Center has operated since 1984 to define and teach improv to generations of students. The second wave includes ImprovOlympic and ComedySportz. Their very different variations on classic improv, both inspired by the work of British teacher/director Keith Johnstone, are based on a sports metaphor and the creation of "teams" of players. ImprovOlympic follows the teachings of the late improv guru Del Close in exploring psychological and artistic patterns through the Harold, a unique brand of long-form improv. By contrast, ComedySportz focuses on short, fast, comic improv games designed to appeal to a family audience. Both theatres currently offer training programs and performance opportunities in Chicago.

By the late 1980s to 1990s, a significant third wave of improv comedy began to evolve, made up of independent groups who challenged the rules and sometimes exclusive membership practices of more established theatres. Leading the movement was The Annoyance Theatre, whose anarchic style brought new energy to the improv community. Also key to the third wave was the emergence of troupes that offered an alternative to the predominantly white male perspective of many companies. Groups such as Jane, Sirens, Red, Oui Be Negroes, Black Comedy Underground, Stir-Friday Night, ¡Salsation! and GayCo Productions helped women, people of color, and gays and lesbians find their voices in improv. Stir-Friday Night, for example, found many of its early gigs through university student groups whose members were hungry for humor that reflected their own experience. One collegiate reviewer wrote, "Of the very few Asian performers in the entertainment industry, most play serious, Asian-oriented stereotypical roles...However, Stir-Friday Night proved to the audience that Asian comedy can be funny...The actors do not appear removed, but more familiar, like the John Kim down the street...I understood the humor as an extension of my background and my history."

As the millennium drew to an end, the improv world was again in flux. Nationwide awareness of improv had grown rapidly throughout the 1990s, fostered by festivals, the Internet, college and university troupes, television programs and films. Most new arrivals enrolled in classes at one or more of the city's "Big Three" improv theatres: Second City, ImprovOlympic or the Annoyance Theatre. Each school of improv has something distinctive to offer. Students learn classic improvisation technique at Second City, the Harold and other long-form skills at ImprovOlympic, and creative confidence at the Annoyance. But the boundaries separating important troupes or waves has begun to blur. Players often belong to several troupes at once—

dividing their time among established companies and freelance endeavors. While some players seek opportunities to move up the ladder, hoping to be discovered by talent scouts, others have rededicated themselves to the collaborative ideals of improv. The Playground is an improv co-op founded in 1997 with this mission statement: "We believe that the value of improv goes beyond mere entertainment; rather, in a society filled with isolating and fragmenting influences, improv holds a societally valuable message: It demonstrates how teamwork, trust and support can make something wonderful out of absolutely nothing."

The Next Generation of Improv

The future of Chicago improv, the (fourth or fifth) waves of the future will be shaped by the tremendous increase in improv's reach and accessibility and the growing impact of technology on the dissemination of improv technique and philosophy far beyond Chicago. Not only are improv companies developing in many cities, but the Internet has enabled improvisers everywhere to be in daily contact with one another. The fertile intersection of improv and technology has possibilities we cannot fully anticipate. Today's fledgling improvisers can attend (and organize) improv festivals, refer to improv pages on the Internet, and even see modified versions of improv on television.

At the grassroots level, hundreds of troupes are formed each year on college campuses. Mission IMPROVable's Aaron Krebs explains the seasonal pattern of college improvisers' migration to Chicago: "[They arrive] every June, right after school and then again in September. Kids that worked all summer to save up to move out here like we did. The generation before us, last year, some people came from Florida State, from North Carolina and from New Jersey…It's like a graduation. It's becoming a bigger and bigger thing in colleges and more and more people want to do it. It's just going to expand."

Many players believe that improv's next wave consists of its rapid growth and recognition outside Chicago. Eager students poured into Chicago in seasonal floods, but an increasing number of veterans were flowing out again, looking for ways to use their skills in less improv-saturated, more lucrative arenas. Chicago became a hub for the improv diaspora.

While improv festivals draw some students to Chicago, they are also an effective means of disseminating ideas and even decentralizing improv activity throughout the country. In 1994, the Kansas City festival (later called Spontaneous Combustion) was the first large regional event to bring troupes together from all over North America for workshops, panels, and performances. More important, players could meet informally to share games, techniques, anecdotes and opinions. In the latter half of the '90s, festivals were held in Austin, Portland, Minneapolis, Aspen and New York with varying degrees of success. In 1998, Frances Callier and Jonathan Pitts organized the first Chicago Improv Festival, a six-day extravaganza that showcased Chicago troupes, Chicago alumni, and other companies from New York, Minneapolis and Los Angeles. Offerings included workshops with respected teachers and directors, including such improv luminaries as Keith Johnstone and the late Del Close. Callier hoped to make people understand that improv was not merely a technique or acting skill, but "an art form in and of itself." That festival has become an important annual event.

According to some players, the next wave of improv is its growing presence on the Internet, on television, and in film. By the mid '90s, the Internet had become an increasingly important part of improv subculture. Players exchanged information, traded games, advertised performances, made contacts and solicited students through newsgroups like alt.comedy.improvisation. By decade's end, every self-respecting improv troupe had its own Web site, and the quality of a site's design began to have an impact on a troupe's success (though occasionally sites were better than performances). Troupes post photos, reviews, and tour availability on their Web pages, and use the Internet to send press releases directly to an editor's desk. National improv festivals owe their success and rapid growth to the Internet, where organizers advertise, post registration forms and recruit troupes.

Improv Online

Internet resources for improvisers have proliferated, including The Improv Page, The New Improv Page, The Chicago Improv Page, Improv Resource Center Chicago, The Living Playbook, and many more. Some sites are highly personal and idiosyncratic, while others list games, groups, or festival information. In 1998, a Webzine called YESand began publishing news and feature articles on a monthly basis, and also hosting a bulletin board/discussion list where players post messages under the categories General, Plugs, Casting, Improv Theory, or Silliness. One discussion began by mourning the death of comedian Madeline Kahn, moved into a debate about gender roles in improv, and ended with the successful launch of the Funny Women Improv Festival in Chicago, now in its third year of supporting and encouraging women improvisers and comedians. Improv performance has been broadcast over the Internet through streaming video, and several versions of online improvisation, or interactive theatre, are gaining in popularity.

Whose Line to Saturday Night Live

The Chicago improv community has a decades-long love-hate relationship with television. Second City's role as talent source for "Saturday Night Live" brought it prestige, giving recognition to the art form. But many dedicated players believed that real improvisation was incompatible with television. Television would never capture the spontaneity, audiences wouldn't feel the connection, and network executives would never take the chance

The late '90s, however, saw several new attempts at bringing improvisation to the screen. Comedian Drew Carey hosted the American version of Britain's "Whose Line is it Anyway?," a half-hour mock competition among four comic improvisers. "Whose Line" features some of the most basic gimmick games popular at ComedySportz and other short-form companies. While "Whose Line" seems to provide a certain amount of genuine spontaneity, syndicated shows such as "Kwik Witz" and "Random Acts of Comedy" were far less successful.

In 1998, a special Chicago audition was organized for casting agents from "Whose Line." More than a dozen of the best improvisers from Second City, ImprovOlympic and the Annoyance were there, but not one was cast for the show. ImprovOlympic producer Charna Halpern explained in a NEW CITY interview: "What they are really looking for are stand-up people who can do some quick one-liners, and then, buzz, the time is up." Nevertheless, many players credit "Whose Line" for increasing public awareness of improv as an entertainment form distinct from stand-up. Although women rarely appear on the show, African-American performer Wayne Brady has become a role model for a growing number of black improvisers and has gone on to star in his own summer variety show that includes some improvised sections.

While these shows are based on short-form improv, it remained for cable station Comedy Central to televise the long-form. The Upright Citizens Brigade (UCB), a band of guerillas "dedicated to undermining society through the proliferation of chaos," was in fact a group within ImprovOlympic that developed a unique form of interactive sketch comedy. The players created scenes through improvisation, then devised a show in which characters and themes would overlap and finally "come full circle" as they might in a Harold. The core group of UCB moved to New York, where they opened their own improv performance and training center and created several seasons of television programs. Loyal fans were outraged when Comedy Central canceled the show in 2000, but The Upright Citizens Brigade continues to teach and perform in New York and around the country.

A group of Second City alumni created "Strangers With Candy," an "afterschool special" parody briefly paired with"Upright Citizens Brigade" in Comedy Central's line-up, but also recently canceled. Most improvisers, however, found their training suited them more for writing than for acting. Adam McKay moved from ImprovOlympic's The Family to the Second City mainstage, to "Saturday Night Live" as a writer, writing supervisor, then short film coordinator. Tina Fey followed a similar path in 1999, becoming the first female head writer in "Saturday Night Live"'s 25-year history.

Other Chicago improvisers could be found on the writing staffs of "The Martin Short Show," "Mad TV," MTV's "The Blame Game" and "Mr. Show," "The Drew Carey Show," "The Conan O'Brien Show," new animated series, and many others. In the same period, improvisational acting was highlighted in film, including the high-profile *Blair Witch Project, Waiting for Guffman,* and the critically acclaimed films of Mike Leigh. Most recently, cable station TNN (the National Network) picked up "Lifegame," an improvised show based on an adaptation of a Johnstone improv structure. First an off-Broadway show, "Lifegame" features a team of improvisers who spontaneously create scenes based on the lives of "real people" who agree to be interviewed on stage. In the television version, celebrities are often the interviewees, and the scenes are more directed—though still improvised. Another test of the compatibility of improv and television is underway.

World Domination

As improv troupes proliferate in America and around the world, popular awareness of the form increases. (The New Improv Page lists troupes in 34 states and the District of Columbia, and 34 countries in Europe, Asia, Australia, North and South America. Short-form predominates, but long-form is taught in California, New York, and elsewhere.) Longtime improv performer and teacher Lillian Francis speculates, "I bet that the fifth wave is going to be—you will say 'improv' to someone and they know what it is. They will not say, 'oh, you mean like stand-up.' Your average Joe will know what improv is."

Improv Training

ComedySportz

2851 N. Halsted
Chicago, IL 60657
773/549-8080

A - First level of training consisting of fundamentals and games.

AA - Advanced scenework techniques and more games.

AAA - Intensive work on Styles, Music, Characters, Dialects and advanced scene work.

Minor League Performance Level- Students workshop and perform an eight week run of their own ComedySportz style show

---

ImprovOlympic

3541 N. Clark
Chicago, IL 60657
773/880-0199
773/880-9979 - fax

Long Form Improv - Six levels, geared towards performance, classes run eight weeks

Mainstage: 100 - Proscenium

Low Sodium Entertainment

3741 N. Kenmore #2
Chicago, IL 60613
773/549-3250

Second City

1616 N. Wells
Chicago, IL 60614
312/664-3959
312/664-9837 - fax
www.secondcity.com

Conservatory - The art of improv, Second City revue style

Improv for Actors - For experienced performers with little improv training or as a brush-up course

Writing - Techniques of comedy writing for beginning and advanced writers

Beginning - Foundations of improv for students with limited theatre or improv experience

---

The Improv Playhouse

847/968-4529
www.improvplayhouse.com

The Improv Playhouse, Libertyville. Foundational through advanced improvisation, Story Theater, radio drama, beginning through advanced dramatic arts classes for adults and youth. Staff are arts professionals from premier improv and drama programs. Professional performance opportunities available to students. Sponsor of ComedySportz North Suburban High School League. Several north suburban locations. Contact David Stuart. Call 847/968-4529.

Old Town School of Music

4544 N. Lincoln Ave.
Chicago, IL 60625
773/728-6000
www.improvplayhouse.com

Beginning, Intermediate and Advanced Improv for adults including regular performances, as well as kids and teen classes.

Improv-Friendly Theatres

These theatres either offer improvised shows or are known for using improv as a major force in creating new works.

Annoyance Theater
3747 N. Clark
Chicago, IL 60613
773/929-6200
www.annoyance.com

ComedySportz
3210 N. Halsted - 3rd Floor
Chicago, IL 60657
773/549-8482

Free Associates
Susan Gaspar - Artistic Director
2936 N. Southport #210
Chicago, IL 60657
773/296-0541
www.thefreeassociates.com
See listing in Theatre section.

ImprovOlympic
3541 N. Clark
Chicago, IL 60657
773/880-0199
773/880-9979 - fax

Players Workshop's Children's Theatre
Stephen Roath - Artistic Director
2936 N. Southport
Chicago, IL 60657
773/929-6288
773/477-8022 - fax
www.playersworkshop.com

WNEP Theater Foundation
Jen Ellison - Artistic Director
Mark Dahl - Managing Director
817 W. Lakeside #807
Chicago, IL 60640-6641
773/334-8661 x1
members.aol.com/WNEP

Improv Groups

Baby Wants Candy
773/880-9993

Billy Goat Factory
773/477-9651

Broken Pilgrims in Gothic Sneakers
1925 W. Newport #F
Chicago, IL 60657-1025
312/974-2110

The Playground
773/871-3793
www.the-playground.com
See listing in Theatre section.

ComedySportz
2851 N. Halsted
Chicago, IL 60657
773/549-8080
See listing in Theatre section.

Detonate Productions
1410 W. Belle Plaine #1
Chicago, IL 60613
773/549-8190

Oui Be Negroes
1432 W. Lunt #208
Chicago, IL 60626
773/274-4563
www.ouibenegroes.com

Free Associates
Susan Gaspar - Artistic Director
2936 N. Southport #210
Chicago, IL 60657
773/296-0541
www.thefreeassociates.com
See listing in Theatre section.

ImprovOlympic
3541 N. Clark
Chicago, IL 60657
773/880-0199
See listing in Theatre section.

Low Sodium Entertainment
3741 N. Kenmore #2
Chicago, IL 60613
773/549-3250
See listing in Theatre section.

Chapter 9

Running a Small Theatre Company

Brouthil & Frothingham, "Artist Descending a Staircase"

Rehearsal/Rental Spaces

About Face Theatre
1222 W. Wilson - 2nd Floor West
Chicago, IL 60640
773/784-8565
Mainstage: 100 – Thrust

Act One Studios, Inc.
(see our ad in...)
640 N. LaSalle #535
Chicago, IL 60610
312/787-9384
www.actone.com

American Theater Company
1909 W. Byron
Chicago, IL 60613
773/929-5009
www.ATCWEB.org
Mainstage: 137 - Thrust

The Artistic Home
1420 W. Irving Park
Chicago, IL 60613
773/404-1100

Arts Center at College of DuPage
425 22nd St.
Glen Ellyn, IL 60137
630/942-3008
www.cod.edu

Apollo Theater
916 S. Wabash #503
Chicago, IL 60605
312/461-9292
www.apollochicago.com

Athenaeum
2936 N. Southport
Chicago, IL 60657
773/935-6860
http://athenaeum.livedomain.com
cfoster29@surfbest.net
Mainstage: 976
Studio: 55
Stage 3: 80

Attic Playhouse
410 Sheridan Rd.
Highwood, IL 60040
847/433-2660
www.atticplayhouse.com
Mainstage: 94 - Black Box

Bailiwick Repertory
1229 W. Belmont
Chicago, IL 60657
773/833-1090
www.bailiwick.org
Mainstage: 150
Studio: 90
Loft: 25

Belle Plaine Studio
2014 W. Belle Plaine
Chicago, IL 60618
773/935-1890

Breadline Theatre Group
1802 W. Berenice
Chicago, IL 60613-2720
773/327-6096
www.breadline.org
Mainstage: 40 - Black Box

CenterLight Sign & Voice Theatre
3444 Dundee Rd.
Northbrook, IL 60062
847/559-0110 x237
www.centerlighttheatre.com

Chase Park
4701 N. Ashland
Chicago, IL 60640
312/742-7518

Chicago Actors Studio
1567 N. Milwaukee
Chicago, IL 60622
773/645-0222
773/645-0040 - fax
www.actors-studio.net

Chicago Cultural Center
78 E. Washington
Chicago, IL 60602
312/744-3094
www.ci.chi.il.us/culturalaffairs/

Chicago Dramatists
1105 W. Chicago
Chicago, IL 60622
312/633-0630
www.chicagodramatists.org
Mainstage: 77 - Proscenium

Chicago Shakespeare Theater
800 E. Grand
Chicago, IL 60611
312/595-5656
www.chicagoshakes.com
Studio: 200 - Proscenium

Chopin Theatre
1543 W. Division
Chicago, IL 60622
773/278-1500
Mainstage: 220 - Black Box
Studio: 100 - Black Box

Circle Theatre
7300 W. Madison
Forest Park, IL 60130

ComedySportz
2851 N. Halsted
Chicago, IL 60657
773/549-8080
www.comedysportzchicago.com

Corn Productions
2620 N. Lawndale
Chicago, IL 60647
312/409-6435
Mainstage: 60 - Thrust

Court Theatre
5535 S. Ellis
Chicago, IL 60637
773/702-7005
www.courttheatre.org
Mainstage: 251 - Thrust

Curious Theatre Branch
2827 N. Lincoln
Chicago, IL 60657
773/327-6666
jemlunar@enteract.com

Des Plaines Theatre Guild
1752 E. Greenleaf
Des Plaines, IL 60018
773/388-0495

Duncan YMCA
Chernin Center for the Arts
1001 W. Roosevelt
Chicago, IL 60608
312/738-7980

Mainstage: 220 - Proscenium

Studio: 125

Festival Theatre
P.O. Box 4114
Oak Park, IL 60303
www.oprf.com/festival/

Mainstage: 300

Griffin Theatre
5404 N. Clark
Chicago, IL 60640
773/769-2228

Mainstage: 125 – Thrust

ImprovOlympic
(see our ad on page 57)
3541 N. Clark
Chicago, IL 60657
773/880-0199

Mainstage: 100 - Proscenium

Irish American Heritage Center
4626 N. Knox
Chicago, IL 60630
773/282-7035 x17
www.irishamhc.com

Mainstage: 600 – Proscenium

Lifeline Theatre
6912 N. Glenwood
Chicago, IL 60618
773/761-0667
www.lifelinetheatre.com

Links Hall
3435 N. Sheffield
Chicago, IL 60657
773/281-0824

Mainstage: 75—Black Box

Live Bait Theater
3914 N. Clark
Chicago, IL 60613
773/871-1212
www.livebaittheater.org

Lookingglass Theatre Company
2936 N. Southport
Chicago, IL 60657
773/477-9257
www.lookingglasstheatre.org

Lucid Theatre Productions
941 W. Lawrence
Chicago, IL 60640
773/761-4901

Marriott Theatre
10 Marriott Dr.
Lincolnshire, IL 60069
847/634-0204

Mainstage: 882 - In-the-Round

Mary-Arrchie Theatre
731 W. Sheridan
Chicago, IL 60613
773/871-0442

National Pastime Theater
4139 N. Broadway
Chicago, IL 60613
773/327-7077
Mainstage: 65

The Neo-Futurists
5153 N. Ashland
Chicago, IL 60640
773/878-4557
www.neofuturists.org
Neo-Futurist Performance Workshop
Mainstage: 149 - Thrust

New American Theatre
118 N. Main St.
Rockford, IL 61101-1102
815/963-9454
www.newamericantheater.com
Mainstage: 282 - Thrust
Studio: 90

North Island Center
8 E. Galena Blvd. #230
Aurora, IL 60506
630/264-7202
www.paramountarts.com
Paramount Arts Centre: 1888
Copley Theatre: 216

Northlight Theatre
9501 Skokie Blvd.
Skokie, IL 60077
847/679-9501 x8
www.northlight.org
Mainstage: 850
Second Stage: 354 - Proscenium

Noyes Cultural Arts Center
927 Noyes
Evanston, IL 60201
847/491-0266
847/328-1340 – fax

The Playground
3341 N. Lincoln
Chicago, IL 60657
773/871-3793
www.the-playground.com

Porchlight Theatre
2936 N. Southport
Chicago, IL 60657
773/325-9884
www.porchlighttheatre.com

Pheasant Run Dinner Theatre
4051 E. Main St.
St. Charles, IL 60174
630/584-6300
www.pheasantrun.com
Mainstage: 272 - Proscenium

Profiles Theatre
3761 N. Racine
Chicago, IL 60613
773/549-1815
Mainstage: 52 – Proscenium

Red Hen Productions
2944 N. Broadway
Chicago, IL 60657
773/728-0599
www.redhenproductions.com

A Red Orchid Theatre
1531 N. Wells
Chicago, IL 60610-7752
312/943-8722
www.a-red-orchid.com

Roadworks
1144 W. Fulton Market #105
Chicago, IL 60607
312/492-7150
www.roadworks.org

Schadenfreude
7016 N. Glenwood
Chicago, IL 60626
773/271-5318
www.schadenfreude.net

Second City
1616 N. Wells
Chicago, IL 60614
312/664-3959
312/664-9837 - fax
www.secondcity.com

Shattered Globe Theatre
2856 N. Halsted
Chicago, IL 60657
773/404-1237

Sheil Park
3505 N. Southport
Chicago, IL 60657
312/742-7826

Stage Actors Ensemble
656 W. Barry - 3rd floor
Chicago, IL 60657
773/529-8337
theperformanceloft.com

Stage Left Theatre
3408 N. Sheffield
Chicago, IL 60657
773/883-8830
www.stagelefttheatre.com
Mainstage: 50 - Black Box

Steppenwolf Theatre Company
758 W. North - 4th floor
Chicago, IL 60610
312/335-1888
www.steppenwolf.org

Strawdog Theatre
3829 N. Broadway
Chicago, IL 60622
773/528-9889
www.strawdog.org
Mainstage: 74 - Black Box

The Theatre Building
1225 W. Belmont
Chicago, IL 60657
773/929-7367
773/327-1404 - fax

Theatre of Western Springs
4384 Hampton
Western Springs, IL 60558
708/246-4043
www.theatrewesternsprings.com
Mainstage: 415 - Proscenium
Studio: 130

TimeLine Theatre
615 W. Wellington
Chicago, IL 60657
773/281-8463
www.timelinetheatre.com
Mainstage: 90

Timestep Players Educational Children's Theatre Company
P.O. Box 16442
Chicago, IL 60616
773/736-7077
www.timestepplayers.com

TinFish Productions
4247 N. Lincoln
Chicago, IL 60618
773/549-1888
www.Tinfish.org
Mainstage: 80 - Black Box

Tommy Gun's Garage
1239 S. State
Chicago, IL 60605
312/461-0102
www.tommygunsgarage.com

Trap Door Theatre
1655 W. Cortland
Chicago, IL 60647
773/384-0494

Mainstage: 35 – Proscenium

Under the Ginkgo Tree (Bed & Breakfast)
Gloria Onischuk
300 N. Kenilworth
Oak Park, IL 60302
708/524-2327
708/524-2729 - fax

A spacious home ideally used for filming, photo shoots, etc.

Victory Gardens Theatre
2257 N. Lincoln
Chicago, IL 60614
773/549-5788
www.victorygardens.org

Mainstage: 195 – Thrust

Studio: 60 (2)

Vittum Theatre
773/278-7471 x172

Mainstage: 299—Proscenium

Wellington Avenue United Church of Christ
615 W. Wellington
Chicago, IL 60657
773/935-0642

Wing & Groove Theatre Company
1935 1/2 W. North
Chicago, IL 60622
773/782-9416 x2

Mainstage: 50-55 - Black Box

WNEP Theater Foundation
3210 N. Halsted - 3rd floor
Chicago, IL 60657
773/755/1693
igotgwat@aol.com
www.wneptheater.org

Mainstage: 60 - Black Box

Women in the Director's Chair
941 W. Lawrence #500
Chicago, IL 60640
773/907-0610
www.widc.org

A Guide to Forming a Not-for-Profit

Step 1: Research, Plan and Think, Think, Think.

The first step is to define your purposes and goals. Do you simply want to limit your personal liability should an accident occur at one of your events, or are you primarily interested in obtaining tax-exempt status in order to attract funding from the many private foundations which fund only tax-exempt, nonprofit organizations? Are you organizing to produce a single project or do you intend to generate ongoing activities in the community? Do you know who will serve on your board of directors (you must have at least three directors), and do you know who will have the right to control and direct the activities of your nonprofit corporation? How will you raise funds in support of your activities, and do you plan to sell goods or services which are related (or unrelated) to the purpose of your nonprofit corporation? The answers to these and similar questions will determine the form and structure of your organization.

Nonprofit Financial Center (www.nonprofitfinancial.org), located at 111 W. Washington Street, Suite 1221, Chicago, IL 60602-2706, offers a number of useful handbooks (including one on creating an Illinois nonprofit company) and sponsors training sessions to educate nonprofit companies on topics such as responsible financial management, raising money, legal reporting and public disclosure requirements.

IRS (www.irs.ustreas.gov) by clicking the section on "Tax Info For Business," or you can go directly to the specific IRS Web page which provides information on tax-exempt organizations (www.irs.ustreas.gov/prod/bus_info/eo). From the IRS site you can download "Publication 557," a 55-page booklet which discusses the rules and procedures for seeking to obtain exemption from federal income tax under §501(a) of the Internal Revenue Code.

Step 2: Obtain Professional Advice.

Few things will ruin your day as quickly as having to withdraw a foundation funding proposal or having to tell a donor that her contribution to your nonprofit corporation is not tax deductible because the IRS declined your application for tax-exempt status. A one-time reading of all 55 triple-columned, single-spaced pages of IRS Publication 557 together with roughly 150 pages of the Illinois General Not For Profit Corporation Act of 1986 (codified as 805 ILCS 105/101 and available at www.legis.state.il.us) may not be sufficient to enable you to steer clear of potential traps.

Lawyers For The Creative Arts, 213 W. Institute Place, Suite 401, Chicago, 60610 (312/649-4111), itself an Illinois nonprofit corporation, provides low-cost legal assistance in support of the creative arts. If you are truly without funds, either the LCA or one of its volunteer attorneys may be able to assist you.

Small Business Opportunity Clinic of the Northwestern University School of Law (312/503-8576), located at 357 E. Chicago Avenue, Chicago, IL 60611, provides law school students who perform the majority of the legal services (www.law.nwu.edu/small-business).

Step 3: Setting Up Your Illinois Nonprofit Corporation.

Now that you have defined your purpose and goals and have reviewed the application process with a professional, you are ready to prepare your incorporation papers and hold your first meeting of directors. Once you've done your homework and enlisted the aid of a professional, the process looks deceptively easy.

The first stop is the Illinois Secretary of State Web site (www.sos.state.il.us), from which you can download a variety of forms and learn the cost of each filing. Finding the nonprofit forms page is a bit confusing, but it can be located either by using the Not-For-Profit form page URL (http://www.sos.state.il.us/depts/bus_serv/forms.html) or by clicking the following sequence of hot links: click "Services" on the Secretary of State home page; click "For Business" on the Services page; click "Download Business Services Forms" on the Business page; and click "Not-For-Profit Forms and Fees" on the Download Business Services Forms page.

Step 4: The Follow-Up.

The list of required post-filing actions is extensive, but here are a few. *Within 15 days* after you receive your certified Articles of Incorporation from the Secretary of State, you must file the certified Articles with (and pay a filing fee to) the recorder of the county in which the registered agent of the nonprofit corporation has its office. Additionally, *you must file* an application to obtain a federal tax identification number for the corporation. The directors of the new nonprofit corporation *must promptly adopt bylaws and elect officers,* upon proper notice. If you have decided to have members, it is recommended that you promptly schedule a first meeting. Be aware that certain charitable organizations are also required to register and to file annual reports with the Office of the Illinois Attorney General.

Step 5: Federal and State Tax Exemptions.

Unfortunately, creation of an Illinois nonprofit corporation, by itself, *does not entitle your organization to any form of tax exemption.* Even worse, not all nonprofit entities will qualify for an exemption from federal income taxes (see Publication 557, mentioned above, to determine whether your organization qualifies for tax-exempt status). Even if you qualify, the application process for obtaining tax-exempt status often takes six months or longer! So, if tax-exempt status is essential to the operation of your nonprofit, plan accordingly.

The filing fee alone for applying for tax-exempt status can be as much as $500 (if your organization's gross receipts have been or are likely to be more than $10,000 per year). The Application for Recognition of Exemption requires you to provide detailed information, such as:

- A detailed narrative description of your organization's activities—past, present and planned;
- The name, address and title of each officer and director;
- The Federal Employer Tax Identification Number of the organization;
- A copy of your organization's Articles of Incorporation and Bylaws; and
- Financial Statements (including a detailed breakdown of revenue and expenses) for the current year and for each of the prior three years, or if organized less than one year, proposed budgets for the next two years.

Also keep in mind that once you have filed your application, it is not uncommon for the IRS to contact you to request more specific or additional information.

Other Helpful Organizations for Business Managers

Arts & Business Council of Chicago (A&BC). There are many facets to the A&BC, all of which operate under the common goal of enhancing management and leadership capabilities of arts organizations by uniting them with the business world. Two programs of particular interest are the Business Volunteers for the Arts (BVA) and the Arts Marketing Center.

According to Deborah Obalil, assistant director of the Arts Marketing Center, the "BVA is designed to provide pro-bono management assistance to arts organizations." The program recruits experienced business professionals, provides extensive training that teaches them to apply their knowledge and skills to the arts, and then matches the volunteers with small to mid-sized not-for-profit arts organizations as pro-bono consultants.

There is an application process (including a nominal fee) required to participate in the BVA program. Only organizations that have maintained 501(c)3 status for at least two years will be considered.

The Donors Forum of Chicago, which strives to "to promote and support effective and responsible philanthropy," serves as an informational and networking hub for grantmakers, funders, foundations, not-for-profit organizations and market researchers.

If you are researching new grants, the Donor's Forum Library is where you want to go. It houses the largest collection of philanthropic and not-for-profit resources, such as private and corporate foundation directories, grant lists, foundation annual reports and giving guidelines.

Workshops currently offered by the Forum include: The ABCs of Proposal Preparation & Writing, an introductory course for not-for-profits applying for funding from private foundations or corporations; Major Gift and Capital Campaign, which introduces participants to the basic fundraising concepts underlying major gifts and capital campaigns; and Securing Support from Individuals, which teaches basic techniques in soliciting funds from private individuals. Workshops are typically all-day events that range in price from $100 to $140.

Arts Bridge operates three programs—the Incubator Program, Art Works and the Alternative Business Center—that strive to connect "emerging and underserved cultural groups with arts management expertise and a professional business environment."

The Incubator Program is the organization's "signature program, it is what Arts Bridge was initially established to do." The program is a residential business training center that provides members technical service (annual business planning, individual management consulting, workshops), administrative support (computer training/assistance, clerical support, bulk purchasing, receptionist services), onsite Arts Bridge staff members, facilities (furnished offices, resource library, conference room, kitchen), and equipment (computers, printers, internet access, Xerox, fax, telephone, postage meter). Highly competitive, the program only harbors approximately six to eight groups at a time from various artistic backgrounds ranging from theatre and dance to the visual arts. Depending upon the individual needs and development of the groups, the program length can range from two to six years. The rigorous application/selection/interview process alone takes from six months to a year to complete.

Helpful Organizations

Arts and Business Council of Chicago
Arts Marketing Center
70 E. Lake #500
Chicago, IL 60601
312/372-1876
312/372-1102 - fax
www.artsbiz-chicago.org

Arts Bridge
2936 N. Southport
Chicago, IL 60657
773/296-0948
773/296-0968 - fax
www.artsbridge.org

Association of Consultants to Nonprofits
P.O. Box 2449
Chicago, IL 60690-2449
312/580-1875
www.ACNconsult.org

Center for Communication Resources
Nalani McClendon
1419 W. Blackhawk
Chicago, IL 60622
773/862-6868
773/862-0707 - fax
www.bham.net/soe/ccr

Chicago Department of Cultural Affairs
Richard Vaughn - Director of Legal Affairs
312/742-1175
www.ci.chi.il.us/CulturalAffairs

Community Media Workshop at Columbia College
600 S. Michigan
Chicago, IL 60605
312/344-6400
312/344-6404 - fax
www.newstips.org

CPA's for Public Interest
222 S. Riverside Plaza - 16th floor
Chicago, IL 60606
312/993-0393
312/993-9432 - fax
www.icpas.org/cpaspi.htm

Cultural Facilities Fund
78 E. Washington #250
Chicago, IL 60602
312/372-1710
312/372-1765 - fax

Department of Revenue
Gladys Alcazar-Anselmo
312/747-3823
www.ci.chi.il.us/Revenue

Donors Forum of Chicago
208 S. LaSalle #735
Chicago, IL 60604
312/578-0175
312/578-0158 - fax
www.donorsforum.org

Executive Service Corps of Chicago
30 W. Monroe #600
Chicago, IL 60603
312/580-1840
312/580-0042 - fax
www.esc-chicago.org

Illinois Alliance for Arts Education
200 N. Michigan #404
Chicago, IL 60601
312/750-0589
312/750-9113 - fax
www.artsmart.org

Illinois Arts Alliance
200 N. Michigan #404
Chicago, IL 60601
312/855-3105
312/855-1565 - fax
www.artsalliance.org

Illinois Arts Council
100 W. Randolph #10-500
Chicago, IL 60601
312/814-6750
312/814-1471 - fax
www.state.il.us/agency/iac

IT Resource Center
Sarah Oaks - Marketing Director
29 E. Madison #1605
Chicago, IL 60602
312/372-4872
312/372-7962 - fax
www.npo.net/itrc

Lawyers for the Creative Arts
213 W. Institute #401
Chicago, IL 60610
312/944-2787
312/944-2195 - fax
www.cityofchicago.org/culturalaffairs/CulturalProgramming/Lawyers.html

League of Chicago Theatres
228 S. Wabash #300
Chicago, IL 60604
312/554-9800
312/922-7202 - fax
www.chicagoplays.com

The League promotes Chicago's theatre industry through marketing, advocacy, and information services. Programs include Hot Tix, Chicago Theater Guide, Play Money Gift Certificates, Cooperative Advertising and the Annual CommUNITY Conference. The League coordinates the annual Non-Equity general Auditions in May/June and also hosts the annual theatre industry conference with workshops and seminars open to the public.

Nonprofit Financial Center
111 W. Washington #1221
Chicago, IL 60602
312/606-8250
312/606-0241 - fax
www.nonprofitfinancial.org

Pre-Paid Legal Services, Inc.
9242 W. National Ave.
West Ellis, WI 53227
414/329-3047

Season of Concern
203 N. Wabash #2104
Chicago, IL 60601
312/332-0518
312/372-0272 - fax
members.aol.com/sochicago/

The Support Center
3811 N. Lawndale #100
Chicago, IL 60618
312/648-0995
773/539-4751 - fax
www.supportcenter.org/sf/

Demystifying Grant Writing

With this there grows
In my most ill-composed affection such
A staunchless avarice.

By Kelly Kurtin

Cash flow. There's no doubt that every theatre company, from an upstart group mounting Mamet in a garage to a troupe that uses 700-seat digs in a Broadway grand palais, needs it. The question, then, is how—how to get the money you need to buff up your budget and put out the kind of productions you want. Theatre companies—especially non-Equities who might not have strong subscriber cache—can revel in the fact that there are people out there who make funding your business their business.

It comes down to grant writing. Mere mention of the "G" word is enough to set a managing director's heart into frenetic palpitations. Questions ("Where do I start?" or "What information do I need to provide?" or "Is a foundation really going to be interested in our dadaist approach to Auntie Mame?") are common. Luckily, there are a few simple suggestions to jump-start the grant application process.

Before you read on, keep on mind that there is a difference between private (foundation) money, corporate gift money and bucks that come from the federal or state government. In addition to having a somewhat more labor-intensive application process, corporate and federally allocated money is quite often given on a project basis. It might be designated for specific programs, not simply for ongoing general operating expenses. Theatre companies find, then, that arts-focused private funders are the ones to flock to when it comes to bolstering an overall budget. Keep in mind though that every donor is different. In the words of Jason Heeney from the Mayer and Morris Kaplan Family

Foundation, "When you've seen one foundation, well...you've seen one foundation." The bottom line: Do your research and you'll find a good fit.

Step One: Establishing Goals and Researching Funders

Figuring out what grants to apply for is a bit like solving a puzzle. You first have to examine all of the pieces—staffing issues, budget allocations, upcoming projects—in order to really document what direction your company is headed in. Are you looking to expand, or perhaps get a permanent home? Possibly your goals are more artistically inclined.

Barbara Kemmis, the director of library services for the Donors Forum of Chicago (a great local link when it comes to fostering relationships between funders and non-profits), stresses the importance of involving a company's board of directors in these vital questions. "When you're looking into applying for grants, especially for the first time, make sure that you have an organizational plan and that there is board involvement," she stresses. "[The board] should understand that this is the path you want to take. They should be aware of the company's direction. After all, you put yourself under greater scrutiny when you apply for grants."

It all comes down to the theatre's mission. The board (if one exists) should be clear on this. And funders, especially, want to know who you are and where you plan to be even 10 years from now. Think about the big picture.

After a good bout of brainstorming, it's time to get your hands on some leads. A great place to start is the Donors Forum. Along with hosting workshops and publishing some pretty helpful publications, the Forum boasts the Midwest's largest collection of resources on philanthropy, nonprofit management and fundraising. Its library is open to the public, and staffers offer free weekly training on how to get the most out of its materials.

Most people find the Forum's searchable databases of foundations to be beneficial. Be aware, though, that while the Forum offers computer use free of charge, many databases can be accessed by subscription only (which comes at a small price, in most cases). You'll want to take some time to analyze all options. "Make sure the foundation fits your program area and even your geographical area," says Kemmis. "Then write your own prospect list, but keep it at a manageable number...don't overload yourself."

Kemmis recommends narrowing your selection to between 12 and 15 potential funders. These "finalists" should be asked to send you their guidelines. Kemmis cautions against starting any paperwork until you have a full understanding of all stipulations and deadlines. This may mean placing a phone call to the foundations and, in some cases, getting hooked up with a program officer who can work with you through the entire application process. "That way you're not applying to a faceless organization. There's been contact before," she asserts.

Step Two: Writing the Grant

So, you've got contacts and are ready to start writing. Daunting? Sure. Worth it? Definitely. Again, different foundations look for different things, so it's important to read through individual guidelines carefully and be realistic about your chances. Jason Heeney of the Kaplan Foundation admits that out of the 120-some arts organization funding requests he receives each year, Kaplan is able to fulfill about one half of them.

"It is a pretty bulky process," he says. "We look for a cover letter, proposal narrative (a description of activities and programs), a mission statement, budgets, other fundraising commitments, a list of potential supporters, an audit, a list of the board of directors and a summary of contributions."

The most critical thing to remember, Heeney notes, is to be honest. "We're equally compelled by an organization that has struggled to survive than one that has had huge success," he says. Brevity, too, is important. And when it comes to compiling information, what is more "no-no" than "gotta-do" is adding elaborate touches for extra oomph. "We don't like videos," he says. "No fancy binders, and proposals don't have to be hand-delivered."

Laura Samson, program officer for the WPWR Channel 50 Foundation, agrees that a true understanding of a company's goals is more important than the way things are packaged. "Chicago has an endless supply of new, small companies, and that's one of the strengths of our community," she says. "But with all these theatres, we need to realize what sets company 'A' apart from company 'F.' I need to feel what your niche is."

If an application manages to distinguish itself—and if it falls within a foundation's guidelines—then you can bank on funding officers giving it a good read. "We give the proposals due diligence," says Heeney. "We try to be respectful of the grant-making process, and we might get out to them…initiate a site visit."

These "site visits" are common practices among funders. Some pre-planned visits may entail an officer stopping by your office to check out the administrative side of things. It also could mean an unannounced drop-by. Be aware that a potential funder could be filling one of the audience seats during any performance. Many funders, the Kaplan Foundation included, want to experience the spirit of the organization first-hand.

To that end, foundations often expect that somebody very embedded in the company's artistic coil—somebody with first-hand, intimate experience with the theatre—will be the one writing the grant. "I'd tend to not get a professional…a third party…to do it. There are things that they just won't be able to tell us, like theatre-earned income or amount of income from ticket sales," says Hope Cooper, an arts officer for the Kaplan Foundation. "Get someone from within the organization. They are the heartbeat. They know what's going on."

Yet even while an inner view is vital to the success of the application, it's always a good idea to let an outside pair of eyes scan through everything before it's submitted. Even the best of writers need editors, and a bit of proofreading for simple grammar and spelling mistakes may be the difference between a grant given and a grant denied.

Step Three: Submitting the Proposal (a.k.a. "The Waiting Game")

Once your proposal package is completely finished and the time is right, send it certified mail (unless specified otherwise by the granting organization). You're obviously going to be spending a lot of time on this, and you wouldn't want all your efforts to be wasted just because the postal service went awry.

Now the wait begins—and it can get long. Thankfully, that's because funders are probably making every effort to give your application ample consideration. Take this time to relax—without becoming completely idle, that is. While you don't have to busy yourself with constantly calling to check the status of your application, there are some quick and thoughtful things you can do to stay on a potential funder's mind. "Put foundations on your mailing list," Cooper recommends, noting that keeping funders informed leaves them with a favorable impression of the theatre.

Step Four: And the Answer Is…

There is bound to be good news. And, unfortunately, there is bound to be bad news. If all goes well, though, you may just end up with that much needed cash flow every director, ensemble member and technician has been dreaming of. It's not uncommon for a grant officer to call you personally if the grant is given. This, without a doubt, is definitely a reason to break out the bubbly for a theatre company party. But remember to remain strategic—even in the face of success. Write an immediate thank you note (you'd be surprised at how few grant writers actually do this) and read through your responsibilities to the funder at length. There will be audits to prepare, receipts to file and a lot of record keeping in store.

In most cases, a program officer will be there to assist you in the reporting process. Contact with this "mentor" varies depending on the foundation, and there are things you can do to maintain a good relationship with officers in the interim.

"What matters to me is direct, straightforward communication," says Samson. "Make sure I know about what's going on. E-mailing reviews is a relatively easy way to keep people informed." Samson also notes that inviting a grant officer to an opening night performance is another way to open up the lines of communication. "It's those personal experiences that matter," she says.

And what if a grant is not given? You may not have the money, but you do have an excellent opportunity to get some helpful feedback about your application. It's wise to write to the foundation and ask for comments. Program officers are usually happy to comply. Chances are, there are steps you can take to make an application stand out more in the future. "Persistence has its benefits," says Samson. "If I can watch [a company's] development through time, I'll have a better idea of what they're all about."

Luckily, new grant opportunities are cropping up all the time. One "no" is not an end to the application process. Look at it as just one more step to reaching a final goal. Revise, reevaluate and really pay attention to the kind of foundations that you're reaching out to. Chances are, they will reach back—check in hand—sooner than you realize.

By Julie Franz Peeler

There's nothing more exciting than striking out on your own and building your own theatre company. It's tempting to think that if we throw all of our efforts into what goes on the stage, people will magically recognize superiority and show up in droves. But, like any small business, there are thousands of details to tend to outside of artistic excellence that can make or break your business, especially when it comes to attracting, and keeping, audiences.

Much of that has to do with thinking longer term than the next show. It's hard when you're starting, since you're literally financing things from show to show, so this article will focus on things that hopefully are easy and inexpensive, but will help set the stage for long term success.

There are as many wrong definitions of marketing as there are stars in the sky. Marketing is not just promotions, and it's not sales. It's not posters or a good review or a direct mail piece. It's developing a deep understanding of your customer and how they relate to your artistic product. It's customer-focused, and it includes thinking through issues regarding product, price, place and promotion. It's understanding the relationship between your artistic product and the customer. Here are five basic audience development issues to think through as you consider starting your own theatre company.

First, make absolutely sure you're theatre company really is unique. Chicago is full of actors and theatre companies. To Joe Consumer perusing the Chicago Tribune Friday Arts Section in search of something to do, you're just one of hundreds of arts listings. People buy on uniqueness and trust. You can communicate uniqueness in your marketing materials; you build trust with artistic excellence.

In making sure you're really unique, ask yourself why you couldn't have just joined another theatre company. Why, artistically, did you have to strike out on your own? What do you do that no other theatre company does? And answer the question as if you're explaining it to your mom and her friends. (Most ticket buyers and arts decision-makers are women.) In other words, use consumer language, or language the common person can understand.

"Ensemble theatre" is one of my favorite phrases since no one but us theatre professionals has any understanding of what it means; it only describes how you're organized, and it's a fact, not a consumer benefit. Tell your mom how and why what she sees on the stage will be different from something out there already. Focus your communications pieces—posters and fliers—on benefits, not just facts. It's a fact that you're presenting a certain play on a certain night at a certain time and location. But how will that benefit the customer? Most consumers are unfamiliar with the standard repertory. Tell them what the show is about. Is it a comedy, drama, mystery or musical? Which specific emotions will it stir?

Second, now that you can describe your uniqueness, spend money to have a logo designed by a professional. Having a single, distinct visual image is paramount in the consumer's ability to recognize you in an instant. And it stays with you forever. With a few minor revisions and updates, the Hubbard Street Dance Chicago logo hasn't changed dramatically since their inception. Neither has Steppenwolf's or Victory Gardens'.

Once you've got a logo, put it on everything, including signage. So many arts organizations slap together their space without developing signage to help patrons find it. We call that the "we're hiding" theory of arts management. There's a theatre company in Cincinnati that moved, but didn't put a map on its season brochure. I guess they were trying to ditch their subscribers! On the other hand, Brooklyn Children's' Museum is several blocks from the train station. They got a grant to put street banners all along the way from the station to the museum. Can't miss 'em now.

Third, budget for marketing and promotions. Again, it's tempting to put all your money and effort into the artistic product, then leave nothing for promotion. It's like throwing the most elaborate birthday party in the world, but forgetting to budget for invitations. Typically, when first starting out, you'll need about 25 percent of your budget devoted to audience development.

Fourth, take advantage of free promotional opportunities. This means developing a strong press relations program, and habitually updating newspaper and Web site entertainment listings.

Deborah Popely of Deborah Popely & Company in Des Plaines touts the following as the "Seven Secrets of Highly Successful Publicists:

- Have a smart media strategy that targets publications that reach your audience, includes a unique story angle, looks beyond the usual media, and puts you at the right place at the right time.
- Pitch a creative story angle, not just the fact that you're mounting a new production.
- Provide a well-written presentation of that creative story.
- Provide strong visuals to help make the story come alive.
- Be fearless and persistent in pitching story ideas.
- Have a well-researched, up-to-date media list.
- Have a service orientation toward the media (you're solving their need for fresh ideas, they're not solving your need for publicity).

And, don't overlook free listings. The TRIBUNE and SUN-TIMES are great, but focus too on your neighborhood newspaper, and newsletters from neighborhood organizations like Neighbors Associations and religious organizations. Most of your initial audience will come from a 5-10 minute walk or drive. Make the time to consistently send updates listings to the state tourism and city tourism Web sites. They're seen by millions during the year, many of whom are locals.

Fifth, and finally, get the name, address and phone number of every audience member. It's easier and less expensive to retain a current customer than to get a new one. Why start at ground zero for each show when you can, for less time and effort, invite past audience members, then build a larger audience from there? Use personal letters, newsletters, press releases, etc. to keep your audience informed. Treat them like one of the family, since your most loyal audiences will actually believe they "belong" to your theatre. Hold special receptions or "meet the director" nights to break down the fourth wall and help them become more intimately involved with you and your group.

Time and again, The Arts Marketing Center works with arts groups to help develop new audiences. More times than not, we end up having to go back and "fix" these five areas of marketing and audience development. But if you're contemplating founding your own company, now is the time to get it right from the start.

PR/Marketing

Carol Fox & Associates
1412 W. Belmont
Chicago, IL 60657
773/327-3830
773/327-3834 - fax

GSA Advertising
211 E. Ontario #1750
Chicago, IL 60611
312/664-1999
312/664-9017 - fax

Jay Kelly
Off Loop Marketing
2254 W. Grand
Chicago, IL 60612
312/633-1992
312/633-1994 - fax

K.D.-P.R.
K.D. Kweskin
2732 N. Clark
Chicago, IL 60614
773/248-7680
773/883-1323 - fax

Margie Korshak, Inc.
875 N. Michigan #2750
Chicago, IL 60611
312/751-2121 • 312/751-1422 - fax

MMPR
Michelle Madden
1636 W. Summerdale #1
Chicago, IL 60640
773/784-8347
773/784-8599 - fax

PitBull PR
Don Hall
3210 N. Halsted - 3rd. Floor
Chicago, IL 60657
773/755-1693
igotgwat@aol.com

PitBull PR offers the small theatre owner:

-Press Releases and Follow-up

-Graphics Design for posters, postcards and ads

-Web Design and Web Banners

-Flexible Pricing

Running a Theatre

He hath honored me of late, and I have bought
Golden opinions from all sorts of people,
Which would be worn now in their newest gloss,
Not cast aside so soon.

By Susan Hubbard

According to companies who can attribute great success to an active board as well as experts at Chicago's Arts and Business Council, theatre companies must already have key elements in place before they can even begin contemplating recruiting a board. Your company must ask and internally agree upon a number of apparently simple but critical questions:

1. Who are you? What defines you as a theatre company? In marketing terms, this is known as your "brand" identity. It must be clarified for a potential board member before they can decide whether your company is the right cause for them. Can you say who you are in no more than a couple of well-turned phrases?

2. What is your mission? Why do you exist? A potential board member must feel that their most passionately held values are embodied and upheld by your organization.

3. Who do you serve? This is your audience, otherwise known as your constituency. You must know three key things about them: Who are they, what do they need, and how is your company uniquely positioned to serve them?

4. What is your vision for the future? Do you know where you want to

be as a company in five years? In ten?

5. What is missing to get you where you want to be? What people, resources, space and equipment do you need? A potential board member will need to know in order to gain a clear picture of what their role is to be in your success.

6. What is your articulated battle plan for filling in those gaps? Part of a board member's responsibility is to oversee and scrutinize your plan.

7. Finally, who are the people who can help you fill the gaps and carry out the plan?

If you can answer these questions, you can begin to think about recruiting your board.

Chiefly, you need a board to help govern your company and support it financially. According Matt O'Brien, producing director of Irish Repertory of Chicago, "When you get to the point where you are looking at your work as a long-term business to make a living from, you have to ask how can we as a theatre develop our product to become an asset to the Chicago community?"

That, says O'Brien, takes a highly developed and articulated idea of what your company can uniquely contribute to Chicago theatre. And it takes money.

"I don't have the connections," says Melissa Vickery-Bareford, managing director of Lifeline Theatre. "I don't know the more affluent theatre-goers, or have the influence to get the kinds of sponsorships, or the expertise in physical structures, accounting or marketing that our board members possess."

Lifeline's board most recently led a campaign that raised over $100,000 to renovate their theatre space in Rogers Park. But the board's commitment to the company was there from the very beginning in 1983. "One of the first things our early board did," says Vickery-Bareford, "was take it upon themselves to raise funds to hire key people full-time. It has been a big plus to have the board take on the responsibility for specific types of expertise. It frees us to focus on the work, on the programming, and where we are going artistically."

"If you want to go the not-for-profit route," says Ken DeWyn, director of development for Chicago Shakespeare Theatre, "a board is essential."

The board, says DeWyn, is the primary fundraising group in your organization. "Most people don't realize that in a capital campaign, 90 percent of your campaign goal comes from 5-10 percent of your giving base. This is one of the reasons why boards are increasingly important. It is your board that drives your major gift work. Their contacts provide your company access to the top 10 percent of the wealth population in your region. As an organization, you have to be willing to expend the resources and the personnel to support their efforts."

The general rule is that board members must have a passion for the organization they serve and can either give resources, get resources, or both. "You may have heard of the three W's every organization wants and needs on its board," says DeWyn. "They are wealth, work, or wisdom."

At Chicago Shakespeare Theatre, 70 percent of contributions to their current campaign are coming from the board and board networking and fully half of that contribution comes directly from the 36 member board itself. "This kind of success entails responsibility," says DeWyn. "As your board grows, you have to be sure you have the staff and the resources to effectively work with these dedicated volunteers."

According to Michelle Cohen, the On Board program director at the Arts and Business Council, when you are considering board recruiting, look first at who currently is part of your organization. This includes your audience, your ensemble members, your volunteers and any "friends" of the organization. "My strategy would be to tell smaller companies to tap into their audiences more," says Cohen. "Sometimes organizations have as their mission serving specific populations, yet there is no one inside the organization representing that population. But those are the very people who know about the needs of that population, who can speak to and improve the programs you're doing."

DeWyn confirms her strategy. "Look within your own ranks for that start-up leadership. Who currently volunteers for you, is involved and interested, who has the passion and the ability to contribute to the organization? Initially, it is friends and family. Some of those earliest board members can become your longest-term board members because of their sense of ownership. And as time goes on, those supporters often increase their capacity to contribute many times over."

To begin then, you need a handful of people with the experience, means or interest to contribute to your company and who are willing to identify and cultivate others who can be brought into your company's community.

Case Study: Irish Repertory of Chicago

Matt O'Brien formed Irish Repertory of Chicago, an out growth of Splinter Theatre Group, in 1998. "After awhile, it's no fun to produce on a small scale," he says of Splinter's inability to cultivate a large and consistent audience base. "Because no one will come to see what you produce on a small scale." Splinter Group needed to define their audience, and to do that they needed to bring their own identity as a company into focus. "We were drawn to Irish and Irish-American writers. We were in love with the language, and we were interested in doing work that showcased designers, writers and directors, as well as actors. We believed that our interest would be matched in Chicago by interest in Irish and Irish-American cultural life." The group looked for "a specific project as a benchmark for what we would become," says O'Brien. They found it in Marina Carr's award-winning play, The Mai, which had never been produced here.

The company took two years to plan and develop the project that would define their new identity. Meanwhile, they expanded their audience reach. They had an exhibit at each Irish-American Heritage Center event and created a Web site with the kind of links that if you type in "Irish" and "Chicago," Irish Repertory Chicago is the first link that comes up. They also bought mailing lists specifically composed of Irish-origin names.

"Half the deal is to get yourself and your company name out there in such a way that you have that instant recognition," says O'Neill. "The point is to get people familiar with your product."

Finding the board resources to make the show happen began as a grass-roots effort. "Once we knew who we were, it was about finding the connections out there and then laying into it," says O'Brien. "Our people networked. They would go out and find new people, and those people would find new people. As potential board members, we looked to approach people who were already involved in charitable work and who had a connection to what we were doing. Then we had the bright idea to call up Lois Weisberg at the Chicago Cultural Center and tell her about what we were doing, and she said, 'I'll call Maggie.'" And Mrs. Maggie Daley became the honorary chair of Irish Rep's Founders Committee, a board devoted strictly to fundraising. "It took us seven years of mucking it up to figure it out," says O'Brien.

Irish Rep's success had to do first with defining themselves as a company and then defining their mission and their audience. O'Brien notes that in smaller, younger theatre companies often the whole mission is really about individual expression rather than long-term community development. "I've been in Chicago theatre for 20 years and seen literally 300 companies come and go. They last three to four years and maybe they've done what they've set out to do, which is to get their people on the stage and further their careers. But if you want to be around for the long term, you need to develop a community."

Irish Rep's inaugural season opened in May 2000 and has consistently played to 85 percent capacity, garnering rave reviews and thousands of subscribers. "For seven years before, Splinter group never got any "marquee" board members who could help take us where we needed to go to make an impact on the community. Like other groups, we were a bunch of artists in our early 30s whose primary identity was as designers and directors. We had to reshape to become Irish Rep. "

Due to its success, Irish Rep's board will have to grow to meet the needs of the company's expanding future. By the end of spring 2002, the company's annual budget will have grown from 80-90K pre-'98 to 650-750K. One third to one half of this budget will have to be brought in from outside revenue.

Identity and Mission: Lifeline Theatre

"Lifeline's KidSeries was founded very early on—in 1986—well before other theatres embraced the concept," says Vickery-Bareford. The focus on kids and family has helped to define Lifeline. Child-friendly programming spills over into the mainstage with one show a year having a strong child element that also appeals to adults.

"A lot of our board members got involved specifically because of this focus," says Vickery-Bareford. "And we have kids who started with our KidSeries, continued through our mainstage Kids and Family program, and who now regularly attend our mainstage productions." Conversely, parents of kids who attended KidSeries have become mainstage regulars. With KidSeries and its related programming, Lifeline fulfilled an audience need, defined what they were about as a theatre, and established audiences from whom they could draw their board.

Now, Lifeline is reaching out to the 70,000 people who live near them in Rogers Park. They've hosted neighborhood organizations and businesses at special events and are planning to launch a specially priced subscription next year for people living in their zip code area.

"Our board and our staff really work together," says Vickery-Bareford.

"We have a new business plan that we created last year with the help of the BVA (Business Volunteers for the Arts), a program out of the Chicago Arts and Business Council. It cost us $25 to apply and get a volunteer. I strongly recommend that theatre groups tap into this terrific resource."

With the help of the BVA volunteer, Lifeline has been focusing on where they want to be in five years and planning both financially and artistically. "The simple fact of just planning our season two years in advance has added so much stability," says Vickery-Bareford. We are able to plan programs, plan the marketing. As an organization, we're looking forward more than ever before."

Lifeline's current board members came from their audience. Part of their responsibility is to bring new membership into the Lifeline community. "We have Board Nights, where we can all meet each other, three to four times a year. If the new folks show interest, we ask them to join a committee. A benefit committee is really ideal. That way, there is a specific event with a specific end that they can help with to see how we all fit. We've gotten away from just asking people right away to join the board. We like to say we're trying to date people before we marry them!"

Finding the Right Fit

The dating/marriage analogy in relation to board recruiting is echoed Cohen. "We like to help organizations understand the special role of the board by saying that the difference between being a volunteer for an organization and being on its board is the like the difference between dating and a marriage. It has to do with the level of commitment. Being on the board entails a bigger time commitment, it entails a financial commitment, and there is a legal side in a board member's role. There's accountability there that isn't on a volunteer level. If volunteering is like dating, recruiting a board member is a lot like hiring an employee or preparing for a marriage."

Cultivating a board member should be a kind of courtship—gradually bringing them in and getting them excited about what your company is doing. But the prospective board member's own values and passions will be the defining factors in their decision to join your board. Also important are size and structure of the organization and its organizational culture. How do the people inside your company relate? Are they businesslike or casual, democratic, or charged by a fiery core of leaders? Does your company thrive on new ideas? or does it like to take its time mulling them over? If the latter, and you're recruiting a board member who likes to hit the ground running, that recruit will probably wind up feeling frustrated and undervalued.

A Chicago success story, Chicago Shakespeare Theatre (CST), was operating out of a one-bedroom apartment on Broadway 11 years ago. Today it has a new seven-story home on Navy Pier with a 525-seat theatre. An estimated 120,000 people attended the 2000-2001 season and their annual budget grew from three million to eight million in just two and a half years. The company couldn't have gotten there without their board.

"What you've done with your mission statement and your vision and your plan is created a prospectus for your own success," says DeWyn. "Anybody can put on a play. How have you defined your mission? Is it outreach to the community, educational, supportive of new work or of local artists? A clearly defined mission is necessary to make you distinctive in the Chicago theatre scene."

Nearly 20 years ago when CST began, no major theatre in Chicago was devoted to a continuing exploration of the Shakespeare canon. Barbara Gaines, CST's founder and artistic director, started a workshop among her friends devoted to the art of performing Shakespeare. They put on their first performance of Henry V upstairs in a bar. But they invited key individuals from the community and from that first audience were drawn the first board members, some of whom are still with the company today.

"All of this was possible because Barbara[Gaines] had a big vision," says DeWyn. "She had a mission of Shakespeare for Chicago. Somehow Shakespeare had to get around the misrepresentation people had of him, be released from the ivory tower and plunked back into the public square where he belonged. This was an idea people could rally around. Theatre companies should strive to brand what it is you're going to do and be."

Communicating that to your prospective board members is important. There has to be clarity about what you are and how potential board members fit in as well as enough flexibility to optimize the different strengths that they bring.

"Identifying your brand comes back to the idea of serving an audience," says DeWyn. "It really gets to the heart of philanthropy to ask what it is you're doing and for whom. When you can define it and communicate it to your potential board members, you help inspire the passion and the loyalty that comes from engaging their highest values. We like to say that Chicago Shakespeare is there above all to make Shakespeare accessible. That's why the new location at Navy Pier fits in with our mission so well. With such a location, we're able to serve a very broad demographic. Shakespeare used to perform among the populace. He would approve of what we're doing."

Susan Hubbard developed and managed the Managing Institutional Advancement program at the University of Chicago's Graham School.

He hath honored me of late, and I have bought
Golden opinions from all sorts of people,
Which would be worn now in their newest gloss,
Not cast aside so soon.

By Carrie L. Kaufman

The **Joseph Jefferson Awards,** or Jeffs as they're commonly called, originated in 1967 when four actors got together to honor the best and brightest actors in Chicago. Six awards from seven theatres were given out at the first ceremony in 1968. Thirty-three years later, the Jeffs are split into three different sections, which give out almost 100 awards a year.

Equity Awards

The Equity wing of the Joseph Jefferson Awards judges theatres that have contracts with Actors Equity Association.

Local Equity theatres are judged from August 1 to July 31, with an awards ceremony in late October or November. They are formally called the Joseph Jefferson Awards. What an Equity actor, director, etc. wins that night is a Jeff Award.

And they only win one. For a few years, the Jeff Committee tried giving multiple awards in each category, which is what they do for the non-Equity Citations. But a consultant the committee hired told them that the community overwhelmingly preferred to be singled out.

"At the end of the day, they still really thought the value of the award was more significant if it were for single winners," says current Jeff Committee chair Joan Kaloustian.

Some of those single winners can be from lower tier Equity theatres. Since Equity instituted its new tier system in the mid-90's, a CAT N theatre, which produced a show with only one Equity actor at a very low pay scale, can compete with a major LORT or CAT V theatre that has a budget in the millions and actually come out on top. This has done much to obliterate the distinctions between Equity and non-Equity theatre and also to showcase the remarkable work by people and theatre companies that are non-union—something that is unique to Chicago.

Non-Equity Citations

The Citations wing of the Joseph Jefferson Awards, instituted in 1973, is for non-Equity theatres. Citations are judged from April 1 to March 31, with a ceremony in early June. That ceremony is called the Joseph Jefferson Citations. The Jeff Committee is very careful to keep the word "award" away from non-Equity theatre. They structure the non-Equity ceremony to be non-competitive. There are "honorees," who may be called "winners," but there are absolutely no "losers." Of course, with the multiple recipients structure, there have been instances in which four out of the five people nominated have been "honored" with citations, leaving a very clear "loser."

Non-Resident Productions

About seven years ago, the Jeff Committee began giving awards for touring productions, such as *Show Boat, Ragtime* and *Aida.* Frankly, these awards have little credibility in the theatre community and are often looked upon—rightly or wrongly—as opportunities for the Jeff Committee to get free tickets to the hot post- or pre-Broadway shows.

That may be a bit unfair, and it may be more of a reflection on the gripers than the Committee. The Jeff Committee argues that they support the theatre community and that the bigger shows—especially when they take up long-term residence—are part of that community. That sentiment sticks in the craw of many small, struggling artists.

There's also the argument that many of these non-resident shows cast out of Chicago and a good deal of the actors may be local. In fact, some of the producers may be too. Shouldn't they be honored? Have they somehow given up their community status by taking or producing a big show?

Eligibility

The Jeff Committee rules for eligibility are Byzantine. Barely anyone in Chicago theatre outside the committee understands them, and I dare say there are some people on the committee who would have trouble reciting every single rule. But if you work through the complexities, a remarkably fair, and strangely beautiful, system emerges.

There are two sets of rules. One qualifies theatres and shows to be judged. The other details exactly how a show is recommended—or not.

Qualification

For an **Equity** show to be **Jeff eligible,** it must be produced at a theatre within a 30 mile radius of the corner of State and Madison and in the state of Illinois. Some theatres outside of 30 miles, such as Marriott Theatre in Lincolnshire, were Jeff eligible before this rule was in place and have been grandfathered in. There is no waiting period for a new Equity theatre to begin being judged.

For **non-Equity** theatres, the rules are a bit more stringent. You just can't do the Judy and Mickey thing in a storefront somewhere and expect the Jeff Committee to come. The producing non-Equity theatre must have been in existence for at least two years and have produced at least four productions during those two years, with at least two productions in the preceding year. To keep their eligibility, they have to keep producing at least two Jeff-eligible shows a year (see below). And non-Equity theatres have to be in the city of Chicago, unless grandfathered in. (Circle Theatre in Forest Park was grandfathered in about 10 years ago when the rules changed.) So if you start a new theatre company in your hometown of Naperville (which wouldn't be a bad idea, considering there would be little competition and vast audiences), you can't be Jeff eligible. Likewise, if you start a theatre company here and gain a great reputation and maybe even win some Jeffs and you decide to move it to Naperville, you will lose your Jeff eligibility.

For an individual production to be Jeff eligible, it must have a minimum of 18 performances. In addition, it must have at least two consecutive weekend performances, with at least one weekend night performance per week available to Jeff members.

The Jeff Committee does not judge children's theatre, nor does it judge performance art. Late night shows—which are quite standard in Chicago—are also not eligible. Curtain for an eligible show must be no later than 9:30 p.m. This is not because the Jeff Committee does not like these things (many of them go to ineligible shows just for fun); it's that they have to draw the line somewhere.

For judges to come to a theatre's opening night (or opening weekend) performance, the theatre must put in its request a minimum of three weeks before opening night or the 25th of the preceding month. They would prefer you get them in before the 25th, when the assignments are made. All requests must be in writing.

If the theatre is doing a co-production with another theatre, both theatres must be Jeff eligible. It doesn't matter how long the first theatre has been in existence—or how many Jeff Citations or Awards it has won in the past—if it hooks up with a brand new theatre company, the Jeff Committee won't come.

These rules were instituted as a sort of filter. While there is much good theatre in Chicago, there is a lot of bad theatre here too and, frankly, the Jeff members don't want to waste their time. They figure that if a company has been able to attract audiences and stay afloat for two years, it must be doing some good stuff. Similarly, they feel that if a company is willing to take the risk of putting up an Equity bond and pay its actors, they probably aren't fly-by-night.

Of course, this means that some really good theatre can't be nominated for a Jeff. But it doesn't mean a new theatre isn't on the Jeff's radar screen. Many members show up to good shows by new theatre companies that aren't yet Jeff eligible.

Nominating Process

Over the last few years, some theatres (namely Goodman, Steppenwolf, Marriott's Lincolnshire and Victory Gardens) haven't been happy with the Jeff voting procedures. Too often, they said, good shows or good performances or good design elements would slip through the cracks. So after a couple of years of studies and negotiations, the Jeff Committee and the theatres—represented by the League of Chicago Theatres—came up with a system to include theatre professionals in the judging system. The Advanced Technical (AT) Team adds two theatre professionals to the opening night judges. That's all. It does not add any judges after opening night. Since the AT Team has come on board, more elements that might have slipped through the cracks have been caught, but there are still cracks. And some theatres have still been slighted.

New AT Team Rules

Under the new rules, seven judges, not five, are sent out for opening night. Five of them are Jeff Committee members, chosen are random just like before. The other two—the AT Team members—are theatre professionals who are not members of the Jeff Committee. They are chosen at random by the League. No one AT Team member can judge more than five Equity and five non-Equity shows a year, which ensures broad participation from theatre professionals. Those seven judges must call in their votes by 9 a.m. the next day, after which the theatre is notified as to whether or not it is recommended.

For an Equity show to be recommended under the new rules, five of the seven judges have to vote positively. After that, there must be four or more votes for one single element (like direction) and three or more votes for another single element (like lead actor).

"That's ratcheting up the requirement from what it was," says Kaloustian. "That was part of the goal, to make sure the term 'Jeff Recommended' carried a little more weight."

There are a couple of exceptions to this rule. One is if the show has three or fewer people in the cast. In that case, the criteria is that one single element of the production has to receive four or more votes. They wave the second, three-vote standard.

The other exception is when at least 20 positive votes for anything are cast by five of the seven judges. So if a show got 21 positive votes, but no one element got four positive votes, it still gets recommended—but only if five of the seven judges cast those positive votes. If four judges make those 21 positive assessments, the show is still not recommended.

For non-Equity theatres, the criteria are a bit more relaxed. Five out of seven judges have to vote positively, but a show only needs four votes for a single element to be nominated. The three votes for another single element are not necessary for non-Equity shows. A non-Equity show can also be nominated if the production gets a total of 15 votes from at least five judges.

"It's more difficult for folks with teeny, teeny budgets to get technical nominations," says Kaloustian. "When you're spending $3.12 to build a set, your expectations are that it's not going to look like the Goodman."

Once the show is recommended for Equity or non-Equity, the rest of the Jeff Committee is informed and must see the show within 60 days of opening night. They are not told which categories were the ones that garnered the positive votes. They fax, e-mail or mail in their votes in each category after they've seen each show. Those votes are tabulated. The recipients of the most votes in each category are put onto a final ballot, which is sent out to each of the members at the end of the August 31 (for Equity) or March 31 (for non-Equity) judging season. Those final ballots are the nominations for each category.

After those award and citation nominations are made, the committee sends in those final ballots for the winners or recipients. The results of that vote are announced at either the November Awards or the June Citations.

Structure

The Jeff Committee is made up of 45 people dedicated to the theatre industry in Chicago. Quite simply, they love theatre. They see upwards of 125 shows a year and in the busy seasons—around September/October and February/March—they see around six shows a week. Many even see two shows a day on weekends when it's busy.

"This is a labor of love for people. You've got to love it if you're doing it for 125 nights a year with no compensation," says Kaloustian.

As with any awards, there are people who don't like the Jeffs or who discount them. Funny though, Jeff Awards and Citations always seem to show up on people's resumés and in ads for shows or theatres. Over the years, the committee has been criticized for not being made up of theatre professionals, but truly how many working theatre professionals have time to see other people's work six nights a week?

Currently, over half the Jeff Committee is or has been involved in theatre professionally. Some are teachers, some are actors and playwrights. A couple of critics are on the committee. And there are a good many producers, some still active. Some committee members, says Kaloustian, still have their Equity cards.

Jeff Committee members get a single comp for non-Equity shows and two comps for Equity shows. Frequently, says Kaloustian, members will just use the one comp no matter what the show. Spouses tend to get a bit theatre weary, and the Jeff Committee members tend to go see theatre with each other. But, she adds, they don't talk about the show amongst themselves. I've even tried to engage Jeff Committee members at intermission in conversations about the show and have gotten a nod and a vague answer at best. Wish I could say the same for some groups of critics I've seen at intermission.

The Jeff Committee, no matter what their formal training, is always trying to learn more about theatre and the crafts that come together to make a show. Each meeting they have a speaker or program designed to help them learn more about stage crafts. Designers have taught them about the elements that are not supposed to be noticed. They have talked with directors and dramaturgs. And one cannot discount the point that no matter what one knows about theatre before joining the committee, they learn a hell of a lot after seeing 125—often mediocre—shows. I wonder if many theatre artists have that kind of education.

To contact the Jeff Committee, call 773/388-0073.

Chapter 10

Living

The Journeymen, "Lillies"

By Susan Hubbard

Actors know that keeping their minds and bodies fit is just as important as taking a class in improv, scene study or on-camera work. But many actors believe they've found further secret ingredients to artistic success.

Yoga

"Anything that gets you focused and 'in the flow' is good for acting," says Gretchen Sonstroem, an actress and a yoga instructor at Act One. "The spiritual aspect of yoga, the meditation, really enhances relaxation and is vital to creativity. So much of creativity has to come from a place that accepts who we are in the moment and where we are in the moment. That's what meditation is all about."

Sonstroem began practicing yoga only casually. Then she got a role in *Deermaster* at Writer's Theatre in Glencoe. Based on the Flaubert-Georges Sand correspondence, *Deermaster* requires the two-person cast to perform uninterrupted for an hour and 45 minutes. "Yoga turned out to be the key," says Sonstroem. "I started noticing that on the days I did yoga, the physical stamina was there, and the breath to talk that much and keep the throat relaxed. But even more, on those days I was more emotionally connected to the role and to the audience."

The reasons? Theory holds that the practice of yoga activates the body's sources of spiritual and physical energy, called chakras. The entire nervous system is organized around seven chakras. "The tradition is that as you work with yoga and become more subtle, your energy starts to move up the chakras to the sixth or penultimate chakra, near the eyes," says Sonstroem. "It is believed that when this chakra is activated, that's when you get the master artists."

There are many forms of yoga. Experienced practitioners often advance to Ashtanga, a physically demanding form that builds power, strength and flexibility. Practicing celebrities include Gwyneth Paltrow, Madonna and Sting. Sonstroem introduces aspects of Ashtanga in her class.

Yet controlled breathing, the breathing that comes with meditation, is considered the most subtle form of control. "People think it's the easiest but it's actually the highest level. The physical stuff is just preparation for meditation based on breath," says Sonstroem. It's okay if students never reach these higher levels. She adds, "In yoga, as in acting, you go from where you are and from there you naturally, organically grow. That's what I love about it."

In Yoga for Actors, students learn basic poses, breathing exercises, and meditation. "I introduce ideas about achieving a state of being that helps creativity," says Sonstroem. "After that, it's really up to the individual to apply them outside of class for rehearsal or in a performance. I find that actors in particular are very open to the more spiritual side."

Fitzmaurice

Jim Johnson, actor and former faculty member at DePaul's Theatre School, believes he's found his secret of creative success in Fitzmaurice. He is a certified Associate of Fitzmaurice Voicework. Based on yoga poses, Fitzmaurice uses physical stressing to induce and control emotional states.

The main element of Fitzmaurice, adapted from bioenergetics, is tremoring. "The practitioner puts a part of their body in flexion—the hand, the foot or the heel, for example," says Johnson. The pose causes the body to shake in a way that most of us experience only under extreme trauma. "After a car wreck, for example, you walk away shaking," he explains.

During tremoring, students often have very strong emotional responses and learn that the physical and emotional stresses correlate. As in Rolfing, the theory is that we hold emotional memories in different parts of our bodies. "In Fitzmaurice, most people have a position or two that are big triggers," says Johnson. Through training, practitioners gain control over flexing and the resulting emotions. "The psychological aspect is that you are getting used to being in an extreme emotional state," says Johnson. "Then the technique is to 'sound,' or 'sigh out sound' while tremoring. It gets sound more into the body, throughout the body." Practitioners learn to speak "with the whole body."

"They get used to expressing with their voice what they're experiencing in an extreme emotional state," says Johnson. "That's invaluable for the actor."

Students can begin to practice Fitzmaurice after a single one-on-one session. Over a longer period, benefits increase as students destructure old habits and restructure new, more effective ones.

Feldenkrais

Bill Burnett, actor-director and assistant professor of Voice and Speech at DePaul, also works with a technique linking body and emotions. Burnett is a certified practitioner of the Feldenkrais Method. He describes it as "the one regularly ongoing transformative practice I've found. It keeps giving me new possibilities.

"It's very beneficial for the actor since it deals with the whole instrument, and the actor is his or her instrument. If you become more fully acquainted with your instrument and its various possibilities, then you've got something you can work with."

The emphasis in Feldenkrais is on noticing how a movement is done, especially with awareness of how the skeleton is moving. "You see, for instance, if people are leading with parts of their body or if they are restricted in some way or have injuries," says Burnett. "Working with an individual over time, you begin to identify patterns of movement where some of them are efficient and some are not." A series of guided movements helps students, through their skeletons, gain awareness that ultimately affects the central nervous system.

"A lot of things break loose for people. Perceptually their senses become more alive. And they experience various kinds of emotional release," says Burnett. "It helps them become very aware of how they're moving to express what they mean to express."

Burnett recently directed *Anna Karenina* with student actors at DePaul. Throughout the process they worked extensively with Feldenkrais before rehearsals and some shows. Burnett is proud of the results. "What I saw on stage were actors more grounded and balanced in their person and with a quiet poise and authority," he says.

Famous practitioners of Feldenkrais include Peter Brook, Whoopi Goldberg and Mike Nichols.

Tai Chi

Dan Guidara, a founding member of the Mary-Arrchie Theatre Company, is an advocate of a centuries-old form of martial arts, Tai Chi Chuan. Guidara choreographed the company's Tai Chi segment at the end of the Jeff award-winning *Tracers* in 1997.

"Tai Chi movement involves the entirety of yourself," says Guidara.

"The goal is to achieve perfect balance of yin and yang and get to the original source, the chi or breath."

Tai Chi is reputed to free up energy, increase concentration, balance and endurance, and strengthen the immune system—important in the often stressful life of the actor.

Students begin with a series of slow, harmonious movements named after events or forces in nature. Grasping the Sparrow's Tail is a series of movements derived from a tale wherein a master, practicing in the garden, grasped a sparrow as it flew past. Holding it in his open hand, he prevented it from flying away not by force, but by anticipating and thwarting the sparrow's movements with his own. Embrace Tiger and Return to Mountain is another common movement used to conclude practice sessions.

"In Tai Chi, the style of movement is never from the periphery, but always from the center of the body or tan-tien," says Guidara. "This is the seat of chi, primal life energy, which can be understood as breath. You are to move like you're a river or like a snake, your whole body moving together." Tai Chi is also called the Small Nine Heavens in reference to the body's nine joints from the foot to the opposite wrist. As practitioners move, all nine joints should move together.

The style of movement increases blood flow to the body and enhances the ability of the nervous system to react faster. At a certain level of competency, says Guidara, it enables practitioners to feel their opponent's intention before they even move. "Tai chi is about accumulating your opponent's action and attacking his stillness," he says.

Actor Rob Johansen, who appeared in *The Action Against Sol Schumann* at Victory Gardens, did 10 minutes of Tai Chi before each performance. "No matter what the day's been, it brings me to a nice grounding and gets me ready to be open to the story I'm about to tell," he says.

Capoeira

Rather than focusing inward, actors might want to try something Plasticene member Sharon Gopfert finds "spiritually invigorating and communal." Capoeira (pronounced cap-we-ra) is "an African-Brazilian dance-performance art form," says Gopfert. "It was brought from Africa to Brazil by slaves who practiced it as a way to defend themselves against their masters. They made what was a form of physical fighting look like dance so they could practice it with impunity."

The origins of Capoeira are shrouded in legend. In Africa, youths tending animals were forbidden to practice it because it was believed it would steal their souls. In Cuba, a version is used to commune with spirits of the dead.

Practitioners of modern-day Capoeira call it "a celebration of life." Each game is improvised in a circle with players in the middle and everyone on the periphery egging them on or engaging in their own mock battles. While there is no actual physical contact, no blocks, each game is a kind of physical conversation with players anticipating and countering the movements of others. Players make use of trickery, fake-outs, and "major attitude" as they brilliantly deploy what would be deadly kicks if they were to find their mark.

Gopfert is part of Capoeira group Ginjarte, formed in 1991. She got involved two years ago and learned various classic steps and to play the required African-origin instruments.

"I wanted to put myself in a place of learning with something new and something I knew little about," she says. Some of the physical benefits are strength, endurance, quickness, and strategic response. But Gopfert stayed with it for other reasons. "It's a way of life. The way of the capoerista is very communal. It's about banding together and laughing in the face of adversity." Gopfert regularly socializes and spends hours practicing with her game partners, who come from very different backgrounds, countries and jobs.

"For women, it's really good. It's about putting up that confidence. Capoeira puts us in a physical place we're not used to being. You're constantly improvising, responding with your body. It makes you incredibly alert and sensitive to other people." Gopfert calls it "the perfect balance to hard work, rejection and low pay." In other words, the life of the actor.

Legal, Tax and Insurance

Accountants and Tax Preparers

American Express Tax and Business Services
Craig Minnick
30 S. Wacker #2600
Chicago, IL 60606
312/634-4318
312/207-2954 - fax

Bob Behr
Resumes by Mac
4738 N. LaPorte
Chicago, IL 60630
773/685-7721
773/283-9839 - fax

David P. Cudnowski, Ltd.
70 W. Madison #5330
Chicago, IL 60602
312/759-1040
312/759-1042 - fax
www.lawyers.com/talentlaw

David Turrentine, E.A. Income Tax Service
3907 N. Sacramento
Chicago, IL 60618
773/509-1798
773/509-1806 - fax

Gerald Bauman & Company
75 E. Wacker Drive #400
Chicago, IL 60601
312/726-6868
312/726-3683 - fax

H. Gregory Mermel
2835 N. Sheffield #311
Chicago, IL 60657
773/525-1778
773/525-3209 - fax

H&R Block
179 W. Washington
Chicago, IL 60602
312/424-0268 • 312/424-0278 - fax
www.hrblock.com

James P. Pepa, C.P.A.
651 Hinman Ave. #3S
Evanston, IL 60202
847/491-1414
847/491-0740 - fax

Jay-EMM Acct/Tax/Consulting
4835 Main St.
Skokie, IL 60077
847/679-8270

Joel N. Goldblatt, Ltd.
100 N. LaSalle #1910
Chicago, IL 60602
312/372-9322
312/372-2905 - fax

Katten, Muchin & Zavis
525 W. Monroe #1600
Chicago, IL 60661
312/902-5200
312/902-1061 - fax

Mangum, Smietanka & Johnson, L.L.C.
35 E. Wacker #2130
Chicago, IL 60601
312/368-8500

Weiner & Lahn, P.C.
900 Ridge Rd. #F
Munster, IN 46321
708/895-6400

Attorneys

Chicago Bar Association Lawyer Referral
321 S. Plymouth
Chicago, IL 60604-3997
312/554-2000
312/554-2054 - fax
www.chicagobar.org

Chicago Volunteer Legal Services
100 N. LaSalle #900
Chicago, IL 60602
312/332-1624

David P. Cudnowski, Ltd.
70 W. Madison #5330
Chicago, IL 60602
312/759-1040
312/759-1042 - fax
www.lawyers.com/talentlaw

Joel N. Goldblatt, Ltd.
100 N. LaSalle #1910
Chicago, IL 60602
312/372-9322
312/372-2905 - fax

Dale M. Golden
25 E. Washington #1400
Chicago, IL 60602
312/201-9730
312/236-6686 - fax
www.dalegoldenlaw.com

The Law Office of Dale M. Golden is a general law practice for the special legal needs of creative artists, entertainment professionals, and companies. It provides a full range of services to the entertainment industry, including negotiation and drafting of contracts, copyright and trademark licensing, business formation, and litigation.

Katten, Muchin & Zavis
525 W. Monroe #1600
Chicago, IL 60661
312/902-5200
312/902-1061 - fax

Fred Wellisch
1021 W. Adams #102
Chicago, IL 60607
312/829-2300
312/829-3729 - fax

Jay B. Ross & Associates P.C.
838 W. Grand #2W
Chicago, IL 60622-6565
312/633-9000
312/633-9090 - fax
www.jaybross.com

JoAnne Guillemette
311 S. Wacker Dr. #4550
Chicago, IL 60606
312/697-4788
312/697-4799 - fax

Lawyers for the Creative Arts
213 W. Institute #401
Chicago, IL 60610
312/944-2787 • 312/944-2195 - fax
www.cityofchicago.org/culturalaffairs/CulturalProgramming/Lawyers.html

---

Mangum, Smietanka & Johnson, L.L.C.
35 E. Wacker #2130
Chicago, IL 60601
312/368-8500

Peter J. Strand
McBride, Baker & Coles
500 W. Madison - 40th floor
Chicago, IL 60661-2511
312/715-5756

Pre-Paid Legal Services, Inc.
9242 W. National Ave.
West Ellis, WI 53227
414/329-3047

Timothy S. Kelley
Attorney at Law
55 E. Washington #1441
Chicago, IL 60602
312/641-3560

Tom Fezzey
600 W. Roosevelt Rd., Ste. B1
Wheaton, IL 60187
630/909-0909
630/839-1923 - fax
www.lawyers.com/fezzey

William Borah and Associates
IBM Plaza, Ste. 2905
330 N. Wabash
Chicago, IL 60611
708/799-0066

Insurance

Myers-Briggs and Company, Inc.
125 S. Wacker #1800
Chicago, IL 60606
312/263-3215
312/263-0979 - fax

Paczolt Financial Group
913 Hillgrove
La Grange, IL 60525
708/579-3128
708/579-0236 - fax
www.paczolt.com

Ronald Shapero Insurance Associates
Health Insurance Specialists
260 E. Chestnut #3406
Chicago, IL 60611
312/337-7133

Movie Theatres (Cool and cheap ones)

Davis Theatre
4614 N. Lincoln
Chicago, IL 60625
773/784-0893

Esquire Theater
58 E. Oak
Chicago, IL 60611
312/280-0101

Facets Multimedia
1517 W. Fullerton
Chicago, IL 60614
773/281-9075
773/929-5437 - fax
www.facets.org

Logan Theatre
2646 N. Milwaukee
Chicago, IL 60647
773/252-0627

Music Box
3733 N. Southport
Chicago, IL 60613
773/871-6604
www.musicboxtheatre.com

The Vic Theatre (Brew & View)
3145 N. Sheffield
Chicago, IL 60657
312/618-VIEW
www.victheatre.com

Three Penny Theatre
2424 N. Lincoln
Chicago, IL 60614
773/935-5744

Village North
6746 N. Sheridan
Chicago, IL 60626
773/764-9100
www.villagetheatres.com

Village Theater
1548 N. Clark
Chicago, IL 60622
312/642-2403

Health and Fitness

Acupuncture

Advance Center
Dr. Michael Luban
55 E. Washington #1310
Chicago, IL 60602
312/553-2020
312/553-5128 - fax

American Acupuncture Association
65 E. Wacker
Chicago, IL 60601
312/853-3732

Chicago Acupuncture Clinic
Dan Plovanich, Dipl. Ac.
3723 N. Southport
Chicago, IL 60613
773/871-0342
773/871-0348 - fax

Chiropractic Chicago
Dr. Ellisa J. Grossman
407 W. North
Chicago, IL 60610
312/255-9500

East Point Associates, Ltd.
Mary Rogel & Unsoo Kim
1525 E. 53rd #705
Chicago, IL 60615
773/955-9643
773/955-9953 - fax

Franklin D. Ing
2451 N. Lincoln
Chicago, IL 60614
773/525-2444
773/525-9989 - fax

Graham Chiropractic
Dr. Betty E. Graham
5344 N. Lincoln
Chicago, IL 60625
773/769-6666
773/334-1696 - fax

Progressive Chiropractic Rehabilitation & Wellness Center
2816 N. Sheffield
Chicago, IL 60657
773/525-WELL
773/525-9397 - fax
www.progressivechiro.net

Dr. Kevin Regan
Holistic Practitioner
55 E. Washington #1630
Chicago, IL 60602
312/578-1624
312/578-8717 - fax
www.doctorkev.com

Seaman Chiropractic Center
4941 W. Foster
Chicago, IL 60630
773/545-2233
773/545-8383 - fax

Dr. Briana S. Skarbek
513 Waukegan Rd.
Northbrook, IL 60062
847/509-0005

Ton Shen Health Inc.
2131 S. Archer Avenue, Suite B&C
Chicago, IL 60616
312/842-2775
312/842-1553 - fax

Wellspring Integrated Medecine
1565 Sherman Ave.
Evanston, IL 60201
847/733-9900
847/733-0105 - fax
www.mirocenter.org

AIDS Resources

Harambee Wellness Center
1515 E. 52nd - 2nd floor
Chicago, IL 60615
773/925-6877

Horizons Anti-Violence Hotline
773/871-2273

Horizons Community Service
Gay and Lesbian Hotline (6-10 pm)
773/929-4357

Howard Brown Health Center
4025 N. Sheridan
Chicago, IL 60613
773/388-1600

Stop AIDS
3651 N. Halsted
Chicago, IL 60613
773/871-3300
773/871-2528 - fax
www.howardbrown.org

Test Positive Aware Network
1258 W. Belmont
Chicago, IL 60657
773/404-8726
773/404-1040 - fax
www.tpan.com

Chiropractors

Advance Center
Dr. Michael Luban
55 E. Washington #1310
Chicago, IL 60602
312/553-2020
312/553-5128 - fax

Belmont Health Care
Lena Granlund
2110 W. Belmont
Chicago, IL 60618
773/404-0909

Chicago Chiropractic Center
30 S. Michigan #400
Chicago, IL 60603
312/726-1353
312/726-5238 - fax

Chicago Neck and Back Institute
5700 W. Fullerton #1
Chicago, IL 60639
773/237-8660
773/237-3159 - fax

Chiropractic Chicago
Dr. Ellisa J. Grossman
407 W. North
Chicago, IL 60610
312/255-9500

Chiropractic Health Care
Dr. Peter Georgiou
911 W. Belmont
Chicago, IL 60657
773/665-4400

Chislof Chiropractic Center
7448 N. Harlem
Chicago, IL 60631
773/763-0400

Graham Chiropractic
Dr. Betty E. Graham
5344 N. Lincoln
Chicago, IL 60625
773/769-6666
773/334-1696 - fax

Greater Chicago Chiropractic
Dr. Dale Zuehlke
561 W. Diversey #221
Chicago, IL 60614
773/871-7766
773/871-0781 - fax

Franklin D. Ing
2451 N. Lincoln
Chicago, IL 60614
773/525-2444
773/525-9989 - fax

Dr. Craig H. Jacobus
Lifelink Medical Center
64 Orland Square Dr. #116
Orland Park, IL 60462
708/873-5868
708/873-5884 - fax

Dr. Kevin Regan
Holistic Practitioner
55 E. Washington #1630
Chicago, IL 60602
312/578-1624
312/578-8717 - fax
www.doctorkev.com

Dr. Briana S. Skarbek
513 Waukegan Rd.
Northbrook, IL 60062
847/509-0005

Progressive Chiropractic Rehabilitation & Wellness Center
2816 N. Sheffield
Chicago, IL 60657
773/525-WELL
773/525-9397 - fax
www.progressivechiro.net

Seaman Chiropractic Center
4941 W. Foster
Chicago, IL 60630
773/545-2233
773/545-8383 - fax

Stiles Chiropractic Offices
48 E. Chicago
Chicago, IL 60611
312/642-1138

Counselors

A Creative Change
Honora Simon, Ph.D.
541 W. Diversey #208
Chicago, IL 60614
312/939-9394
312/939-9594 - fax
www.reducestress.com

Abraham Lincoln Center Screening & Support
(specializes in children)
1950 W. 87th
Chicago, IL 60620
773/239-7960
773/239-0272 - fax

Ann L. Hammon, M.D.
550 W. Surf #101C
Chicago, IL 60657
773/296-2195

Associated Psychologists and Therapists
77 W. Washington #1519
Chicago, IL 60602
312/630-1001
312/630-1342 - fax
www.psychologists.org

Chicago Women's Health Center
3435 N. Sheffield
Chicago, IL 60657
773/935-6126

Community Counseling Center of Chicago
Mental Health Center
4740 N. Clark
Chicago, IL 60640
773/769-0205
773/769-0344 - fax

Community Counseling Centers of Chicago
4740 N. Clark
Chicago, IL 60640
773/728-1000
773/728-6517 - fax

Dance Therapy Center
Fine Arts Building
410 S. Michigan
Chicago, IL 60605
312/461-9826
312/461-9843 - fax

Kate DeVore, M.A.
4451 N. Hamilton
Chicago, IL 60625
773/334-7203
www.KateDeVore.com

Also listed under speech therapy in Actors Tools.

Do you feel ready to make a shift in your life, but in need of guidance? You have the answers, and I can help you clarify them in a safe, loving and supportive environment. I offer a combination of counseling, bodywork and an eclectic set of healing modalities. I am a Reiki Master also certified in Vibrational Healing.

Great Lakes Psychological Providers
111 N. Wabash #1408
Chicago, IL 60602
312/443-1400
312/443-1307 - fax

Gerald Greene, Ph.D.
500 N. Michigan #542
Chicago, IL 60611
312/266-1456

Harambee Wellness Center
1515 E. 52nd - 2nd floor
Chicago, IL 60615
773/925-6877

Howard Brown Health Center
4025 N. Sheridan
Chicago, IL 60613
773/388-1600

Hartgrove Hospital
520 N. Ridgeway
Chicago, IL 60624
773/722-3113 • 773/722-6361 - fax

Institute for Psychoanalysis
122 S. Michigan #1300
Chicago, IL 60603
312/922-7474
312/922-5656 - fax

Jason Simpson and Group Solutions
888/415-1530
mirconnect.com/doc/simpson.html

Ruth Landis, Inc.
(See our ad on page 69)
773/991-7777
773/463-3683 - fax

Build inner safety so that creativity flows naturally and spontaneously while preparing technically for auditions (monologues, on-camera, cold-reading) and performance experience. As a longtime acting coach and certified body-psychotherapist and hypnotherapist, Ruth help you explore mind/body/emotion awareness around performance anxiety, blocks, creating ease with self, using work rooted in Alexander, Feldenkrais, and Gestalt therapy. Ruth coaches actors, is in private practice, and has taught at Victory Gardens, Northwestern, Columbia and Roosevelt University.

Panic Anxiety Recovery Center
680 N. Lake Shore #1325
Chicago, IL 60611
312/642-7954
312/642-7951 - fax

Patricia Martinez
4072 N. Sheridan #3D
Chicago, IL 60613
616/469-1151

Dr. Steigman
4433 W. Touhy #552
Chicago, IL 60646
847/675-7544

Health Clubs

Bally Total Fitness
2828 N. Clark
Chicago, IL 60657
773/929-6900
www.ballytotalfitness.com

Chicago Fitness Center
3131 N. Lincoln
Chicago, IL 60657
773/549-8181
773/549-4622 - fax
www.chicagofitnesscenter.com

Gold Coast Multiplex
1030 N. Clark
Chicago, IL 60610
312/944-1030
312/944-6180 - fax
www.gcmultiplex.com

Gorilla Sports
2727 N. Lincoln
Chicago, IL 60614
773/477-8400
773/477-8476 - fax

Know No Limits
5121 N. Clark
Chicago, IL 60640
773/334-4728

Lehmann Sports Club
2700 N. Lehmann
Chicago, IL 60614
773/871-8300
773/871-3506 - fax
www.lehmannsportsclub.com

Mint Condition Wellness and Training Center
1111 Pasquinelli Dr. #450
Westmont, IL 60559
630/455-9525
www.InMintCondition.com

A personal trainer is an investment in your health and well-being...choose the best! One-on-One Personal Training in a private, professional setting. Located in the Oak Brook area near the intersection of Rt. 83 & Ogden Ave. Don't you deserve to be in Mint Condition?

Let Julie Fulton, RD, LD, and the West Suburban Dietetic Association 1999 Recognized Young Dietitian of the Year help you modify your eating habits to achieve and maintain your desired weight, control or prevent specific medical conditions, or just eat better.

One on One Fitness Personal Training Service, Inc.
Michael Sokol
312/642-4235 • 312/642-7686 - fax

Webster Fitness Club
957 W. Webster
Chicago, IL 60614
773/248-2006 • 773/248-3195 - fax
www.websterfitness.com

Women's Workout World
208 S. Lasalle
Chicago, IL 60604
312/357-0001

World Gym
909 W. Montrose
Chicago, IL 60613
773/348-1212

World Gym
150 S. Wacker
Chicago, IL 60606
312/357-9753
312/357-0577 - fax
www.worldgymchi.com

World Gym - Hyde Park
1451 E. 53rd St.
Chicago, IL 60615
773/363-1212
773/363-2010 - fax
www.worldgymchi.com

YMCA
801 N. Dearborn
Chicago, IL 60610
800/935-9622

Health Food Stores

Advance Nutrition Center
55 E. Washington - Lobby
Chicago, IL 60602
312/419-1940

Life Spring
3178 N. Clark
Chicago, IL 60657
773/327-1023 • 773/327-1030 - fax

Sherwyn's
645 W. Diversey
Chicago, IL 60614
773/477-1934

Whole Foods Market
1000 W. North
Chicago, IL 60622
312/587-0648
www.wholefoods.com

Whole Foods Market
3300 N. Ashland
Chicago, IL 60657
773/244-4200
www.wholefoods.com

Hypnotists

A Creative Change
Honora Simon, Ph.D.
541 W. Diversey #208
Chicago, IL 60614
312/939-9394
312/939-9594 - fax
www.reducestress.com

Associated Psychologists and Therapists
77 W. Washington #1519
Chicago, IL 60602
312/630-1001
312/630-1342 - fax
www.psychologists.org

Gerald Greene, Ph.D.
500 N. Michigan #542
Chicago, IL 60611
312/266-1456

Dr. Steigman
4433 W. Touhy #552
Chicago, IL 60646
847/675-7544

Sun Center
1816 N. Wells - 3rd floor
Chicago, IL 60614
312/280-1070
www.home.earthlink.net/~suncenter

World Hypnosis Organization, Inc.
2521 W. Montrose
Chicago, IL 60618
773/267-6677

Massage

American Massage Therapy Association
Illinois Chapter
708/484-9282
708/484-8601 - fax

Back to One
5342 N. Winthrop
Chicago, IL 60640
773/561-5893

Bodyscapes, Inc.
Massage Therapy Clinic
1604 Sherman Ave., Ste. 210
Evanston, IL 60201
847/864-6464

Karen L. Bruneel
4770 N. Lincoln #6
Chicago, IL 60625
773/769-1133
773/769-1134 - fax

Chiropractic Chicago
Dr. Ellisa J. Grossman
407 W. North
Chicago, IL 60610
312/255-9500

Chislof Chiropractic Center
7448 N. Harlem
Chicago, IL 60631
773/763-0400

Diamond Beauty Clinic
151 N. Michigan #1018
Chicago, IL 60601
312/240-1042

Greater Chicago Chiropractic
Dr. Dale Zuehlke
561 W. Diversey #221
Chicago, IL 60614
773/871-7766
773/871-0781 - fax

Hair Loft
14 E. Pearson
Chicago, IL 60611
312/943-5435

Leslie Kahn
Licensed Massage Therapist
1243 N. Damen
Chicago, IL 60622
773/276-4665

Know No Limits
5121 N. Clark
Chicago, IL 60640
773/334-4728

Mario Tricoci Hair Salon & Day Spa
900 N. Michigan
Chicago, IL 60611
312/915-0960
312/943-3138 - fax

Massage Therapy Professionals
3047 N. Lincoln #400
Chicago, IL 60657
773/472-9484
773/472-8590 - fax

Massage Works
4039 N. Lavergne
Chicago, IL 60641
773/777-2396

Progressive Chiropractic Rehabilitation & Wellness Center
2816 N. Sheffield
Chicago, IL 60657
773/525-WELL
773/525-9397 - fax
www.progressivechiro.net

Rodica European Skin & Body Care Center
Water Tower Place - Professional Side
845 N. Michigan #944E
Chicago, IL 60611
312/527-1459
www.facialandbodybyrodica.com

Anna Sas European Facials
Barbara's Skin Care
645 N. Michigan #420
Chicago, IL 60611
312/943-4728

Seaman Chiropractic Center
4941 W. Foster
Chicago, IL 60630
773/545-2233 • 773/545-8383 - fax

Sun Center
1816 N. Wells - 3rd floor
Chicago, IL 60614
312/280-1070
www.home.earthlink.net/~suncenter

Wellspring Integrated Medecine
1565 Sherman Ave.
Evanston, IL 60201
847/733-9900
847/733-0105 - fax
www.mirocenter.org

Meditation

Peace School
3121 N. Lincoln
Chicago, IL 60657
773/248-7959
773/248-7963 - fax

Vajrayana Buddhist Center
1116 Lake St. - 3rd Floor
Oak Park, IL 60301
708/763-0132
www.vajrabc.org

Zen Buddhist Temple
(Chinese Culture Academy)
608 Dempster St.
Evanston, IL 60202
847/869-0554

Naprapaths

Belmont Health Care
Lena Granlund
2110 W. Belmont
Chicago, IL 60618
773/404-0909

Chicago National College of Naprapathy
3330 N. Milwaukee
Chicago, IL 60641
773/282-2686 • 773/282-2688 - fax
www.naprapathy.edu

Karen L. Bruneel
4770 N. Lincoln #6
Chicago, IL 60625
773/769-1133
773/769-1134 - fax

Lake Shore Naprapathic Center
3166 N. Lincoln #410
Chicago, IL 60657
773/327-0844

Nutritionists

Advance Center
Dr. Michael Luban
55 E. Washington #1310
Chicago, IL 60602
312/553-2020
312/553-5128 - fax

Dr. Craig H. Jacobus
Lifelink Medical Center
64 Orland Square Dr. #116
Orland Park, IL 60462
708/873-5868
708/873-5884 - fax

Lake Shore Naprapathic Center
3166 N. Lincoln #410
Chicago, IL 60657
773/327-0844

Mint Condition Wellness and Training Center
1111 Pasquinelli Dr. #450
Westmont, IL 60559
630/455-9525
www.InMintCondition.com

A personal trainer is an investment in your health and well-being...choose the best! One-on-One Personal Training in a private, professional setting. Located in the Oak Brook area near the intersection of Rt. 83 & Ogden Ave. Don't you deserve to be in Mint Condition?

Let Julie Fulton, RD, LD, and the West Suburban Dietetic Association 1999 Recognized Young Dietitian of the Year help you modify your eating habits to achieve and maintain your desired weight, control or prevent specific medical conditions, or just eat better.

Dr. Kevin Regan
Holistic Practitioner
55 E. Washington #1630
Chicago, IL 60602
312/578-1624 • 312/578-8717 - fax
www.doctorkev.com

Rose Quest Nutrition Center
200 N. Michigan #404A
Chicago, IL 60602
312/444-9234

Physicians

ARR/Alternative Reproductive
2000 N. Racine
Chicago, IL 60614
773/327-7315
773/477-0287 - fax

Center for Human Reproduction
750 N. Orleans
Chicago, IL 60610
312/397-8200
312/397-8394 - fax

Chicago Women's Health Center
3435 N. Sheffield
Chicago, IL 60657
773/935-6126

Harambee Wellness Center
1515 E. 52nd - 2nd floor
Chicago, IL 60615
773/925-6877

Howard Brown Health Center
4025 N. Sheridan
Chicago, IL 60613
773/388-1600

University Family
1953C N. Clybourn
Chicago, IL 60614
773/348-1414
773/348-1477 - fax

University of Chicago Physicians Group
4640 N. Marine
Chicago, IL 60640
773/564-5333
773/564-5334 - fax

Women's Health Resources
3000 N. Halsted #309
Chicago, IL 60657
773/296-3500

Religious Groups

AGLOChicago
Archdiocesan Gay & Lesbian Outreach
711 W. Belmont #106
Chicago, IL 60657
773/525-3872

Chicago Genesis
A Creative Christian Collective
773/275-3490

Congregation Or Chadash
656 W. Barry
Chicago, IL 60657
773/248-9456

Dignity Chicago
(Roman Catholic)
3023 N. Clark - Box 237
Chicago, IL 60657
773/296-0780
www.dignitychicago.org

Grace Baptist Church
1307 W. Granville
Chicago, IL 60660
773/262-8700

HAVURA
Jewish Community Group
7316 N. Tripp
Lincolnwood, IL 60712
847/679-8760

Holy Trinity Lutheran Church
1218 W. Addison
Chicago, IL 60613
773/248-1233
www.holytrinitychicago.org

Second Unitarian Church/Unitarian Universalist
656 W. Barry
Chicago, IL 60657
773/549-0260 - office
www.2uchicago.org

The Ethical Humanist Society of Greater Chicago
7574 N. Lincoln Ave.
Skokie, IL 60077
847/677-3334
www.ethicalhuman.org

Vajrayana Buddhist Center
1116 Lake St. - 3rd Floor
Oak Park, IL 60301
708/763-0132
www.vajrabc.org

Wellington Avenue United Church of Christ
615 W. Wellington
Chicago, IL 60657
773/935-0642
773/935-0690 - fax

Tai Chi

Dance Center of Columbia College
1306 S. Michigan
Chicago, IL 60605
312/344-8300
312/344-8036 - fax
www.colum.edu

Discovery Center
2940 N. Lincoln
Chicago, IL 60657
773/348-8120
773/880-6164 - fax
www.discoverycenter.cc

Dan Guidara
3052 N. New England Ave.
Chicago, IL 60634
773/745-6442

Hedwig Dances
Administrative Offices
2936 N. Southport #210
Chicago, IL 60657
773/871-0872
773/296-0968 - fax
www.enteract.com\~hedwig

Weight Control

A Creative Change
Honora Simon, Ph.D.
541 W. Diversey #208
Chicago, IL 60614
312/939-9394
312/939-9594 - fax
www.reducestress.com

Professional Weight Clinic
200 E. Ohio #501
Chicago, IL 60611
312/664-2255

Weight Watchers
800/651-6000
www.weightwatchers.com

Women's Workout World
208 S. Lasalle
Chicago, IL 60604
312/357-0001

Yoga

Belle Plaine Studio
2014 W. Belle Plaine
Chicago, IL 60618
773/935-1890
773/935-1909 - fax

Bodyscapes, Inc.
Massage Therapy Clinic
1604 Sherman Ave. Ste. 210
Evanston, IL 60201
847/864-6464

Dance Center of Columbia College
1306 S. Michigan
Chicago, IL 60605
312/344-8300
312/344-8036 - fax
www.colum.edu

Global Yoga and Wellness Center
1823 W. North
Chicago, IL 60622
773/489-1510

Hedwig Dances
Administrative Offices
2936 N. Southport #210
Chicago, IL 60657
773/871-0872
773/296-0968 - fax
www.enteract.com\~hedwig

North Shore School of Dance
107 Highwood
Highwood, IL 60040
847/432-2060
847/432-4037 - fax
www.northshoredance.com

NU Yoga Center
3047 N. Lincoln - 3rd floor
Chicago, IL 60657
773/327-3650
www.yogamind.com

Peace School
3121 N. Lincoln
Chicago, IL 60657
773/248-7959
773/248-7963 - fax

Sivananda Yoga Center
1246 W. Bryn Mawr
Chicago, IL 60660
773/878-7771
www.sivananda.org/chicago

Temple of Kriya Yoga
2414 N. Kedzie
Chicago, IL 60647
773/342-4600
773/342-4608 - fax

Tracy Vonkaenel
4057 N. Damen
Chicago, IL 60613
773/279-8879

Yoga Circle
Gabriel Halpern - Director
401 W. Ontario - 2nd floor
Chicago, IL 60610
312/915-0750
www.yogacircle.com

Grooming and Appearance

Cosmetic Surgery

Associated Plastic Surgeons
Dr. Otto J. Placik
680 N. Lake Shore #930
Chicago, IL 60611
312/787-5313
847/398-1784 - fax

Chicago Hair Institute
Ron Corniels
20 E. Ogden
Hinsdale, IL 60521
630/655-9331
630/655-9381 - fax

Dr. Diane L. Gerber
680 N. Lake Shore #930
Chicago, IL 60611
312/654-8700

Liposuction Institute of America
Dr. Leon Tcheupdjian
1700 W. Central Rd.
Arlington Heights, IL 60005
847/259-0100
847/398-3855 - fax
www.lipodoc.com

New Dimensions Centre for Cosmetic Surgery
60 E. Delaware - 15th floor
Chicago, IL 60611
312/440-5050
312/440-5064 - fax
www.nd-plasticsurgery.com

New Image Specialists
James M. Platts, Jr., M.D.
34 E. Oak #400
Chicago, IL 60611
312/951-2694
312/951-6492 - fax

Raymond Konior, M.D.
1 S. 224 Summit #310
Oakbrook Terrace, IL 60181
630/932-9690
630/932-8125 - fax
www.thenewyoudoc.com

Wafik A. Hanna, M.D.
12 Salt Creek Ln. #225
Hinsdale, IL 60521
630/887-8180
630/887-8188 - fax

Dentists

Belmont Dental Care
3344 N. Lincoln
Chicago, IL 60657
773/549-7971
773/348-7544 - fax

Dr. Craig Millard, D.D.S., P.C.
30 N. Michigan #920
Chicago, IL 60602
312/726-5830
312/726-7290 - fax

Dr. David B. Drake
739 W. Belmont
Chicago, IL 60657
773/248-8813
773/248-8898 - fax

Dr. Glenn Ulffers, D.D.S.
1001 N. Clark
Chicago, IL 60610
312/337-1318
312/642-5166 - fax

All phases of general dentistry emphasizing cosmetics including bleaching, porcelain veneers, and crowns. All done in a friendly environment in order to make the apprehensive patient comfortable. Nitrous oxide analgesia is available for those who are most fearful.

Dr. Gray Vogelmann
155 N. Michigan #325
Chicago, IL 60601
312/819-1104

Dr. Ieva Wright
333 N. Michigan #2900
Chicago, IL 60601
312/236-3226 • 312/236-9629 - fax

Dr. Jeffrey Gaule
3120 N. Ashland
Chicago, IL 60657
773/281-7550
773/281-0808 - fax

Dr. Joseph S. Toups
25 E. Washington #1325
Chicago, IL 60602
312/263-6894

Dr. Marianne W. Schaefer
4801 W. Peterson, Ste. 502
Chicago, IL 60646
773/777-8300
www.the-toothfairy.com

Dr. Martin Lieberman & Dr. William T. Tetford
5419 N. Sheridan #105
Chicago, IL 60640
773/728-9200

Dr. Roger M. Wills
30 N. Michigan #1414
Chicago, IL 60602
312/332-7010
312/332-1812 - fax

Gold Coast Dental Associates
Dr. Jeffrey Weller
1050 N. State - Mezzanine
Chicago, IL 60610
312/654-0606
312/654-1606 - fax

Lincoln Park Columbus Dental Associates
2551 N. Clark #700
Chicago, IL 60614
773/348-7008
773/348-5810 - fax

Lincoln Park Cosmetic and General Dentistry
424 W. Fullerton
Chicago, IL 60614
773/404-0101

Marion Street Dental
Dr. Linda A. Oster
127 N. Marion St. - Ste. 2
Oak Park, IL 60302
708/386-4222

Michelle Rappeport, D.D.S.
3056 N. Southport
Chicago, IL 60657
773/935-4960

Ravenswood Dental Group
1945 W. Wilson
Chicago, IL 60640
773/334-3555
773/334-5771 - fax

Wrigleyville Dental Group
1353 W. Cornelia
Chicago, IL 60657
773/975-6666

Electrolysis

Amber (last name???)
1471 W. Irving Park Rd.
Chicago, IL 60613
773/549-3800

Carol Block Ltd.
Permanent Hair Removal
70 E. Walton - 2nd floor
Chicago, IL 60611
312/266-1350
www.carolblockltd.com

Water Tower Hair Removal
845 N. Michigan #963W
Chicago, IL 60611
312/787-4028
312/787-4092 - fax
www.purelaser.com

Salons

Alfaro Hair Design
3454 N. Southport
Chicago, IL 60657
773/935-0202

Curl Up and Dye
2837 N. Clark
Chicago, IL 60657
773/348-1000
773/348-2802 - fax
www.curlupdye.com

Diamond Beauty Clinic
151 N. Michigan #1018
Chicago, IL 60601
312/240-1042

Femline Hair Designs, Inc.
3500 Midwest Rd.
Oakbrook, IL 60522
630/655-2212

J. Gordon Designs, Ltd.
2326 N. Clark
Chicago, IL 60614
773/871-0770
773/871-2514 - fax

Hair Loft
14 E. Pearson
Chicago, IL 60611
312/943-5435

Marianne Strokirk Salon
361 W. Chestnut
Chicago, IL 60610
312/944-4428
312/944-4429 - fax
www.mariannestrokirk.com

Mario Tricoci Hair Salon & Day Spa
900 N. Michigan
Chicago, IL 60611
312/915-0960
312/943-3138 - fax

Media Hair & Makeup Group
Maureen Kalagian
708/848-8400

Molina Molina
54 W. Maple
Chicago, IL 60610
312/664-2386

Nancy Angelair Salon
1003 N. Rush
Chicago, IL 60611
312/943-3011

Niko's Day Spa
2504 N. Clark
Chicago, IL 60657
773/472-0883

Paul Rehder Salon
939 N. Rush
Chicago, IL 60611
312/943-7404

Philip James
710 W. Diversey
Chicago, IL 60614
773/248-9880

Salon Absolu
1216 W. Belmont
Chicago, IL 60657
773/525-2396

Southport Hair Studio
3430 N. Southport
Chicago, IL 60657
773/477-9319

Timothy Paul Salon
200 E. Delaware
Chicago, IL 60611
312/944-5454
312/944-5460 - fax

TRIO Salon Ltd.
11 E. Walton St.
Chicago, IL 60611-1412
312/944-6999
312/944-9572 - fax
www.triosalon.com

"Chicago models turn to TRIO...for many of the shortest, coolest looks seen on the hottest new faces in town...(TRIO) has been recognized nationally for its creative and technical works...(the) name (being) synonymous with flattering, precision cuts and picture perfect stylings."
MODERN SALON

Trio Salon Ltd.
1913 Central St.
Evanston, IL 60201-2227
847/491-6999
www.triosalon.com

Skin Care

Anna Sas European Facials
Barbara's
645 N. Michigan #420
Chicago, IL 60611
312/943-4728

Channings Day Spa
54 E. Oak
Chicago, IL 60611
312/280-1994
312/280-1929 - fax
www.channings.com

Femline Hair Designs, Inc.
3500 Midwest Rd.
Oakbrook, IL 60522
630/655-2212

Hair Loft
14 E. Pearson
Chicago, IL 60611
312/943-5435

Mario Tricoci Hair Salon & Day Spa
900 N. Michigan
Chicago, IL 60611
312/915-0960
312/943-3138 - fax

Nouvelle Femme
1151 Wilmette Ave.
Wilmette, IL 60091
847/251-6698

Rodica European Skin & Body Care Center
Water Tower Place - Professional Side
845 N. Michigan #944E
Chicago, IL 60611
312/527-1459
www.facialandbodybyrodica.com

Salon Absolu
1216 W. Belmont
Chicago, IL 60657
773/525-2396

Syd Simons Cosmetics, Inc.
6601 W. North Ave.
Oak Park, IL 60302
877/943-2333
www.sydsimons.com

Public Service Phone Numbers

ArtLaw Hotline
312/944-ARTS

Attorney General
312/814-3000

Chicago Park District
312/747-2200

CTA/PACE Information
312/836-7000

Equal Employment Opportunity Commission
Chicago, IL
312/353-2713

IRS Taxpayer Information
Chicago, IL
800/829-1040

League of Chicago Theatres Hotline
900/225-2225

Police (Non Emergency)
Chicago, IL
311

Post Office Information
312/654-3895

Women's Bureau
U.S. Department of Labor
233 S. Dearborn #1022
Chicago, IL 60604
312/353-6985
312/353-6986 - fax

Writer's Biographies

Jonathan Abarbanel is the senior writer for PERFORMINK, Chicago's trade newspaper, and the theatre editor for the WINDY CITY TIMES, a Chicago weekly paper. He also is an award-winning theatre critic for NORTH SHORE MAGAZINE and National Public Radio Affiliate WBEZ; a senior contributor to CHICAGO FOOTLIGHTS; and a featured columnist for BACKSTAGE, the national trade weekly. He is a member of Dramatists Guild and the American Theatre Critics Association.

Christine Gatto has been involved with "The Book" since the first edition four years ago. Currently, she is completing her MFA in acting at Pennsylvania State University. Upon graduation, she will be returning to her native Chicago, where she has acted with many theatre companies, including Stage Left, Bailiwick, SummerNITE, Powertap, and Trapdoor, to name a few. Additionally, she holds a BFA in acting from Northern Illinois University.

Jenn Goddu writes criticism for THE READER and is a regular contributor to PERFORMINK.

Susan Hubbard is a writer, filmmaker, fundraiser and educator living in Chicago. She worked with Chicago's top fundraisers to develop an executive education program, Managing Institutional Advancement, for the University of Chicago's Graham School. Experts and students in that program provided countless affirmations of the board-building practices suggested by the theatre companies in the grant writing article.

Carrie L. Kaufman is the publisher of PERFORMINK Newspaper, PERFORMINK Books and PI Online. She's won a couple of journalism awards and is beloved by her staff and various child relatives.

Kelly Kurtin has been writing about the Chicago arts scene for four years. She is the senior editor of WHERE CHICAGO MAGAZINE, for which she covers theatre, museums, music and dance. She also writes for STAGEBILL, UR CHICAGO, PERFORMINK, chicago.citysearch.com, CHICAGO HOME & GARDEN and SOMA. She was the editor of the CHICAGO OFFICIAL VISITORS GUIDE and now writes frequently for ILLINOIS NOW!, the travel magazine of the Illinois Bureau of Tourism. Kelly is a graduate of the Beginning Improvisation Program of The Second City and is currently a student at Improv Olympic.

Mechelle Moe is the editor of PERFORMINK newspaper, PI Online and "The Book: An Actor's Guide to Chicago" (fifth edition). She also serves as the executive director of The Hypocrites theatre company. As an actor she as worked with The Hypocrites, Lifeline, Prop, The Factory and A Red Orchid.

Rachael Patterson serves as the director of The Audition Studio where she has been teaching audition technique for film, industrials and commercials for 12 years. Formerly a partner in Brody/Patterson Casting, she cast numerous films, television pilots and commercials. Rachael trained at the American Conservatory Theatre in San Francisco. Along with Carol Dibo and The Audition Studio North, Rachael organizes workshops and seminars for teens on Chicago's north shore. She is a private coach and teaches film workshops at universities. Recently, she has begun offering workshops for commercial directors in order to help them communicate more clearly with actors in auditions and while on set.

Julie Franz Peeler, Director, National Arts Marketing Project Julie is an accomplished market researcher and marketing strategist in both the for profit and non-profit arena. She worked actively with the arts and funding communities to develop the four programs of the Arts Marketing Center. While working at major international advertising agencies, she developed growth plans for Fortune 500 clients, as well as for the U.S. Olympic Committee. She holds a BA in Journalism from Loyola University of Chicago and a Masters in Management in Marketing and Non Profit Management from the Kellogg Graduate School of Business at Northwestern University.

Dr. Amy Seham is an assistant professor of Theatre and Dance at Gustavus Adolphus College in Minnesota. She was artistic director of Performance Studio theatre and Free Shakespeare on the Green in New Haven, Connecticut, where she also taught and performed improv and improvisational playwriting. Her book, "Whose Improv Is It Anyway? Beyond Second City" (University of Mississippi Press), traces the history of improv comedy in Chicago and also takes a look at questions of race and gender in improv.

Ben Winters previously lived in Chicago where wrote regularly for PERFORMINK and was a theatre critic and columnist at NEWCITY. Now Ben lives in New York City, where he is associate editor at Theatremania.com. His writing on theatre, books, politics, and various other stuff has appeared in publications like STAGEBILL, the CHICAGO TRIBUNE the NATION, IN THESE TIMES and NYLON MAGAZINE.

CTA eL Train System

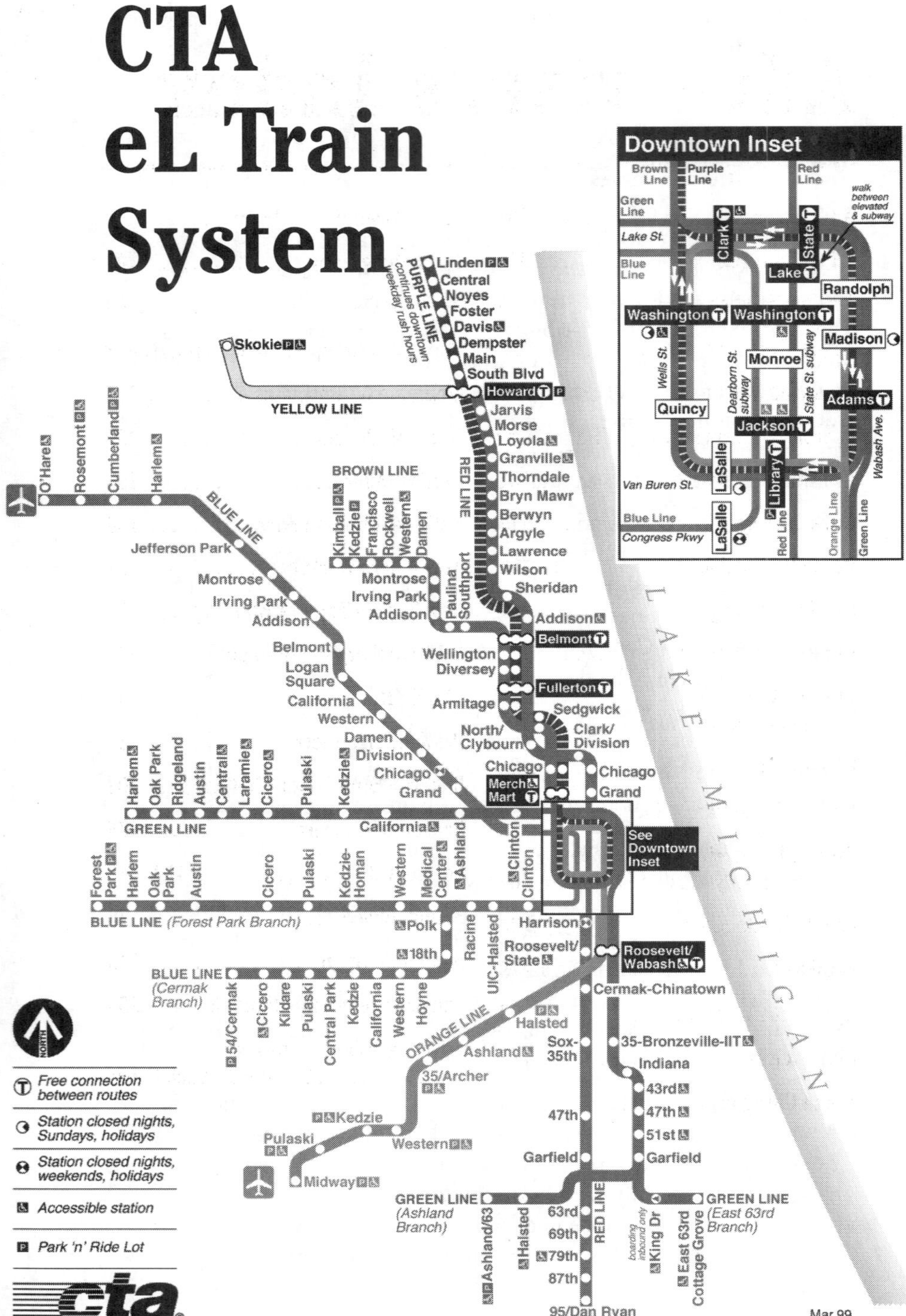

Advertisers Index

Order more copies of

The Book: An Actor's Guide to Chicago!

Every religion has its text, Chicago theatre has *The Book!*

Name ____

Business Name ____________________________________

Address ____

City ________________________ St ____ Zip ________

Phone ____

Fax ____

e-mail ____

website _______________________________________

___ Send me a copy of the 2002 edition of "The Book: An Actor's Guide to Chicago" for $15 plus a $5 shipping and handling fee. I have enclosed my check or money order for $20, which includes the $5 shipping and handling fee. Please bill the credit card number below for $20.

___ Send me both a subscription to PerformInk and "The Book: An Actor's Guide to Chicago" for a total of $51.95 ($36.95 for a subscription and a discounted subscriber price of $10 for "The Book," and a $5 shipping and handling fee.

___ I have enclosed my check or money order for $____________.

___ Please bill the credit card number below for $____________.

Visa/MasterCard/Discover #____________________, Exp. ______

Send to:
PerformInk, 3223 N. Sheffield - 3rd floor
Chicago, IL 60657